THE FREEDOM TO D

In the wake of the events of September 11th 2001, it is disturbingly clear that no government or individual can afford to ignore religious fundamentalism. Religious faith in the modern world is a political statement, from the hot spots of Al Qaeda's Afghanistan to the religious tensions and explosive violence igniting the streets of Israel, Palestine, India and even the urban centres of the USA and Europe. But how does fundamentalism function across cultural and social boundaries? Are all faiths equally susceptible to it? How can we recognize fundamentalism, and is it always by its nature harmful or wrong?

Under the auspices of top international commentators, *The Freedom to Do God's Will* considers the global impact of fundamentalism on religious traditions including Hinduism, Buddhism, Mormonism, Christianity, Judaism and Islam. With special reference to human rights issues, women's rights and the influence of social factors, it brings a new dimension to a field of study often dominated by purely religious or political perspectives, while effectively challenging received ideas about the violence and conservatism of fundamentalist movements. Revealingly illustrated with original case studies, ten investigative essays from a multicultural panel of experts, each with specific local and academic knowledge of the faiths and issues they discuss, offer an intimate and highly specific portrait of why and how fundamentalism occurs. Essays include:

- **Scott Appleby** on religions, human rights and social change
- **Chakravarthi Ram-Prasad** on Hindu nationalism, violence and governance in India
- **Alice Shalvi** on repression in the modern Jewish state
- **Sharifah Zaleha binti Syed Hassan** on women, Islam and inclusion in Malaysia

Introduced and edited by experts in human rights policy-making, and giving essential practical guidance for professionals working in related areas, *The Freedom to Do God's Will* provides a comprehensive, sensitive and topical overview of fundamentalism's many faces, and of our collective roles in understanding and responding to it.

Gerrie ter Haar is Professor of Religion, Human Rights and Social Change at the Institute of Social Studies in The Hague, and Deputy Secretary-General of the International Association for the History of Religions. She has written widely on religious developments in Africa, and is also the author of *Halfway to Paradise: African Christians in Europe* (Cardiff, 1998).

James J. Busuttil, former Director of the British Institute of Human Rights and legal adviser with the US Department of State, is Associate Professor of International Law and Organisation at the Institute of Social Studies and editor of the bi-monthly *Human Rights Case Digest*. He is Chair of the Working Group on Religion, Conflict and Peace, based in The Hague.

THE FREEDOM TO DO GOD'S WILL

Religious fundamentalism and social change

*Edited by Gerrie ter Haar
and James J. Busuttil*

London and New York

First published 2003 by Routledge
11 New Fetter Lane, London EC4P 4EE

Simultaneously published in the USA and Canada
by Routledge
29 West 35th Street, New York, NY 10001

Routledge is an imprint of the Taylor & Francis Group

© 2003 Gerrie ter Haar and James J. Busuttil for selection and
editorial material; individual contributors their contributions.

Typeset in Sabon by Wearset Ltd, Boldon, Tyne and Wear
Printed and bound in Great Britain by TJ International Ltd, Padstow,
Cornwall

British Library Cataloguing in Publication Data
A catalogue record for this book is available from the British Library

Library of Congress Cataloging in Publication Data
A catalog record for this book has been requested

ISBN 0-415-27034-0 (hbk)
ISBN 0-415-27035-9 (pbk)

CONTENTS

CONTENTS

CONTRIBUTORS

Nancy T. Ammerman is Professor of Sociology of Religion at Hartford Seminary, Hartford, Connecticut, USA. She is the author of three books published by Rutgers University Press: *Bible Believers: Fundamentalists in the Modern World* (1987), *Baptist Battles: Social Change and Religious Conflict in the Southern Baptist Convention* (1990), and *Congregation and Community* (1997). She is the editor of two volumes of papers and has published numerous scholarly articles and chapters, including on fundamentalism.

Abdullahi Ahmed An-Na'im is Charles Howard Candler Professor of Law at Emory University in Atlanta, Georgia, USA. He was Executive Director of Human Rights Watch/Africa from 1993 to 1995. He is the author of *Toward an Islamic Reformation: Civil Liberties, Human Rights and International Law* (Syracuse: Syracuse University Press, 1990), which has been translated into Arabic, Indonesian and Russian. He is the editor of six volumes on human rights and has published extensively on human rights, Islamic law and politics. He is currently director of two major research projects, one on women and land in Africa and the second on Islamic family law.

R. Scott Appleby is Director of the Kroc Institute for International Peace Studies and Professor of History at the University of Notre Dame, South Bend, Indiana, USA. He is also Director of the Cushwa Center for the Study of American Catholicism. From 1988 to 1993 he was co-director of the Fundamentalism Project sponsored by the American Academy of Arts and Sciences, which resulted in a five-volume series published by Chicago University Press (1992–95), of which he is the co-editor. He is the author of two books, the most recent of which is *The Ambivalence of the Sacred: Religion, Violence and Reconciliation* (Lanham, MD: Rowman & Littlefield, 2000) and is the editor of several others.

James J. Busuttil is Associate Professor of International Law and Organization at the Institute of Social Studies in The Hague, The Netherlands. He was previously Director of the British Institute of Human Rights in London and Lecturer in Law at the University of Essex. Before that, he worked as a practising lawyer in New York City and Washington, DC. He is Chair of the Working Group on Religion, Conflict and Peace, based in The Hague. He is the editor of the bi-monthly *Human Rights Case Digest*, published by Kluwer Law International in The Hague.

Gerrie ter Haar is Professor of Religion, Human Rights and Social Change at the Institute of Social Studies in The Hague, The Netherlands. She is Deputy Secretary-General of the International Association for the History of Religions. She is the author of three books on religion in Africa, including *Spirit of Africa: The Healing Ministry of Archbishop Milingo of Zambia* (London: Hurst & Co., 1992), which has been translated into French and Italian. Her most recent book is *Halfway to Paradise: African Christians in Europe* (Cardiff: Cardiff Academic Press, 1998), which has recently been republished in Africa (Nairobi: Acton Publishers, 2001). She is also the editor of three volumes of essays.

Chakravarthi Ram-Prasad is Lecturer and Director of Graduate Research in the Department of Religious Studies, Lancaster University, Lancaster. He is the author of *Knowledge and Liberation in Classical Indian Thought* (Basingstoke: Palgrave Macmillan, 2001) and *Advaita Epistemology and Metaphysics: An Outline of Indian Non-realism* (Richmond: Curzon Press, 2002). He has written extensively on Indian and comparative analytic philosophy, and also on religion and politics, and classical Hinduism. He has taught at the National University of Singapore, and held research fellowships at the universities of Oxford and Cambridge.

H.L. Seneviratne is Professor of Anthropology at the University of Virginia, Charlottesville, Virginia, USA. He is the author of *Rituals of the Kandyan State* (Cambridge: Cambridge University Press, 1978) and *The Work of Kings: The New Buddhism in Sri Lanka* (Chicago: The University of Chicago Press, 1999). He is the editor of *Essays in Honour of Victor Turner* (*South Asian Anthropologist*, Special Issue, vol. 4, no. 1, March 1983) and *Identity, Consciousness and the Past* (New Delhi: Oxford University Press, 1997).

Alice Shalvi was the first woman Rector of the Schechter Institute of Jewish Studies, Jerusalem, Israel, has been its Acting President, and is

now Chairperson of its Executive Board. She was a member of the
English Department of the Hebrew University of Jerusalem, from 1950
to 1990. She is the Founding Chair of the Israel Women's Network. She
is the author of three books and has published widely on literature and
on women, feminism and Judaism, and education. She has received
numerous awards in Israel and the United States and been granted hon-
orary doctorates by US and Israeli universities. Born in Germany, she
emigrated to the United Kingdom in 1934 and to Israel in 1949.

Sharifah Zaleha binti Syed Hassan is Professor of Social Anthropology at
the Centre for Social, Development and Environmental Studies in the
Universiti Kebangsaan Malaysia, Selangor, Malaysia. She is President of
the Southeast Asian Association for Gender Studies (Malaysia Branch).
She has co-written a book entitled *Managing Marital Disputes in
Malaysia: Islamic Mediators and Conflict Resolution in the syariah
Courts* (Richmond, Surrey: NIAS-Curzon, 1997), is the editor of a col-
lection entitled *Malaysian Women in the Wake of Change* (Kuala
Lumpur: University of Malaya Press, 1998), and has published papers
and essays elsewhere. She has done fieldwork in Malaysia focusing on
Islamization, modernity and the participation of Muslim women in reli-
gious politics.

Walter E.A. van Beek is Associate Professor of Anthropology at Utrecht
University, Utrecht, The Netherlands. He has done fieldwork in
Cameroon, Nigeria and Mali. He is the author of *The Kapsiki of the
Mandara Mountains* (Prospect Heights: Waveland Press, 1987) and
Africa's People of the Cliffs: The Dogon (New York: Abrams, 2001).
He is the editor of a comparative volume entitled *The Quest for Purity:
Dynamics of Puritan Movements* (Berlin: Mouton de Gruyter, 1988).
Himself a Mormon, he has also published on the cultural aspects of
Mormonism and is currently engaged in a study of the encounter of
Mormonism with Africa.

FOREWORD

At the end of 2001, after the attack on New York City and the Pentagon, no one will doubt that a volume on religious fundamentalism and social change holds, at the very least, the promise of potential relevance. A decade or so before, that would not have been considered all that obvious – at least not by all. For instance, at the Institute of Social Studies – the venue for the conference and expert meeting from which this book arose – academics had for almost 50 years studied societal development and change typically from a perspective that is covered by the label 'structuralist' better than by any other. It is only recently (actually, in 1999) that, with the help of two Dutch development agencies (CORDAID and ICCO) and one international NGO (the World Council on Religion and Peace), a first Chair in the 'superstructural' field (as one might call it) of Religion, Human Rights and Social Change was established. It was under the umbrella of this Chair that the conference was organized.

The conference brought together scholars and practitioners from a variety of disciplines: history, political psychology, religion, anthropology and law/human rights. In itself that is a significant and powerful mix. What is at least as important as this disciplinary diversity is the variety in the cultural and religious backgrounds of the participants. Among the contributors were authors coming from the 'worlds' of Hinduism, Buddhism, Islam and Christianity. That, today, strikes us as rather soothing: most of the current debate, at least in the major media, appears to look at world dynamics as if it could be reduced to a dialectic involving (post-Christian) modernity versus Islam (or parts thereof).

I would like to thank the organizers of the conference and the editors of this volume for their foresight, and for enriching the readers, and especially the ISS community, with their ecumenical approach.

Hans Opschoor
Rector
Institute of Social Studies
The Hague

PREFACE AND ACKNOWLEDGEMENTS

This volume has emerged from a series of public lectures entitled Religious Fundamentalism and Social Change, presented in April–May 2000 at the Institute of Social Studies in The Hague, under the auspices of the Chair in Religion, Human Rights and Social Change. The revised and edited lectures form the core of the book, to which some complementary materials have been added.

In conformity with the objectives of the original lecture series, the book aims at a wide international readership, including both academics and non-academics. The editors have particularly borne in mind the needs of governmental bodies and non-governmental organizations of various sorts, politicians and policy-makers, human rights activists, religious organizations, development workers and others with a professional interest in the subject matter.

The editors would like to thank the Dutch sponsors of the lecture series: NCDO (National Committee for International Cooperation and Sustainable Development), CORDAID (Catholic Organization for Relief and Development), Stichting Katholieke Noden, ICCO (Interchurch Organization for Development Cooperation), ISIM (Institute for the Study of Islam in the Modern World), Haëlla Stichting, NGG (Netherlands Society for the Study of Religions), and the Baha'i community in The Hague.

In addition, the Institute of Social Studies generously contributed time and facilities for the lecture series and the development of this book.

The contributors to this volume were most cooperative in providing revised versions of their chapters and replying to the inevitable editors' queries and requests. In particular, Professor Scott Appleby was generous in allowing us to appropriate as the title of the book the original title of his overview chapter.

The Editors
The Hague
January 2002

1

RELIGIOUS FUNDAMENTALISM AND SOCIAL CHANGE

A comparative inquiry

Gerrie ter Haar

Fundamentalism: What is it?

Religious fundamentalism has a rather short history. The concept has its origins in a Protestant movement that emerged in the early twentieth century in the United States.[1] Its recent significance, however, stems from developments hardly two decades old, starting with the 1979 Islamic revolution in Iran. In retrospect, it may be said that the year 1979 has become a watershed in the world's religious history, to the point that some influential commentators have suggested that the world should now best be considered as divided into distinct and separate cultural areas, each reflecting a specific religious identity.[2] Ten years later, in 1989, the fall of the Berlin Wall and the effective death of communism as a political ideology left traces in all parts of the world, not least because of the opening up of vast areas as potential spheres of influence for religious ideology, notably creating a new arena for the rival Christian and Muslim traditions.[3]

By the year 2000, at the turn of the new millennium, religious ideology was clearly back on the world's political agenda, often in rather unexpected and even frightening ways. The upsurge of religious extremism in various parts of the world, at times accompanied by massive violence, has opened the eyes of people who had considered religion a relic of the past that would naturally disappear as Enlightenment thinking overtook the world. The historical conditions of the late twentieth century seem to have created a particular context of social and cultural change, subsumed in the term 'modernization', that is considered fertile ground for the rise of fundamentalist movements.[4] Yet, as one observer warns us, we should be

1

careful not to confuse two separate issues: modernity as an idea, on the one hand, and the actual effect it has on specific social structures, on the other.[5]

For many people today, the word 'fundamentalism' is automatically associated with Islamic fundamentalism, which is discussed in the opening chapters of this book. But, as Abdullahi An-Na'im insists, Islamic fundamentalist movements are neither new, nor prevalent, nor permanent in Muslim societies. They also do not fit any of a number of popular theories such as those advanced by opinion makers like Samuel Huntington or Francis Fukuyama. In An-Na'im's view, Islamic fundamentalist movements are no more and no less than a spontaneous indigenous response to profound social, political and economic crises. He also argues from a historical point of view that Islamic fundamentalists hold beliefs sufficiently similar to what American Protestants believed when they coined the term 'fundamentalism' for the use of the word to be justified in its application to certain strands of Islam today. Hence, the term 'fundamentalism', though coined in a Christian context, is equally applicable to Islam and may therefore legitimately be used in his view. Further, he emphasizes that today there actually are Islamic movements in North Africa and the Middle East which describe themselves in similar terms. This marks, we may note, a shift in identity construction, moving from self-description to outside imposition and back to self-description, a process which can also be observed in other places. In Malaysia too, for example, fundamentalism has become a self-descriptive term in at least a number of cases, as Sharifah Zaleha demonstrates.[6] Malaysia's brand of fundamentalism has taken its own original course and has actually resulted in the empowerment of women.

But the use of the term 'fundamentalism' is not uncontested, and its meaning has often become so imprecise as to raise the legitimate question whether academics should use it at all. As we have noted above, its original use stems from Christianity, when in the early twentieth century a group of orthodox Protestants in the United States published a series of pamphlets under the title *The Fundamentals* in response to a number of social problems of the time. Hence they referred to themselves as 'fundamentalists', a name they freely chose. This is an important difference from the development of the term in modern times, when the term 'fundamentalism' is almost exclusively used to refer to a type of belief professed by others. This shift from self-definition to outside imposition has serious implications for the relationships between adherents of different faith communities or people born into societies with different religious cultures. In the past and present this has been most clearly visible in the relationship between Christian and Muslim communities. In the popular mind, notably in the West, the concept of fundamentalism has negative connotations and is almost exclusively applied to Islam. In such cases the term is mostly used to refer to the explicit or implicit resistance among Muslim believers to Western cultural and political values. This resistance is often seen in the West as the common denominator in what is otherwise the great variety of fundamentalist expressions.

It is even possible to trace the history of this shift in perception, back to the Iranian revolution under Ayatollah Khomeini in 1979. At that time the word 'fundamentalism' was applied by journalists to describe the nature of the revolutionary process in Iran, and from there it soon became used to refer to other religious groups with certain political interests. Its use in mainstream journalism in this sense is usually traced to a piece published in the British Sunday newspaper the *Observer* on 27 September 1981. In an article in which, with characteristic provocativeness, he compared the Koran with *Mein Kampf*, the British novelist Anthony Burgess wrote of 'the dangerous fundamentalism revived by the ayatollahs and their admirers as a device, indistinguishable from a weapon, for running a modern state'. This article was widely referred to, and soon other commentators began linking the words 'Islam' and 'fundamentalist'.[7] Whereas the original American Protestant fundamentalists had chosen their own description, the fundamentalist label was now imposed by outsiders, notably those journalists and academics who adopted the term in uncritical fashion. Subsequently, 'fundamentalism' has become a general term for a range of rather diverse phenomena.

In spite of the vague and even dubious application of the term 'fundamentalism' in many cases, its existence and usage have become an undeniable social fact. We must therefore ask ourselves how the term may be used in a responsible manner, in other words in such a way that it illuminates rather than obscures the phenomenon under discussion. All the contributors to this book have pondered this question and, though not necessarily coming to the same conclusion, they make it very clear what they mean by it in the specific context in which they are discussing it. In doing so, they underline the importance of contextualization, emphasizing the need for working definitions which are provisional in character, and of avoiding the use of essential definitions of an absolute nature. Hence, each author provides his or her own definition of religious fundamentalism in the particular context under discussion. Interestingly, the political aspect of the matter, that is the political aspirations implied in religious fundamentalism, are not explicitly mentioned in any of these definitions. In fact, in situations where the political aspect becomes dominant, the term 'fundamentalism' is considered inappropriate for understanding the situation at hand. Hence, one should rather use a different term, such as Chakravarhi Ram-Prasad concludes in the case of Hindu 'fundamentalism' in India and H.L. Seneviratne with regard to Buddhist 'fundamentalism' in Sri Lanka. These, the authors argue, are situations which can be better understood in terms of cultural essentialism or ethno-nationalism than anything else. It is significant that in such cases religion becomes a powerful tool in the hands of politicians.

Although the religious factor appears prominent in all forms of religious fundamentalism, fundamentalist movements are first and foremost social movements which, according to An-Na'im, should be judged and evaluated like any other social movement in the past or the present. Fundamentalist movements are at the same time products and agents of social change. It is not religion itself, but social conditions that are the crucial factor in their development. He strongly rejects any claims of religiously-based cultural exceptionalism, insisting that Islamic fundamentalism can and must be understood in the light of insights gained from experiences in other social movements, especially those emerging in similar contexts. Viewed this way, Islamic fundamentalism is just another variant of such movements. There is a parallel to be made in that respect with the developments in India which gave rise to the fundamentalism of *Hindutva*, as described by Ram-Prasad. Where Ram-Prasad explains the rise of the Hindu nationalist movement in primarily political and economic terms, his type of analysis comes close to An-Na'im's social movement approach. But there the similarity ends, as the context that gave rise to *Hindutva* is strikingly original and *Hindutva* itself cannot be properly understood in terms of fundamentalism, given the nature of Hindu religious traditions.

A key issue in the discussion of fundamentalism today, however, has become less what alleged fundamentalists believe, than the means they use. Fundamentalism is today generally associated with the use of violence, which was not implied in the original concept. But militancy alone, a distinguishing feature of religious fundamentalism, is not the same as violence. Yet it is true that various degrees of subtle differentiation between political and religious thought and action may cause the distinction to become blurred. Hence, *Hindutva*, essentially a political movement that makes use of religious resources, and which has indeed been associated with violence, is often mistakenly referred to in the West as a case of 'religious fundamentalism'. From the contributions to this volume it appears that many of the phenomena considered typical of fundamentalist movements are not inherently violent at all but that one important component of fundamentalism, namely militancy, is often confused with violence by observers who have come to believe that all fundamentalist movements are by nature violent, in spite of evidence to the contrary.

Central to the definition of fundamentalism are a number of other characteristics, not including the concept of violence, which are shared by the religious traditions discussed in this book. These can be considered at different levels including ideological or theological, social and cultural ones. In summary, one might say that ideologically the focus is on the past, socially it is on alternative structures, and culturally it is on identity. These characteristics will be discussed in more detail below.

Characteristics of religious fundamentalism

Since social change in itself does not necessarily breed religious fundamentalism, the question becomes what the specific conditions are that have given rise to it in recent times. As Nancy Ammerman explains, the type of social change that is generally referred to as modernization has brought about structural changes that imply a disruption of tradition. Urbanization and technological innovation, ethnic and religious pluralism, and the creation of the nation–state, are some of the most radical changes to have affected societies worldwide in recent times. They have altered the way in which people view themselves and others, and the way in which they view their relationships with one another. Most importantly, these profound changes have affected people's worldviews, and altered their relationship with the divine. As their social and religious identity seems to be at stake, they look to the past in order to find solutions for the present and the future. It appears from the contributions in this volume that this is not a simple reaction, as is often commonly assumed by outsiders, to the notion of fundamentalism. It may also be seen as a constructive and creative attempt to reconsider the position of individuals and societies at a time that old certainties have gone and need to be replaced by new ones. Or, as Seneviratne argues in the case of Buddhism, a return to Buddhist fundamentals might actually be desirable, as these traditionally include, for example, pacifism and the conscious development of non-violent behaviour. He also suggests that fundamentalism would not need to be a negative term if it were used only in the very limited sense of a call for a return to a Buddhist utopia.

Regrettably, such constructive attempts are often undermined by those who resort to violence to achieve their objectives, thus contributing to the notoriety of religious fundamentalists. In reality, the use of violence is limited to small groups of extremists, who are able to create havoc. Some examples discussed in this volume are India and Sri Lanka, even though, as

5

we will come to see, the use of the term 'fundamentalism' is debatable in both cases.[8] In other cases, the damage caused by violence remains limited, such as for example in Israel where violent incidents have occurred in the form of physical attacks by religious fundamentalists against those seen as violating the rules and regulations that govern orthodox Jewish life.[9] It is important to realize, as R. Scott Appleby reminds us, that religious fundamentalists tend to be 'exceptionalists'. That is, they believe that they are living in special times that require a departure from normal standards and procedures, allowing them to abandon a tradition of tolerance and peace and resort instead to intolerance and violence. Since times have changed, old social norms no longer apply.[10]

Appleby, whose authoritative work in conjunction with Martin Marty has become a major source on religious fundamentalisms worldwide,[11] finds that religious fundamentalism, generally speaking, refers to 'an identifiable pattern of religious militance in which self-styled true believers attempt to arrest the erosion of religious identity by outsiders, fortify the borders of the religious community, and create viable alternatives to secular structures and processes'.[12] The word 'pattern' is important here as the different contributions to this volume show how the various elements that form the pattern can be put together in rather different ways, at times adding new elements and leaving out others. Yet, 'family resemblances' are identifiable, as becomes clear from the individual chapters. Considering the various contributions and appreciating the importance of a contextual approach, a number of similarities can be discerned, constituting some of these family resemblances. Thus, significant aspects of religious fundamentalism appear to include, first, a return to traditional values and an accompanying sense of restoration, which may stimulate and contribute to the building of alternative structures; second, the search for a new identity, often at the expense of minority groups; third, a preoccupation with moral concerns that tends to have an adverse effect on the position of women; and fourth, a spirit of militancy with which these objectives are pursued. It is important to note again at this point that militancy does not necessarily include the use of violence and may be limited to less harmful expressions of religious zeal. It is only in recent years, as argued above, that the idea of violence has become attached to the concept of fundamentalism. Yet, the fundamentalists' experience of beleaguerment and their enclave mentality can easily turn a defensive mentality into an aggressive attitude.

Generally speaking, it appears from the contributions in this volume that religious fundamentalism displays a number of characteristics worldwide, irrespective of background and context. Religious fundamentalism, we noted above, is characterized by an evaluation of the past that brings about a sense of restoration. As most authors demonstrate, this is not in any way a general enterprise, but a careful and selective process whereby only those elements are retained which are considered helpful in furthering the specific agenda of religious fundamentalists in their various countries. These agendas, as can be seen from the different chapters in this book, may vary greatly and are dependent on the historical conditions that have led to the type of crisis giving rise to fundamentalist movements in the first place. The basis for this process of selective retrieval is found in a sacred history, often as recorded in sacred texts. It is worth noting here that fundamentalism is not exclusively found in book religions. Today a similar trend can be discerned in oral religions, which may be described as the fundamentalization of traditional religions. One illuminating example is the way in which the traditional religion of the Kikuyu in Kenya has been given new meaning by a particular group of people, notably young Kikuyu men.[13] The aim of members of *Mungiki*, as the movement is known, to revive traditional religious thought and action with political purposes in mind has been met in Kenyan society with both sympathy and hostility, depending on whose interests seem to be at stake.

In all cases, sacred history is positively contrasted with worldly history, in terms which suggest a moral opposition between 'tradition', on the one hand, and 'modernity', on the other. While the former is associated with the central role ascribed to the divine in human society, and hence identified as the source of all good, the latter epitomizes all society's ills and is ascribed to a deviation from original tradition that is believed to have caused moral decay. Morality is a central concern of most religious fundamentalists, and from this proceeds their preoccupation with purity and separation, which becomes visible notably in the role accorded to women. They seek a solution in restoring religion to its central role in public life, which requires a transformation at the individual and social level, either peacefully or by violent means. The notion of theocracy is never far from such an enterprise, confounding religious with political interests. The latter became literally true in one of the cases described in this book, that of Mormonism.[14] It is not often that the Mormon Church (officially: the Church of Jesus Christ of Latter-Day Saints) is considered in discussions about religious fundamentalism, and that is the main reason why it has been included in this volume.

Although all authors in this volume agree on a number of characteristics deemed typical of religious fundamentalism in general, the emphasis depends largely on the exact context in which the phenomenon has emerged. Sharifah Zaleha, for example, drawing on her knowledge and experience of Malaysia, underlines the significance of Islamic fundament-alism as a cultural ideology that advocates a rediscovery of the Islamic past. The notion of the Islamic past is a particularly important one, as the rise of Islamic fundamentalism in Malaysia has to be considered in the context of British colonial rule and related Western cultural domination. The re-orientation of culture along Islamic lines, she argues, has provided a new framework for Malaysian society. The importance of reconstructing cultural identity is underlined by other authors in this book, such as Seneviratne, who shows how in the Buddhist context of Sri Lanka religious fundamentalism has become a modern phenomenon which easily connects to aspects of identity, in this case of the Sinhala majority population. Here, too, religious fundamentalism is described as the tragic culmination of processes related to colonial domination and Western superiority.

Another general element of religious fundamentalism is its objective of empowering people, usually in ways that do not conform to established interests. Empowerment is often based on memories of a glorious past, whether historically accurate or mythical, which are projected into the future and believed to be within reach through transformative action. One reason for the successful implementation of fundamentalist agendas is a deep sense of commitment, generated and sustained through religious ideo-logy. Religious imagery is crucial to such an ideology, which accounts for believers' ability to imagine another world qualitatively different from the present one. The moral foundation for such an alternative society is sought in the past, to be projected onto the future through the present. Although not free from millenarian inclinations, the present is the arena in which the fundamentalist agenda has to be fought.

This process has contributed to myth-formation and a misguided idea about events of the past. In his analysis of the fundamentalization of Bud-dhism in modern Sri Lanka, Seneviratne demonstrates, for example, how the empowerment of Buddhist monks through the reformist ideology of the nineteenth-century religious thinker Anagarika Dharmapala was in fact based on an illusion, as real power in the past lay in the hands of a govern-ing secular elite. He also points to some of the effects of Dharmapala's utopian empowerment project, which has led in effect to many of the social and political ills apparent in Sri Lanka today. Yet, myth formation among religious fundamentalists may also be based on a degree of histori-cal accuracy, as various chapters in this volume show.

An important tool in the empowerment project that seems part of the fundamentalist agenda is its organizational structure. Telling examples are the cases of Malaysia and North America discussed in this volume, where the basic social unit for the effective functioning of religious fundamentalists is the congregation or congregational group. These are often loosely structured and able to act independently within a wider framework. Its political counterpart may be seen in the organization of independent 'cells', such as is believed to be the case with some Islamist networks, including that of the at present much-debated Al Qaeda network of Osama Bin Laden. Another notable aspect of the effectiveness of the fundamentalist agenda is the consideration given to developing practical strategies. This becomes particularly clear in the contributions concerning the participation of Malay women in public life and the successful strategies of Christian fundamentalists in North America, such as in the field of education. In fact, fundamentalist groups in various parts of the world are known for their provision of social and educational services, whether it is the *Shas* Party in Israel or the Muslim Brotherhood in Egypt, to quote only two examples.

It is notable that in African countries with a significant Muslim population fundamentalist groups, generally referred to as 'Islamists', have been particularly active in the areas of health and education, which has earned them a progressive reputation as agents of religious renewal and civil society. Here, the 'fundamentalist' problem may be analysed as an inter-generational conflict, whereby a new Muslim elite challenges the legitimacy of power wielded by an older generation held responsible for various forms of corruption and decay.[15] As elsewhere, so-called fundamentalist movements in Africa are largely led by educated young people, most of whom are only recently urbanized and themselves not necessarily marginal in society. The Islamic Salvation Front (FIS) in Algeria, which was effectively taken over by a younger generation in the 1990s, is an instructive example of such a model. At the same time, it is of interest to note the individual differences in strategies between countries. In Algeria, control of the broad Islamist movement by a new generation has been contested both through the ballot box and through armed insurgency; in Morocco, it happened through control of textual exegesis by modern means: the printed media instead of preaching in the mosque; in Nigeria, Islamist groups have promoted a new interpretation of texts while breaking with traditional community affiliations. In all cases, this has been a process of a younger generation by-passing or superseding old elites. In North Africa in particular, these strategies aim at securing a position for the young new elite within the existing system, rather than aiming at its destruction.[16]

Finally, it is important to realize that fundamentalism is not an instant phenomenon, but a process that develops over time. Fundamentalisms have histories that can be reconstructed, as is demonstrated in this book. An illustrative case is Mormonism. Drawing upon a classical definition of fundamentalism, Van Beek demonstrates how the seeds of fundamentalism were always present in Mormonism, from its very beginnings to the present day. Two trajectories or 'pathways' can be distinguished in that process: a mainstream of Mormon fundamentalization and what is known as a 'second order' fundamentalization. Whereas the first of these paths transformed Mormonism from a church into a modern fundamentalist corporation, often referred to as the 'Mormon corporate empire', the second and narrower path led to a schismatic church reflecting many of the characteristics usually ascribed to fundamentalist movements, notably its discourse on the past and its rejection of modernity. This example also shows that there is no historical determinism at work in such a process, but that different options are open at all times. Everything depends on the specific context and the way in which the various elements that make up a fundamentalist pattern form themselves in it. It is through these elements that the actual outcomes are decided.

Women, human rights and social change

There are a number of recurrent themes in this book, all reflecting major concerns in the debate on religious fundamentalism. Among the most important of these are the position of women according to any fundamentalist ideology and the issue of human rights. Both matters bear a relation to the concept of modernization which, as we have seen, is what at heart motivates the fundamentalist response. Whereas until recently the position of women in most societies, including Western ones, was fixed according to norms and standards which prescribed separate roles for men and women, this has dramatically changed in modern times. In regard to human rights, the 1948 United Nations Universal Declaration of Human Rights has effected an irreversible change. In both cases, there are fundamentalists who appeal to traditional culture, imagined or real, to reverse the processes of change that have placed these issues high on the international agenda today. A most dramatic example is the case of women under the Taliban regime in Afghanistan.

The effect of the fundamentalists' agenda on women in individual countries is an important sub-theme in this book. Several writers have paid attention to it in their discussion of fundamentalist trends in particular religious traditions. In many cases women are excluded from public life by enforced seclusion, based on conservative notions of women's roles in public life and related to religiously grounded ideas about female modesty, decency and purity. Defining fundamentalism as 'a fidelity, often rigid, to religious tradition, ideology or sacred text and the literal (or extremely strict) interpretation of such text', Alice Shalvi shows how the legal enforcement of gender roles, entailing the subordination of women, is a notable characteristic of Jewish fundamentalism.[17] The rigid application of sacred texts, in this case notably the *Torah* and the *Talmud*, and the strict adherence to Jewish tradition advocated by orthodox Jews, severely limit women in their actions. Yet, and rather paradoxically, it appears that orthodox Jewish women have found a way to turn their exclusion into an advantage by using the privacy of their homes to catch up with modern times. Working from home, they use modern means of communication to engage in studies in such a way that their relative isolation gives them access to modern technologies in advance of their husbands. Zaleha demonstrates a somewhat similar process for Muslim women in Malaysia. In this case, rather unusually, religious fundamentalists do not require women to live a secluded life even though they believe, like their counterparts in other religions, that the domestic sphere is women's natural environment. Instead, fundamentalists in Malaysia have engaged in a process of redefining the position of women, both within and outside the domestic sphere. Women's relative freedom in Malaysia to participate in the debate about their proper role in society and to find their own way has had a positive effect on society as a whole, contributing to the country's development. These examples show how at times fundamentalists, who are predominantly but not exclusively men, may make use of traditional resources to improve the status of women.

Muslim women in Malaysia, as we saw, have not been obliged to withdraw from the public sphere and can in fact be found in influential positions in public life. Many have voluntarily adopted the veil as a sign of pride in their own, Islamic, culture. A similar case can be made for women in some Muslim countries in Africa, where it has equally been argued that fundamentalist movements, such as the *izala* movement in Nigeria, enable women to gain access to public space by adopting Islamic dress. In doing so, for example, they may demand the application of *Shari'a* in order to be able to inherit property, work outside the home, or engage in trade.[18] The examples show how varied different types of fundamentalism are, and how differently they may affect the position of women.

By its very nature, however, religious fundamentalism tends to be patriarchal and androcentric, as various authors in this volume demonstrate, and determined by existing power relations. This also has a bearing on human rights, as An-Na'im and Appleby show. In the same way in which he rejects any claims to religious exceptionalism, An-Na'im also rejects any form of exceptionalism in matters of human rights, whether religious or otherwise. In the case of Islamic fundamentalism, for example, women's rights are not considered as human rights; hence women's right to self-determination is constantly violated. This is ironic, for it undermines the legitimate argument that Islamic peoples have a right to self-determination. The same concern applies to religious minorities, whose members run a serious risk of violation of their basic rights, as the examples of fundamentalist responses in India and Sri Lanka notably demonstrate. Yet, as Appleby shows, there is a great potential for peace in the world's religious traditions. He particularly points to the capacity of progressive thinkers and scholars within their own traditions to transform popular attitudes towards the 'Other' and the inherent implications of such evolution of popular attitudes for conflict resolution.[19] The construction of the 'Other' has proved at many times in history a major condition for the most serious violations of human rights, whether religiously or politically motivated.[20]

The main point at issue in the human rights debate, as has often been pointed out, lies in the contrast between a basically secular and a basically religious worldview of people in various parts of the world. A religious view is one that acknowledges the existence of an invisible sphere, distinguished but not separated from the visible one, and believes in its effective power in human life. For a worldwide inculturation of human rights it is vital to take the religious worldview of people into serious account and to find a way to overcome the historical divide in the development of human rights thought and practice. I am referring to the difference between a secular and religious foundation of human rights, a distinction that has become acute since the adoption of the Universal Declaration. An-Na'im in particular has always been adamant that we have no choice but to accept religious discourse, in whatever way it may express itself, since it is a reality for the vast majority of people whose thoughts we want to influence. He argues that if we do not take a stand on religious grounds in favour of human rights, that stand will be taken *against* human rights on grounds which resonate most with believers of respective faith communities.[21] One important condition for successful human rights campaigning is not only to become acquainted with people's views, but also to try and understand the rationale behind them. Today this applies rather urgently to so-called religious fundamentalists.

It is notably in cases where religious fundamentalists seek to further their agenda by violent means that the issue of human rights becomes a burning one. Militancy, we noted already, is an important characteristic of fundamentalist strategies generally, often based on the exclusive claims of specific groups at the expense of other groups. Religious intolerance is only one of the effects of religious exclusivism, the latter being an inherent feature of Christianity and Islam especially, which have been rivals for centuries, but also of Judaism and Buddhism, as the examples in this volume show. Religious exclusivism and its resulting hegemonistic claims are attached particularly to the so-called world religions. Their claim to universality has traditionally been reflected in a missionary zeal and the concomitant need to spread outside their place of origin. This stands in stark contrast with another trend within the world's religions, generally known as traditional or community religions, which are essentially inclusive in nature.[22] They are traditionally characterized by their lack of motivation to broaden their appeal outside the community in which they originally emerged.

This does not mean that traditional religions lack the ability to incorporate newcomers within the community of believers. Rather, the opposite is the case: precisely because they lack a written dogma such religions are usually open in character, very flexible and adaptable, prepared not only to make room for others, but also to actually offer space for this purpose. This is true of people, but above all of ideas, reflecting an attitude conducive to religious tolerance. However, a current process of revitalization of traditional religions has led to the adoption of a number of characteristics which seem to reverse such a trend.[23] The important distinction between an exclusivist and inclusivist approach in religion is also noted by Ram-Prasad when describing some of the changes in Hindu thought that have given rise to acts of violence in recent years. The tendency for religious believers to move from an inclusivist to an exclusivist approach, even where this was traditionally not the case, is perhaps one of the most regrettable consequences of modern social change.

A summary of contents

The order in which the various chapters are presented in this book follows a certain logic. The volume opens with a discussion by Abdullahi An-Na'im of what is seen today as the most significant manifestation of religious fundamentalism and hence the most debated one, namely Islamic fundamentalism. It is followed by Sharifah Zaleha's discussion of the role of women in Islamic fundamentalism, which may be compared with that of women in Jewish fundamentalism as described and analysed by Alice Shalvi. Nancy Ammerman continues with a historical analysis of Christian fundamentalism particularly in the United States, followed by a discussion of the Mormon offshoot of Christianity by Walter van Beek. H.L. Seneviratne and Chakravarhi Ram-Prasad then discuss fundamentalist trends in Buddhism and Hinduism respectively. R. Scott Appleby draws elements of the discussion together, with a special focus on the issue of human rights, one of the main issues of our time. With his attention for human rights he concludes the discussion on the same note as An-Na'im, whose biography he takes as an example of the fundamental compatibility of religion and human rights. In a conclusion James J. Busuttil applies some of the theoretical insights for policy purposes, drawing on the extensive discussions held at a series of expert meetings forming part of the lecture series that gave rise to this volume.

The following contains a short summary of the individual contributions to this volume. Abdullahi An-Na'im in Chapter 2 applies to Islam the idea of fundamentalism, a term he considers appropriate in this context for reasons he explains and illustrates. In fact, he argues, there is nothing new under the sun, and it would be a mistake to consider fundamentalism as constituting a historical rupture. Rather than looking at fundamentalism as a typically religious phenomenon, An-Na'im advocates an analysis of it as a social movement. Social movements inspired or motivated by religious ideology are of all times and places. Although different in motivation and inspiration, in their actions they may be usefully compared with other social movements working in the same or similar conditions. In all cases, An-Na'im argues, such movements are both products and agents of social change in the Islamic societies and communities where they emerge.

As he has made clear on many occasions, An-Na'im does not accept any form of, or claim to, exceptionalism on religious grounds, whether this concerns Islam or any other religious or cultural expression. None of these, he argues as a matter of principle, can be considered so important as to defy general principles of social and political life. Rather than taking a particular situation for granted, we should take a close look at the context in which fundamentalist movements operate with a view to exploring possibilities for transformation which are informed by thorough analysis. In his own study he is primarily concerned with the theoretical question whether Islamic fundamentalism is consistent with its own claims of exclusive representation of Islamic identity, political system and legal order. In his critical analysis he also warns against dismissing Islamic fundamentalism as insignificant in the face of the global triumph of Western liberalism, or exaggerating it into a manifestation of permanent confrontation between Western and non-Western civilizations: it is 'neither the end of history nor a clash of civilizations'. Instead, he proposes a view of Islamic fundamentalism as the legitimate expression of the right to self-determination of Muslim peoples. This is qualified, however, because like any other rights, this is subject to the rights of others. Sudan, his own homeland, is a case in point.

In the final analysis, in which human rights are central, An-Na'im offers a 'framework for constructive interdependence' which seeks and allows for active participation of Islamic fundamentalists, with appreciation for their specific contribution, and provides the full protection of human rights. An-Na'im's approach is an expression of the need to try and solve the human rights dilemma through a new and inclusive interpretation of Islam. Such efforts have to be made from within; they can only be supported from outside. His suggestion to mediate the conflict between the two through the development of a tripartite relationship in terms of synergy and interdependence is not only intellectually creative, but also workable. It offers a new paradigm at a time when this seems most needed.

Sharifah Zaleha in Chapter 3 discusses the role of women in the Islamic reawakening that has taken place in Malaysia in recent times. When this started in the 1970s, it was not the first time that Muslim believers had felt a need to look back to the past to find guidelines for the future. This also happened during colonial times, in the 1920s, when an orthodox Islam emerged in response to the influence of religious modernists. Although the two waves of Islamic fundamentalism in Malaysia – the first one during the 1920s and the second one starting in the 1970s – were rather different in their origins and effects, they both shared a felt need to re-awaken Malaysian society, and notably that part of Malay ethnic origin, to its indigenous Islamic heritage.

The Islamic revival of the 1970s, popularly referred to as *dakwah* or 'to invite one' to Islam, took place at a time of radical social change, including processes of industrialization, urbanization and democratization. These processes of modernization, which arose from British colonial rule, had a profound effect on the role of women in Malaysian society. Zaleha explores the precise nature of this type of social change on different groups of Malay women and on their strategies for participation in public life. As in other Muslim countries, 'the woman question' featured prominently in the fundamentalists' discourse, notably in relation to issues of morality and cultural identity. In that sense, the women's issue formed part of a much wider concern regarding Western domination.

The debate concerning the role of women concentrated on three issues: their personal appearance, their role in public, and their religious contribution. Politics also played its part in this respect, as both the government and political parties contributed to the spread of fundamentalist ideology. Religious activists, including both men and women, engaged in a process of redefining Islamic womanhood. One interesting result was the voluntary 'veiling' of significant numbers of women in rural and urban areas and irrespective of education or other social indicators. For the younger generation of Malay women, who had not lived under colonial rule, veiling was a sign of the pride they took in their own culture, in contrast to that of non-Malays. Unlike in other Muslim countries, Malaysian fundamentalists did not call for women to withdraw from the public sphere. Instead, they encouraged a public debate on the type of activities deemed proper for women. Although the domestic sphere was generally seen as befitting women most, opinions differed with regard to outside employment. In actual fact, therefore, Malay women are free to work outside the home and, due to their increased participation in formal education, we find a significant proportion of women in high positions.

In the realm of religion the situation is rather different, as women have traditionally been excluded from leading positions. However, given the fundamentalists' need to promote Islam, women have become more involved in activities geared to proselytization. As a result, there are active women's sections of fundamentalist movements, often comprising well-educated and professional women, who take the lead in public awareness programmes concerning important social issues, such as with regard to development or youth. Women religious activists, Zaleha argues, are facing new challenges of how to balance the need to assert Islamic woman-hood, reaffirm the progressive elements of Islamic culture in such matters, and create a democratic and just society for women. An interesting new development in this respect is the emergence of a new women's group, *Wanita* JIM, which calls itself 'fundamentalist *and* contemporary', described by Zalefa as a 'reform-minded Islamist feminist group'. It is yet another expression of fundamentalism's modern touch. In today's Malaysia there exists a great variety of Islamic expressions, of an inclusive rather than an exclusive nature. For Muslim women in Malaysia, this is clearly good news.

It is interesting to compare the situation of Muslim women in Malaysia with the experiences of Jewish women in the state of Israel, described by Alice Shalvi in Chapter 4 as a conservative quasi-secular state. Although women have enjoyed equal civil rights since the foundation of the state in 1948, in practice, religious law governs public life in Israel. As a consequence, women are generally discriminated against, since they are denied equal access to the opportunities singled out for men and made to conform to religious law, even if they are not religiously observant. Discriminatory practices, however, mostly affect women from the different orthodox communities that represent modern Jewish fundamentalism.

Jewish fundamentalism, as defined by Shalvi, is not new. Historical research, she argues, reveals recurrent revivals. Contemporary Jewish fundamentalism is just another phase in a centuries-long history. What makes the present phase different, though, is the influence of the late eighteenth-century Enlightenment and the emancipation of Jews in Europe. These two factors, as Shalvi shows, have changed the face of Jewish society and affected the specific expression of Jewish fundamentalism. As a result, modern Israel is a land full of contradictions and paradoxes, which she scrutinizes as these apply to women. While the world will remember Prime Minister Golda Meir as one of the few examples of female political leadership in the world, it may not be aware that at the same time ultra-orthodox rabbis could forbid women in their communities from voting. Or, to quote another paradox, while the secular court system includes several women judges today, not a single woman can be found in the rabbinical courts that regulate much of Jewish life.

But, as Shalvi shows, there is light at the end of the tunnel. In recent years, new skills have equipped women with the knowledge and opportunities to reinterpret Jewish law and practice in such a way as to enable a fruitful blending of tradition and modernity. Through modern means of communication, women from Orthodox communities are able to enter the labour market from the seclusion of their homes. Here we find another paradox: while their menfolk are still concentrating on ancient Jewish texts, Orthodox women have been able to equip themselves with modern technical skills and thus have overtaken their husbands, being much better equipped to deal with the modern world as a result.

Nancy Ammerman in Chapter 5 traces the background and history of Christian fundamentalism, notably in North America. She considers Christian fundamentalism as a response to the situation of disrupted tradition, a typical context for the rise of fundamentalist movements worldwide. She describes and analyses the content of the disruptive change caused by the process of modernization, which provides a challenge to the presuppositions of religious faith.

Rather importantly, she points out that the use of violence which is often connected with the rise of fundamentalist movements is marginal to the life of the movement she describes. She notes how the founding of the organization most representative of this trend in the United States in modern times, known by its own choice as the Moral Majority, coincided with the 1979 Islamic revolution in Iran, widely considered to mark the beginning of a worldwide fundamentalist trend in Islam. In both cases, the world was clearly not prepared for these developments. In America, Ammerman makes clear that, not for the first time in history, this is due to the historical neglect of facts or developments which do not fit easily into the dominant ideology. Although the original movement which gave fundamentalists their name has disappeared, Christian fundamentalism as such has never gone away. While public attention was directed elsewhere, fundamentalist Christians continued building their networks and structures, slowly but steadily.

Their greatest achievement lies in their successful use of modern media, in which they have played a pioneering role. This fits with Ammerman's emphasis on the rhetorical character of fundamentalism, which provides a helpful approach to the understanding of the phenomenon in its broader setting. Fundamentalists generally engage in a number of distinct discourses, notably including a rhetoric of tradition, a rhetoric of boundaries, and a rhetoric of transformation. These 'rhetorical strategies', as Ammerman calls them, allowed for the mobilization of Americans to bring about a type of change in conformity with the doctrines underlying strategies that are not only modern, but also flexible and capable of responding to changing political conditions. For example, the ending of the Cold War, which occupied an essential place in Christian fundamentalist thought, deprived it of its political enemy but at the same time opened new horizons for spreading the fundamentalist message to hitherto inaccessible areas. The successful implementation of fundamentalist strategies makes it important to consider what these are, because, as Ammerman points out, fundamentalists tap a rich vein of social discontent. It would therefore be a mistake to ignore or dismiss them.

Walter van Beek in Chapter 6 presents an unusual case of Christian fundamentalism. Mormonism was originally an American movement that emerged in the nineteenth century, but it has now made inroads worldwide. Its peculiarity (a self-chosen label) lies primarily in two specific aspects that used to characterize the life of the church: commonality and polygamy. For fundamentalist Mormons, who have fallen outside mainstream Mormonism, both aspects are still characteristic of their social and religious life today.

Van Beek draws attention to the '*hijra*-exodus' pattern of Mormon fundamentalism, exemplifying some of the important traits of Christian fundamentalism as discussed in the previous chapter. The rhetorics of tradition, boundaries and transformation can all be found in the history of the Mormon Church, even though they express themselves in a different way from the Moral Majority. Withdrawal and isolation have been the most important strategies for persistent Mormon fundamentalists, in contrast with the adaptation and assimilation strategy of mainstream Mormonism. The paradoxical character of the movement is evident, showing a religious creativity and imagination that are not normally associated with fundamentalism. This is illustrated by a discussion of polygamy or 'plural marriage' in Mormon parlance, originally a central tenet of Mormon doctrine and belief.

Although nineteenth-century Mormonism cannot simply be identified with fundamentalism, as Van Beek shows, some crucial elements were always present. Questions of authority, identity and morality, which are major areas of concern for most, if not all, fundamentalist believers, have been central to Mormon doctrine and practice from the outset. The 'peculiarity' of the Mormon case lay in the way these were moulded and how the results subsequently shaped Mormons' relations with the outside world. Van Beek suggests that it was the political conflict over the foundation of a Mormon theocracy which instigated an actual process of fundamentalization within the movement. He distinguishes a 'first-order' fundamentalization of mainstream Mormonism, and a 'second-order' fundamentalization of some minority groups. While the former is responsible for the growth of Mormonism as a 'fundamentalist corporative empire', the latter has opted for the community as social model and authoritative structure.

H.L. Seneviratne in Chapter 7 discusses the fundamentalization of Buddhism, notably in Sri Lanka, a process in which the role of the Buddhist monk has been of crucial importance. Although the term 'fundamentalism' is problematic in describing Buddhist belief, Seneviratne feels it may be applied in conformity with the general approach which has gained currency in recent years. In this new sense, he argues, religious fundamentalism as a phenomenon easily fades into expressions of group identity, often defined in ethnic, linguistic or regional terms. As an expression of cultural, ethnic and religious–nationalist tendencies, the term 'fundamentalism' may be applied to explain hegemonistic tendencies in Sri Lanka, which are borne by religious sentiments and exclusivist claims. Buddhism in contemporary Sri Lanka exhibits certain traits of fundamentalism in that it strives for the restoration of a utopian past which it sees in Buddhism's beginnings but which in fact, as Seneviratne persuasively shows, is an early twentieth-century invention by the great reformer Anagarika Dharmapala, whose re-definition of the role of the Buddhist monk has been central to the process of fundamentalization in Sri Lanka.

Seneviratne elucidates developments in Sri Lanka by comparing these with Burma and Thailand, which all belong to the same school of *Theravada* Buddhism. The comparison suggests a connection between the emergence of fundamentalist tendencies and the changes that stem from the colonial experience. A religious revival, inspired by Sri Lanka, also occurred in Burma, where the Buddhist clergy became politically active but were later curbed by a military dictatorship. In Thailand, which lacks the colonial experience of Burma and Sri Lanka, Buddhist monks have remained consistently under the political control of the state.

This comparative discussion is illuminating in that it brings out the special character of Buddhist change in Sri Lanka and the central role of the Buddhist clergy. The relationship of the community of monks with the state, Seneviratne shows, is a historical one, although its present form is very recent. To prove his point he explores in depth the change in the role of the Buddhist monk in Sri Lanka under the influence of Dharmapala. This took two directions, one giving rise to the 'pragmatic' Vidyodaya monks, the other to the 'ideological' monks of Vidyalankara. It is the latter trend which has been instrumental in creating a Buddhist fundamentalism in Sri Lanka. The most serious consequence has been the politicization of the monastic calling, and the ensuing identification of Buddhism with the majority population on the island, the Sinhala ethnic group. This leaves no legitimate place for minority groups, unless, as Seneviratne points out, they submit themselves to the hegemony of the Sinhala Buddhists. Today Sinhala is the official language of Sri Lanka and Buddhism in effect is its state religion. The country's ethnic violence has to be understood in this light. But, as Seneviratne also indicates, there are increasing pressures on the Sinhalese majority to return to more tolerant policies, which may arrest or even reverse the current process of fundamentalization.

In Chapter 8 Chakravarthi Ram-Prasad discusses comparable processes of 'fundamentalization' within Hinduism in India. The modern ideology of *Hindutva* is usually referred to in this way, at least in the West. Ram-Prasad, however, considers this an inadequate and unhelpful label to understand modern developments in India. In his chapter, he explains in detail the role and the consequences of Hindu religious thought in the Indian polity, based on his study of the social changes in India that created the conditions for the development of the *Hindutva* ideology. Although derived from Hindu religious thought, *Hindutva* (meaning 'Hinduness'), Ram-Prasad suggests, is best understood as a form of cultural essentialism with nationalist goals. Given the character of both Hindu religious traditions and Hindu nationalism, *Hindutva* can be appropriately understood as a political ideology which builds on the modern Hindu notion of a uniquely Hindu principle of plurality. It is an ideology which identifies Hinduism with the people of the nation–state of India, thus, rather paradoxically, incorporating religious minorities such as Muslims and Christians. To explain *Hindutva*'s hegemonistic claims, Ram-Prasad first relates the history of religious and social change in India, going back to pre-Islamic times. The arrival and presence of Islam have had a crucial influence on the development of *Hindutva* as a nationalist ideology, with British colonialism doing the rest. The latter's attempt to construct a specific Indian identity has not only facilitated *Hindutva* ideology but also helped define its policies towards religious minorities, or in other words non-Hindus.

Ram-Prasad goes on to detail the political history of *Hindutva*, in which the ruling *Bharatiya Janata* Party (BJP) plays a central part, as a requirement for understanding the significance of Hindu nationalism today. He argues that the growth of the BJP, and thus of 'fundamentalist' sentiments, must be ascribed to the failure of the populist strategies of the Indira Gandhi government during the late 1970s, which entailed a reallocation of resources on political grounds, thus creating resentment among the so-called Forward Castes. The *Hindutva* movement skilfully exploited these political failures in the 1980s and 1990s through a form of counter-populism, which in its origins had nothing to do with religious sentiment. One result of this was an explosion of violence, which drew the attention of the world to *Hindutva* ideology and strategy as promoted by Hindu nationalists.

Rather importantly, Ram-Prasad also notes how the realities of Indian politics force Hindu nationalists into a form of pragmatism which effectively constrains their ideological aims. Hindu nationalism, he argues, is essentially motivated by the anxieties and the ambitions of the urban middle class, on the one hand, and a semi-urban and rural constituency, on the other. In both cases, this concerns India's scarce resources. If the material conditions of life improve, argues Ram-Prasad, there will be less pressure to interpret the country's economic conditions in terms of a religio-cultural ideology. In that case, the immediate catalysts for violence will be removed and communal violence hence be eliminated.

In Chapter 9 R. Scott Appleby focuses on the human rights dimension which is inevitable in any discussion of religious fundamentalism and, indeed, of religion more generally today. The spread of 'rights talk', starting in the 1960s, has continued up to this day, affecting all parts of the world. In this renewed discussion of human rights, religious leaders and scholars in particular have taken a critical look at the role of religion. When religion is implicated in situations of conflict, it is often seen to exacerbate rather that reduce passions. Appleby is interested in identifying and mobilizing the peace-building potential of religion, particularly in its organized form, through the community of believers. This is not an easy task, he argues, given the internal and external opposition faced by religious institutions and actors who serve as agents of human rights.

It is easy for religious extremists to destabilize a country, even when they are few in numbers. That makes it all the more urgent, as Appleby suggests, not to simply assume that fundamentalism is basically the same wherever it appears. Instead, we need to study its manifestations one case at a time. Used properly, he argues, the label 'fundamentalism' refers to an identifiable pattern of religious militancy, whose common characteristics he identifies. The salient characteristic of fundamentalism, he believes, is its concern with religious erosion, the response to which may vary greatly, as can be seen throughout the book. In the environments this creates religious actors are uniquely placed to engage in the debate on human rights and to mediate in the encounter between universal and culture-specific elements.

This leads Appleby into a discussion of the universality of moral values, agreement upon the existence of which, he maintains, is a minimum requirement for the functioning of an international legal order. He suggests a middle course between a thoughtless universalism and a narrow-minded culturalism, in order to enhance participation of cultural and religious groups in the formulation of shared moral values. There is an important role in this respect to be played by the religious elites that lead their communities. These elites can, and should, assist their followers in the necessary process of inculturation of universal rights. Appleby rightly puts some of the responsibility also on secular human rights organizations which, through their neglect of religion, have often contributed to strengthening exclusivist tendencies within religious communities. He illustrates his argument with a discussion of various tendencies within Islam, which may vary from religious extremist to extreme liberalist. Strengthening of liberal tendencies in religion has to come principally from within, but if and when that happens, significant progress will be made towards the building of a transcultural regime of human rights. Appleby further reminds us that the location of the human rights idea in humanity itself, rather than in specific cultures and religions, establishes in fact a helpful framework for inter-religious dialogue on human rights. At the core of any human rights regimes, he believes, are religious human rights, most notably religious freedom. Although we should not be blind to the sometimes serious problems this may entail, such as those related to proselytization, that should not be an excuse to reduce such rights. Rather, it should stimulate our efforts to explore and exploit the potentials for peace which are inherent in the same freedom.

In a final contribution, James J. Busuttil in Chapter 10 reflects on the policy implications of the discussions in previous chapters. Attached to this as an Appendix are the papers with policy observations by the individual authors to this volume, as originally produced for discussion in the series of expert meetings held at the Institute of Social Studies in April–May 2000. As Busuttil points out, the aim of this project is not to theorize for academic purposes only, but to show the relevance of academic analysis for those who are called upon to formulate policies in response to the existence and growth of fundamentalist movements.

Conclusion

Religious fundamentalism has gained new attention from the dramatic events during and following the attack on the World Trade Center in New York and the Pentagon in Washington on 11 September 2001. Rightly or wrongly, the fact remains that many people associate these events with a certain type of religious belief. This popular perception shows once more the need for a careful and context-relevant analysis of the role of religion in relation to political violence. It further demonstrates the need for a careful use of terms in the debate on religion and politics. The term 'fundamentalism' should be applied thoughtfully and responsibly, by academics more than anyone. A scholarly use of the term does not always coincide with its popular (or journalistic) use and, if care is not taken, it may confuse rather than illuminate the matter. In this volume, I hope this important scholarly objective has been achieved.

Notes

1 See Chapter 5 in this volume by Ammerman.
2 This idea was notably advanced by Samuel Huntington in his controversial essay 'The clash of civilizations?', *Foreign Affairs*, vol. 72, no. 3, 1993, pp. 22–49. He later elaborated his argument in book form, *The Clash of Civilizations and the Remaking of the World Order*, New York: Simon & Schuster, 1996.
3 This can notably be observed in the independent states that emerged from the former Soviet Union. See, for example, John Witte, Jr and Michael Bourdeaux (eds) *Proselytism and Orthodoxy in Russia: The New War for Souls*, Maryknoll, New York: Orbis Books, 1999.
4 See in this volume Ammerman, p. 94.
5 Mohamed Tozy, 'Movements of religious renewal', in Stephen Ellis (ed.) *Africa Now: People, Policies and Institutions*, London: James Currey, 1996, p. 62.
6 See in this volume pp. 68–9.
7 See *The Guardian*, 20 November 1997.
8 See notably Chapters 7 and 8 in this volume by Seneviratne and Ram-Prasad.
9 See in this volume Shalvi, p. 84.
10 See in this volume p. 200.
11 Martin E. Marty and R. Scott Appleby edited in the early 1990s a series of five volumes on various aspects of fundamentalism, all published by The University of Chicago Press: *Fundamentalisms Observed, Fundamentalisms and Society, Fundamentalisms and the State, Accounting for Fundamentalisms* and *Fundamentals Comprehended*.

12 See in this volume p. 200.
13 See Grace Nyatugah Wamue, 'Revisiting our indigenous shrines through *Mungiki*', *African Affairs*, vol. 100, no. 400, July 2001, pp. 455–67. Compare in this context also Van Beek's reference to the concept of 'the living prophet' on pp. 117–18 of this volume.
14 See in this volume p. 116.
15 Tozy, 'Movements of religious renewal', pp. 58–74.
16 Ibid., especially p. 66.
17 See in this volume p. 76.
18 Tozy, 'Movements of religious renewal', p. 71.
19 See in this volume pp. 220–3.
20 Gerrie ter Haar, *Rats, Cockroaches and People Like Us: Views of Humanity and Human Rights*, The Hague: Institute of Social Studies, 2000.
21 Statement made at an interfaith panel organized during a meeting in May 1994 convened by the Project on Religion and Human Rights. See John Kelsay and Sumner B. Twiss (eds.) *Religion and Human Rights*, New York: The Project on Religion and Human Rights, 1995, p. 89.
22 I have argued this in more detail in Gerrie ter Haar, *World Religions and Community Religions: Where Does Africa Fit In?*, Occasional Paper, Centre of African Studies, University of Copenhagen, 2000.
23 Rosalind Hackett has researched this in the context of Africa, notably Nigeria. See her 'Revitalization in African traditional religion', in Jacob K. Olupona (ed.) *African Traditional Religions in Contemporary Society*, New York: Paragon House, 1991, pp. 135–49.

2

ISLAMIC FUNDAMENTALISM AND SOCIAL CHANGE

Neither the 'end of history' nor a 'clash of civilizations'

Abdullahi Ahmed An-Na'im

Islamic fundamentalist movements are neither new, prevalent nor permanent in Islamic societies. While these movements tend to draw on Islamic
sacred texts and historical traditions in articulating their vision for social
and political change and strategies of popular mobilization, fundamentalism is not the inevitable outcome of those resources. In my view, this
phenomenon should be understood as an indigenous spontaneous response
to profound social, political and economic crises, rather than either pre-
dominant among Islamic societies at any given point in time, or permanent
where it does occur. Like other social movements, Islamic fundamentalism
is a product of the interaction of certain internal and external actors and
factors, and tends to evolve and adapt over time in response to changes in
its local and broader context and re-evaluation of its objectives and strategies. As such, fundamentalist movements should be seen as both products
and agents of social change in Islamic societies and communities. These
movements emerge as a result of certain configurations of factors and
processes in each case, and seek to influence the course of events in favour
of their own social and political objectives.

It should be noted from the outset that there are many approaches to
studying what I define below as 'Islamic fundamentalism'. Some scholars
seek to understand this phenomenon in a historical context, highlight its
policy or security implication, or attempt to predict its demise or decline. I
am not seeking to contribute to these types of analysis, whether in agreement or disagreement. Rather, I am concerned here with the normative
and empirical issues raised by the claim that Islamic fundamentalism is a

legitimate and sustainable expression of the right of Muslim peoples to self-determination.

The premise of this chapter is that Islamic societies are subject to the same principles of social and political life that apply to other human societies. Whether individually or collectively, Muslims strive to secure the same basic needs for food and shelter, security, political stability and so forth, like all other human beings. They also seek to do so under the same or similar conditions, which prevail among all human societies and communities, including the imperatives of social change and adaptation in response to developments affecting individual and collective lives. It is true that social change in Islamic communities is influenced by prevailing understandings of Islam and its role in the public and private life of believers, but that also applies to other believers in relation to their own religious and cultural systems. While the characteristic features of Islam as a religion will affect the ways in which it is understood and practised by Muslims in different settings, that is not so exceptional as to defy the principles of social and political life of human societies in relation to their own religious or cultural frame of reference. In fact, I suggest, some Islamic communities in the Indian sub-continent, for instance, may have more in common with non-Islamic communities of the region who share the same or similar history, colonial experiences and present context, than with Islamic communities of Sub-Saharan Africa with their different experiences and context.

Accordingly, Islamic fundamentalist movements can and should be understood in the light of insights gained from the experiences of other social and political movements, especially those emerging in the same or similar context. In other words, whatever analyses have been developed and verified in relation to such movements in human societies at large is applicable to what might be called the Islamic variety. However, a general principle that has emerged and been verified in this way is that due regard must be taken of such factors as the nature, rationale, membership and so forth, of the particular movement. As I believe is illustrated by events in Sudan briefly discussed below, tactical adjustments in the declared objectives or strategies of an Islamic fundamentalist movement will probably have lasting significant consequences for its ideology and practice, as has happened with other religious or ideological movements. But what can be concluded or predicted in relation to this movement is relative to its specific nature and context, as is true for other social and political movements around the world. This is the approach I recommend for understanding each Islamic fundamentalist movement in its own specific context, in order to appreciate its underlying causes, internal and external dynamics, as well as possibilities of transformation, instead of taking its present position and future direction for granted or casting them in terms of one rigid extreme or another.

In particular, as suggested in the title of this chapter, Islamic fundamentalism should neither be dismissed as insignificant in the face of the final global triumph of Western liberalism, nor exaggerated into a manifestation of permanent confrontation between so-called Western and non-Western civilizations.[1] This mediating perspective is critical for understanding the phenomenon in its specific historical context, whether for scholarly or policy purposes. In the present post-colonial context in particular, it is important to view Islamic fundamentalism as an expression of the right of Muslim peoples to self-determination through the strict observance of *Shari'a* (traditional formulations of the normative system of Islam),[2] whether through its application by the state, or informal communal compliance in social relations and personal life-style. From this perspective, the question is whether Islamic fundamentalism is consistent with its own claims of exclusive representation of Islamic identity, political system and legal order. This is the subject of this chapter, to be addressed from a primarily theoretical perspective, with a brief discussion of the case of Sudan to illustrate my analysis, while emphasizing that final conclusions require closer examination of each specific movement in its own context.

Subject to this caveat about the need for more contextualized analysis, the basic thesis of this chapter is that, despite its strong appeal to disadvantaged or disempowered local populations and the limited success some of these movements may have achieved in a few situations, Islamic fundamentalist movements are counter-productive to the extent that they fail to appreciate the dynamics of social change for their own communities or to develop appropriate responses. To properly appreciate the dynamics of social change, and develop appropriate responses, Islamic fundamentalists would need to drastically redefine and adapt their objectives and strategies in accordance with the present local and global realities of interdependence of all religious and political communities. This is what I call 'framework for constructive interdependence', whereby all religious, ideological, ethnic and other communities cooperate in securing each other's rights through a combination of critical appreciation of the right to self-determination, the protection of human rights at the national level and respect for the rule of law in international relations.

In the next section, I will present a brief clarification of the term 'fundamentalism' as applied to Islamic movements, and an overview of this phenomenon in the history of Islamic societies. In the following section, I will offer a critical evaluation of these movements as means for realizing the right of Muslim peoples to self-determination in the post-colonial context. The case of Sudan is discussed in the next section to illustrate some aspects of my analysis. The final section will be devoted to an elaboration of a proposed framework of constructive interdependence, and its national and international policy implications.

Fundamentalism in Islamic history

The term 'fundamentalism' was coined in the United States in the early decades of the twentieth century, to refer to a Protestant group who published a series of twelve pamphlets between 1910 and 1912 under the title, *The Fundamentals: A Testimony to the Truth*. There is much debate about the appropriateness of using this term, as a product of Western Christian experience, to describe various religio-political movements in the presumably very different context of Islamic societies. But the origin of the term should not preclude its application to movements in the Islamic, Jewish, Hindu or other religious traditions, if they share the same salient features and important traits. The following review of the comparative features of the Islamic variety of today is based on its 'ideal model' as envisioned by its founders from the 1920s to the 1960s.[3] This ideal model is hard to find today anywhere in the world,[4] though it remains the essential frame of reference for current Islamic fundamentalist movements. The drastic change in the nature and operation of these movements clearly illustrates one of the points I wish to make in this chapter, namely, the inevitability of the transformation of these movements as products and agents of social change.

The key characteristic of the American Protestant fundamentalist movement was its firm, principled and militant opposition to the inroads that modernism, liberalism and higher biblical criticism were making into the Protestant Churches, and the supposedly Bible-based culture of the United States at large. That movement called for the defence of a certain form of inherited religiosity, which is based on the literal and categorical belief in, and understanding of, the fundamentals of the Protestant faith. Islamic fundamentalists hold sufficiently similar beliefs in relation to Islam and the *Qur'an* to justify using the term 'fundamentalism' to identify their movements. Moreover, Islamic movements in North Africa and the Middle East do use the corresponding Arabic terms *usuli*, as adjective, and *usuliyya*, as noun (fundamentalist and fundamentalism), to describe themselves and their beliefs as part of a historical tradition that goes back ten centuries, and not as a recent translation of the American term. The call to affirm and implement the 'fundamentals' of the faith, as distinguished from its incidentals, is an established and recurrent theme in Islamic theological and political discourse, as can be seen from the title of a book by al-Ash'ari (died 935): *al-Ibanah 'an Usul al-Diyanah (The Elucidation of the Fundamentals of the Religion)*. Other scholars who emphasized this theme in their work include al-Ghazzali (died 1111), Ibn Taymiya (died 1328) and Ibn Abdel Wahhab (died 1787).

Islamic fundamentalists view themselves as the moral guardians and saviours of their societies, which they condemn as living in a state of apostasy, moral depravity and social decadence. They see Islamic history as one of decline and fall, to be rectified at their hands to achieve complete restoration and fulfilment of the divine design for all of humanity. Islamic fundamentalists also share with fundamentalists of other religions a profound mistrust of all notions of human progress, gradual evolution or historical development, as antithetical to divine action and intervention in the world. As the elect few, they see themselves entrusted with discovering and implementing the will of God through the literal reading of the *Qur'an*, which they hold to be manifestly clear, unambiguous and categorical, irrespective of the contingencies of time and place. In the name of upholding the absolute sovereignty of God on earth, which they claim to know and implement better than other believers, Islamic fundamentalists reject the idea of sovereignty of the people except as the expression of the will of God, as they understand it themselves. To them the state is simply the instrument of implementing the will of God as expressed in the *Qur'an*, not that of the people as reflected in secular constitutional instruments, or political and legal institutions and processes.

The Islamic legitimacy of the state has always been a cause of conflict and civil war since the death of the Prophet Muhammed in 632. The majority of *Sunni* Muslims believe the reign of the first four Caliphs of Medina (the seat of the first Muslim state, in western Arabia) to be an ideal Islamic state and community. But according to *Shi'a* Muslims, the first three of the Medina Caliphs were illegitimate usurpers of the position to which only Ali (the Prophet's cousin who became the fourth Caliph of Medina) and his descendants from Fatima (the Prophet's only surviving child) were entitled. Throughout his reign as the fourth Caliph (656–61), Ali was locked in bitter civil war against the *Umayyad* clan and other factions, including some of his own supporters, known as *al-Khawarij* (the breakaway group), who condemned him for accepting mediation with the *Umayyad*. Upon Ali's assassination by one of the *al-Khawarij* in 661, the *Umayyad* clan established a monarchy that ruled the expanding Muslim Empire from Damascus, Syria, until 750. The *Abbasid* launched their successful challenge to the *Umayyad* dynasty in the name of Islamic legitimacy, but the *Abbasid* state (750–1258) was also a monarchy that ruled from Baghdad, Iraq, more in accordance with political expediency than *Shari'a* principles. The same was true of the other states of various sizes and duration that ruled Islamic societies ever since: from Spain, North and West Africa, Central Asia to India, including the Ottoman Empire that was finally abolished in 1923–4.[5]

The tension between Islamic legitimacy and political expediency was usually mediated at different phases of history through mutual accommodation between *al-umara* (rulers) and *al-ulama* (scholars of *Shari'a*) whereby the former acknowledged the theoretical supremacy of *Shari'a* and the latter conceded the practical political authority of the rulers. Occasionally, some rulers professed commitment to more rigorous implementation of *Shari'a*, as happened during the early *Abbasid* dynasty, the *Ibadi Khariji* kingdom of Tlemsen, Morocco (761–909), *Almoravid* in Morocco and Spain (1056–1147), and the *Isma'ili Shi'a* Fatimate dynasty in parts of North Africa (969–1171). It is difficult to assess the scope and efficacy of those episodes of *Shari'a* application because of the lack of independent and sufficiently detailed historical sources. But it is reasonable to assume that the decentralized nature of the state and the administration of justice at those times in history would not have permitted a systematic and comprehensive application of *Shari'a* as demanded by Islamic fundamentalists in the modern context.

Recent examples of fundamentalist resurgence prior to the present cycle include what is known as the *jihad* movements of the Sahel region of Sub-Saharan Africa.[6] These movements initially began in dispersed places, gradually influenced each other, and culminated in regional campaigns to establish Islamic states. Early examples of *jihad* movements in West Africa include those of Nasir al-Din in Mauritania (1673–7), Malik Dauda Sy in Senegambia (1690s) and Ibrahim Musa, who was known as Karamoko Alfa (died 1751) in Futa Jallon. This movement eventually succeeded in setting up an Islamic state in 1776 under the leadership of Ibrahim Sori. The most successful and influential *jihad* movement in this region was the one initiated by Uthman Don Fodio (died 1817), who began his mission in 1774 and achieved significant military success by 1808. His movement went on to control most of what is now northern Nigeria and northern Cameroon by 1830. This movement, known as the Caliphate of Sokoto, spread to parts of southern Nigeria and Chad, in addition to influencing other *jihads* in Senegambia to the west. Other *jihad* movements in the region include that of al-Hajj Umar (died 1864) in the west, and Muhammad Ahmed 'al-Mahdi' (died 1885) along the Nile valley in the east.

As can be expected, *jihad* movements of the Sahel region of Sub-Saharan Africa varied greatly in their scope, intensity and consequences. Some movements lasted for several decades and succeeded in establishing centralized and effective Islamic states in parts of present-day Nigeria, Volta region, Ivory Coast and Guinea, while others were more in the nature of religious revival with little political or military success. The Islamic orientation of these movements also varied, as Islam for some of them was more of a mobilizing force than a religio-political programme. Some, like those of al-Hajj Umar and Samory Ture (died 1900) forbade dancing and the use of tobacco, alcohol and charms, prohibited pre-Islamic ceremonies and worship, and appointed Muslim scholars to enforce *Shari'a* even in non-Muslim areas under their control. But many *jihad* movements were uprisings of Muslim religious teachers and their followers against local military or landowning elite. While usually driven by local political, economic and security considerations, these *jihad* movements were also confronting the initial stages of European colonialism throughout the region. Like earlier cycles of Islamic fundamentalism, these African movements emerged in the context of societal crisis due to a combination of internal and external factors.

Despite the history of *jihad* movements and present crisis, there is little indication of fundamentalist resurgence in post-colonial Sub-Saharan Africa except in Sudan and Northern Nigeria. However, some Islamic societies may still produce fundamentalist movements in response to their own crisis, and in the name of the collective right of Muslims to self-determination. What does this mean, and can Islamic fundamentalist movements be effective agents of self-determination for their respective societies in the modern context?

The basic difficulty that has frustrated efforts to establish an Islamic state to effectively implement *Shari'a* has been the lack of political and legal institutions to ensure compliance by the state. While the *ulama* were supposed to be the guardians of *Shari'a*, they had no resort except appealing to the moral and religious sentiments of the rulers. Another factor was that the *ulama* were too concerned with safeguarding the unity of their communities and the maintenance of peace and public order to forcefully press their demands on rulers, especially in times of internal strife and external threat.[7] The few scholars who expressly addressed constitutional and legal matters in their writings, like al-Mawardi (died 1058) in *Al-Ahkam al-Sultaniya (Principles of Government)*, and Ibn Taymiya in *Al-Siyasa al-Shari'iya (Islamic Public Policy)* confined themselves to elaborations of what ought to happen, in the form of advice to the ruler, without addressing what should happen when the ruler failed to comply with the application of *Shari'a* as an obligation of the state. Consequently, those episodes of aspirations to an ideal state that would faithfully and impartially implement *Shari'a* as a total way of life were continuously frustrated by the realities of political expediency and security concerns. When the balance tilted too much in favour of the latter considerations, however, the intensity of demands for the application of *Shari'a* would rise, usually in the form of a local or regional fundamentalist movement.

Islamic fundamentalism as self-determination in the modern context

In this section I will elaborate on a few inter-related propositions regarding Islamic fundamentalism as self-determination. First, in my view, Islamic fundamentalists certainly have their own right to self-determination, and to propose themselves to lead their societies in this regard, but that cannot be at the expense of the rights of others, Muslims or non-Muslims alike. The right to self-determination can only be exercised within the framework of the protection of human rights at home, and in conformity with international law abroad. Therefore, to the extent that the ideology or practice of any Islamic fundamentalist movement is inconsistent with these principles, that movement would have to adapt to and comply with these requirements or lose its claim to exercise its own right to self-determination, let alone lead others in that regard. But the manner and dynamics of that internal transformation must be left to the movement itself, in accordance with their right to self-determination. In other words, what is at issue is how to mediate among competing claims to self-determination, and encouraging transformation within social movements themselves in order to facilitate such mediation.

Whatever may be the potential for resurgence of Islamic fundamentalism anywhere in Africa and Asia today, it is clear that the internal and external context within which claims of Islamic identity and self-determination are made today is radically different, in each case, from what it used to be in the pre-colonial era. A primary underlying cause of this transformation of local context in each case is that all Islamic societies are now constituted into nation–states, which are part of global political and economic systems.[8] They are all members of the United Nations and subject to international law, including universal human rights standards. None of these states is religiously homogeneous, politically insulated or economically independent from the non-Muslim world. Even countries that claim to be purely Islamic, like Saudi Arabia, are in fact parties to global economic, security, technological or other forms of interdependence with non-Muslim countries. While the precise consequences of this transformation of local context vary according to the specific circumstances of each society, the fact of its being radically different from what it used to be in the pre-colonial era is common to all of them.

A key element of this transformed context is the principle of self-determination, whether exercised within an existing state or through secession and the establishment of a separate state. As stated by the highly authoritative Declaration of Principles of International Law by the General Assembly of the United Nations:

> By virtue of the principle of equal rights and self-determination of peoples enshrined in the Charter of the United Nations, all peoples have the right to freely determine, without external interference, their political status and to pursue their economic, social and cultural development, and every State has the duty to respect this right in accordance with the provisions of the Charter ...

> Nothing in the foregoing paragraphs shall be construed as authorizing or encouraging any action which would dismember or impair, totally or in part, the territorial integrity or political unity of sovereign and independent States *conducting themselves in compliance* with the principle of equal rights and self-determination of peoples as described above and *thus possessed of a government representing the whole people belonging to the territory without distinction as to race, creed or colour.*[9]

Therefore, the two sides of the coin of self-determination are non-interference in the internal affairs of sovereign states, provided that the state respects the right of its own people to equal rights and self-determination, as indicated in the emphasized part of the Declaration of Principles quoted above.

As it is often associated with claims of minorities to secede from an existing state and establish their own state, much of the policy and scholarly discussion of this principle tend to focus on the legitimacy and viability of claims of secession. As one author put it

> the right to secede is seen as a remedy of last resort for serious injustices, not a general right of groups. . . . Chief among the grievances I identify as providing primary justifying grounds for secession are these persistent and serious violations of individual human rights.[10]

The basic implication of these principles, according to another author, can be seen in terms of

> degrees of self-determination, with the legitimacy of each [claim] tied to the degree of representative government in the state.... If a government is at the high end of the scale of democracy, the only self-determination claims that will be given international credence are those with minimal destabilizing effect. If a government is extremely unrepresentative, much more destabilizing self-determination claims may well be recognized.[11]

In this light, it is clear that the right to self-determination cannot mean that people are completely free to do as they please in their own country. As explained and illustrated below, the right of one people to self-determination is limited by the right of other peoples to their own self-determination as well. It is neither legally permissible nor practically viable for a group of Muslims to force even fellow Muslims, let alone non-Muslims, to accept and implement a specific view of *Shari'a*, whether as a matter of state policy or informal communal practice. This is particularly true due to growing objections to that understanding of *Shari'a*, because it fails to secure complete equality for women with men as a foundational human rights norm. But I will focus in this chapter on the broader issue of self-determination because I take it to include the protection of the human rights of women. Let us consider the negative implications of Islamic fundamentalism for the right of Muslims themselves to self-determination, followed by the more obvious case of non-Muslims.

As mentioned earlier, profound political and theological differences have divided Islamic communities from the beginning in the Arabia of the seventh century, resulting in a series of civil wars within a few decades of the Prophet's death in 632. Those early stages of Islamic history also witnessed the emergence of significant disagreement among Islamic communities over the interpretation and implementation of Islamic sources, leading to the emergence of distinctive religious factions and theological schools of thought (*madhhab*, plural *madhahib*). It should be emphasized here that such clear and significant disagreements among Muslims about major aspects of what subsequently became known as *Shari'a*, were true of the earliest generations of Muslims, and did not emerge later in history as a result of religious decline. In other words, significant disagreement about the content and application of *Shari'a* is inherent to the system itself as understood and practised by believers from the beginning.

Such disagreements are to be expected and celebrated, rather than denounced and denied as Islamic fundamentalism tends to do. Since the *Qur'an* was revealed in an Arabic language, and *Sunna* is believed to represent the ideal model set by the Prophet, who lived in a particular community with its own specific context, there is bound to be disagreement in the interpretation and application of those textual sources in different contexts. In fact, disagreement is logically integral to the authenticity and validity of religious experience itself. One cannot truly and honestly believe unless he or she is also able to disbelieve, and/or change his or her view of what they do believe in.

While this has always been true of Islamic communities, it is likely to become more intensified and widespread under modern conditions of education and communication. As more Muslim men and women are educated enough to know and consider the *Qur'an*, *Sunna* and Islamic history for themselves, and able to communicate with others in different parts of the world about theological and political issues of common concern, there are more opportunities for disagreement as well as agreement. Fundamentalists tend to denounce and deny significant disagreement among Muslims, especially of the earliest generations, because that would repudiate the possibility of a pristine and categorical understanding of Islam, which they claim to know and seek to apply today. Yet, given this historical – now increasing – diversity of views among Islamic juridical and theological schools of thought, as well as popular opinion that may be independent of any of those schools, serious disagreement about the precise principles and policies to be implemented as *Shari'a*, is inevitable. To impose the views selected by the leadership of a fundamentalist movement as a matter of law and official state policy, even if against the beliefs of other Muslims, is a violation of the right of Muslims themselves to self-determination.

The inevitable violation of the right to self-determination of non-Muslims of the same country by Islamic fundamentalist 'ideology' is more obvious because it repudiates the right of non-Muslim citizens to be governed according to their own beliefs, and violates some of their fundamental rights. Both objections arise from the substance of traditional understandings of *Shari'a*, as advocated by fundamentalists, which discriminates against non-Muslims and women. Discrimination on grounds of religion is more drastic for those who are deemed by *Shari'a* standards to be non-believers, like the adherents of traditional African religions in Sudan today, than for People of the Book (mainly Christians and Jews) who are accepted as believers, though not of the same standing as Muslims. But since even People of the Book are not treated as fully equal to Muslims as citizens, their collective right to self-determination and individual rights as citizens of their own country are also violated.[12]

It may be argued that the actual practice of fundamentalists may depart from their ideological claims, but these objectionable aspects of their practice are evident in the official policies of self-proclaimed fundamentalist regimes, like those of Afghanistan, Iran and Sudan. Even if it is true that practice is not consistent with theory, the problem would then be the wide discretion such a policy permits opens the door for selective abuse of power and corruption. If the decision whether or not to discriminate against non-Muslims is left to individual officials of the state in their own discretion, there will be great temptation to abuse that power for corrupt purposes or to settle personal scores, and so forth. Regardless of whether and how that power is used or abused, the potential victims of discrimination will live under constant fear of it befalling them any time. In other words, if fundamentalists are reforming their position on these issues to be more respectful of religious diversity, for instance, then that should be clearly and publicly stated for their own followers to act accordingly, and for non-Muslims to know what to expect.

On the pragmatic side, the human rights of all peoples, including their collective right to self-determination, are sanctioned by a variety of legal, political and other mechanisms, at both the national and international level. At the normative level, the national constitutional and legal systems of the vast majority of Islamic countries guarantee the human rights of all citizens, without distinction on such grounds as sex or religion. Where these systems are lacking in the protection of these fundamental rights at the domestic level, international treaties and institutions provide an independent alternative source of the obligation of the state to respect and protect these rights. In practice, therefore, these arrangements are supported by political and other mechanisms, including protest and even rebellion at home, and economic, security and other pressures abroad. It is clear that existing national and international mechanisms are not working properly in most parts of the world, but they are working enough to be felt and responded to by even the most supposedly insulated Islamic countries like Saudi Arabia. However, the point I wish to emphasize here, for further discussion in the next section of this chapter, is the need to invest in the credibility and efficacy of these national and international mechanisms because they are the best available means for mediating competing claims to self-determination.

The case of Sudan

The present situation in Sudan clearly illustrates the basic point of the preceding analysis, namely, the need to appreciate the reality of the normative and pragmatic limitations of one's right to self-determination by the rights of others. Having been united for the first time through Turco-Egyptian conquest in the 1820s, Sudan was independent between 1885 and 1898, before becoming an Anglo-Egyptian Condominium, in which Britain was the superior partner as it occupied Egypt itself at the time, until independence in 1956.[13] The country was governed as a multi-party parliamentary democracy on the British model, under the 1956 Transitional Constitution, until the first military coup of November 1958. That first military regime, led by General Aboud, was overthrown through the popular civilian uprising of October 1964. The second phase of democratic rule under the 1964 Amended Transitional Constitution was once again interrupted by the 1969 military coup led by General Numeiri. That second military regime transformed itself into a single-party state under the 1973 so-called 'Permanent' Constitution that lasted until April 1985 when it was overthrown, again by a popular revolt that prompted the army to seize power. A transitional government ruled under the second Transitional Amended Constitution of 1985 until it handed power over to an elected government in April 1986. Three years later, the third military coup of June 1989 brought the National Islamic Front (NIF) to power to rule the country as a single-party state, until the regime announced its plans to permit multi-party politics under the 1998 Constitution.

The main issue that has dominated political and constitutional developments in Sudan is the protracted and extremely destructive civil war that has raged in the southern part of the country since 1955, except for 1973–83, when the Addis Ababa Peace Agreement of 1972 was implemented by the Numeiri regime. The current phase of the civil war resumed in 1983, when President Numeiri gradually repudiated that agreement and imposed *Shari'a*. The Sudan People's Liberation Army and Movement (SPLA/M) claims to represent all the marginalized and disadvantaged peoples of Sudan, in the east, north and west, as well as the southern part of the country. But the SPLA/M is also part of the National Democratic Alliance (NDA), together with the main northern political parties, trade unions and some new democratic movements. Some of these northern partners in the NDA have launched their own, limited, military operations in eastern Sudan.

While many direct and indirect causes and factors no doubt contribute to the persistence of the civil war, they can all be seen as reflecting competing visions of the national identity and ideological orientation of the country. Subject to differences within each region, these visions are usually presented as the presumed Arabic–Islamic vision of the North versus an African-secular vision that is attributed to the South. The country's chronic state of transition and instability has not permitted sufficient national deliberation over the meaning and implications of these competing visions, and/or exploration of ways of reconciling and forging them into a unified national identity. However, since 'Arabized' Muslims constitute about two-thirds of the total population and dominate the political and economic life of the country as a whole, any degree or form of national deliberation and/or reconciliation will have to address the constitutional, legal and political role and implications of *Shari'a*.

Earlier plans to adopt an 'Islamic Constitution' were aborted twice by the military coups of 1958 and 1969. Former President Numeiri managed to stay in power during the early 1970s through shifting alliances with various political factions, but eventually decided to declare a unilateral National Reconciliation with all his political opponents in 1977. The Unionist Party refused to accept that initiative, and the *Umma* Party remained ambivalent, but the NIF embraced the opportunity and integrated itself within Numeiri's single ruling party (the Socialist Union). Seeking to pre-empt the mounting threat of the NIF within his own political and governmental institutions, President Numeiri suddenly declared Sudan an Islamic state and sought to impose *Shari'a*, as the primary source of the country's legal system in 1983. That move did not diminish the political isolation of the Numeiri regime, while enhancing the position of the NIF by declaring its own ideology as the official policy of the state.

Numeiri's arbitrary imposition of *Shari'a* as the basis of the legal system of the country proved to be politically impossible for the two main political parties (*Umma* and Democratic Unionist) to reverse when they came to power after the general elections of 1986. This is not surprising in view of the strong Islamic identity of the constituencies of these two parties. While they had managed to claim an Islamic rationale and agenda without implementing *Shari'a* when they were in power during earlier democratic periods, the leaders of these two parties were unable to come out openly against its continued application once it had been imposed by Numeiri. The NIF also played a critical role in pressuring those two main parties into maintaining *Shari'a* rule by representing itself as the 'Islamic alternative'. The NIF was able to play that role by being an active participant in the democratic phase of 1986–9, including being a member of a coalition government in 1988, until it decided to seize exclusive control of the country through the military coup of June 1989. The primary underlying rationale of that coup was declared to be the consolidation and promotion of the application of *Shari'a*, as the sole basis of the country's legal system, and official policy of all other state institutions.

I am not suggesting here that this is the sole motivation of the NIF in seizing power, or the primary reason for its ability to resist all efforts to dislodge its regime since 1989. Indeed, the premise of my whole analysis is the complexity of the causes and dynamics of such developments. It is clear to me that the relative success of the NIF can be better understood in terms of such factors as the personal political ambition of its leaders and their ability to build a stronger, better-funded and more efficient organization than those of other political parties, and the timing of their rise to power in a national and regional context. Nevertheless, I will focus here on the claim of this Islamic fundamentalist movement to implement *Shari'a* because of its relevance to my argument in this chapter, without denying or under-estimating the role of those other factors.

From this perspective, I suggest, the problem is that the implementation of *Shari'a* is inherently incompatible with the unity and stability of the country. As noted earlier, *Shari'a* grants limited rights to People of the Book and none to those it deems to be unbelievers, like the several million Sudanese who adhere to traditional African religions. To implement *Shari'a* is to deny equality of citizenship rights to Christian Sudanese, and any degree or form of citizenship to those who adhere to traditional African religions because they do not qualify as People of the Book, who are recognized as legal persons though not equal to Muslims. Moreover, Muslims are not expected to openly oppose the application of *Shari'a*, as that may be deemed by the state authorities to constitute the *Shari'a* crime of apostasy, punishable by death under section 126 of the 1992 Sudan Penal Code. By excluding non-Muslims from contribution to any debate over the application of *Shari'a*, and intimidating Muslims who may have different views on the matter, the NIF leaders sought to render the application of *Shari'a* an irreversible national reality. However, the persistence of strong national political opposition and continuation of the civil war in the South are apparently frustrating the realization of that objective.

The irony that also seems to support the analysis presented in this chapter is that efforts to implement *Shari'a* have persistently failed in Sudan under successive governments dominated by Muslim Sudanese, who constitute more than two-thirds of the population. In other words, the country is suffering from a protracted and devastating civil war partly because of an agenda that cannot be achieved in any case. Even the NIF, which claims to have seized power through a military coup on 30 June 1989 for the explicit purpose of implementing *Shari'a*, as the sole law of the land, has failed to do so. In particular, neither the brute force of oppression that has been used by the NIF since 1989, nor the political appeal of their propaganda, has succeeded in dispelling strong opposition to this objective by Muslim as well as non-Muslim Sudanese. After more than eight years of exclusive NIF rule, the regime has now found it necessary to enact a Constitution in 1998 which purports to guarantee the human rights of all Sudanese, including non-Muslims who are not entitled to those rights under *Shari'a*, as noted above. The realization of the NIF leadership that their ideologically driven political agenda cannot be realized in any sustainable manner is also clear from their acceptance to negotiate a peaceful end of the civil war on terms that are totally inconsistent with their earlier claims.

It is both difficult and problematic to attribute such a major and complex development to specific causes. For example, what would be the basis of selecting one set of factors or another as a 'cause' of the NIF decision to open up the national political process? How to assess the role or relative importance of one factor or cause, in relation to others? Nevertheless, one can appreciate at least the correlation between this decision and some obvious considerations. It is reasonable to assume, for instance, that it is politically difficult for the NIF to justify the high number of casualities of the civil war, without being able to promise how or when it is likely to end. The huge financial costs of this war constitute a tremendous strain on the national economy, with consequent hardship to the general population. The ideologically driven policies of the NIF, including the manner in which it is fighting the civil war, have resulted in the international isolation of the country. For the first time in its history Sudan was subjected to sanctions, by the Security Council of the United Nations, for being implicated in acts of international terrorism, such as the attempted assassination of President Mubarak of Egypt during a visit to Ethiopia in 1995. This isolation seriously hampered the NIF regime's ability to secure favourable trade terms, development assistance, or to even obtain arms for its side in the civil war. It is also clear that the SPLA and NDA cannot continue to maintain effective military and political opposition to the NIF regime, let alone hope to overthrow and replace it, without considerable international support. That support is unlikely to be forthcoming or sustained at the necessary level if these groups appear to be intransigent or extreme in their demands. These and related factors illustrate the sort of mutual limitations of the right to self-determination for both sides that contribute to the framework of *constructive interdependence* in the present Sudanese context, as discussed below.[14]

It can be argued that the apparent opening up of the national political process is merely a tactical move, intended to confuse the opponents of the NIF regime, both at home and abroad. However, regardless of the 'true intentions' of its leaders, I suggest this publicly declared shift in the NIF position will have lasting ideological implications and practical political consequences for the movement itself in the direction suggested by my analysis. On the one hand, the fact that the NIF regime needed to declare its commitment to human rights, even if only tactically, indicates an appreciation that this is necessary for security and political stability at home, as well as for normal international relations abroad. This concession is also an admission that the strict ideological agenda of the NIF is untenable in practice. Whatever the leadership of the NIF is willing to admit about the ideological implications of this move, its inconsistency with the movement's rationale and objectives will be clear to the majority of its own members. In other words, it will not be possible for the NIF leadership to assert a credible commitment to the application of *Shari'a*, after having abandoned that demand, even if only for the sake of political expediency. This conclusion is supported by comparative reference to the experiences of other social movements with different ideological orientation, as most dramatically illustrated by the collapse of communist regimes in the former Soviet Union and Eastern Europe. Tactical adaptations there for political and economic expediency eventually led to transformation of the whole system. Since Islamic societies are subject to the same social and political life that applies to other human societies, as emphasized at the beginning of this chapter, the nature and dynamics of Islamic fundamentalist movements like the NIF should be understood in a comparative perspective.

In light of the preceding discussion of the realities of normative and pragmatic limitations on the right to self-determination, I will now conclude with an elaboration of the proposed framework of constructive interdependence for mediating such competing claims. Questions to be addressed in the following discussion include: Who defines and implements the balance between competing rights today? Why should Islamic fundamentalists accept that regime, and how can they influence it in favour of their views? How can Islamic fundamentalists exercise their rights to freedom of belief, expression and association, participation in the government of their own country, and so forth, if the content and application of their beliefs have to be negotiated with external forces? In other words, does the regulation of what they can advocate for their own community negate the right of Islamic fundamentalists to self-determination? The reasons for my answer in the negative to this question, and responses to the other questions, are set out in the next section.

Framework for constructive interdependence

To summarize my argument so far, Islamic fundamentalists should not seek to implement *Shari'a*, because that is inconsistent with the protection of the human rights of all the citizens of the country, including the collective right to self-determination of Muslims themselves, which is supposed to be the basis of the demands of these movements. Moreover, this objective cannot be achieved in practice because it will be resisted by Muslim and non-Muslim citizens of the country, as well as the international community at large. Despite the limitations it imposes on Islamic fundamentalists, the proposed framework is in fact consistent with their nature and dynamics as social movements in their own context. But since my argument is premised on what I call a framework for constructive interdependence, let me begin by explaining what this means and how it works in practice.

The point of departure for this framework is the reality of growing global economic, political and security interdependence, with consequent greater possibilities for cross-cultural influence and cooperation. By calling for acknowledgement and addressing this reality, I am not suggesting that it is working fairly and properly for all peoples of the world. On the contrary, I emphasize this reality and its possibilities of struggles for human dignity and social justice as a necessary step towards improving its operation for all concerned. But demands for improvement cannot be taken seriously unless they come from those who accept the legitimacy of the existing system in the first place. It is therefore necessary for Islamic fundamentalists to accept both the reality of interdependence and possibilities of cross-cultural influence, before they can call for some reforms in the actual operation of the system as a whole. Addressing the injustice of the current operation of this global system also needs to be founded on a clear understanding of its nature and consequences. A critical factor in the initial formation and subsequent development of the present global system is, in my view, European colonialism and its dissolution under the principle of self-determination, as it has evolved after the Second World War.

The full impact and implications of colonialism for all concerned societies will remain the subject of much scholarly and political controversy. But it is already clear that colonialism succeeded in imposing the European nation–state model throughout the world, including the application of European conceptions of international law. During the late nineteenth and early twentieth centuries, European powers ensured the dominance of their view of the nation–state as the essential framework for national politics and international relations by imposing their own normative standards and practical determination of the 'recognition' of political entities as 'sovereign' states. Through bitter experience, including two devastating world wars in the first half of the twentieth century, it became clear that this international system is in fact premised on the national unity and political stability of its members. Experience has also shown that national unity and political stability cannot be sustained without the protection of fundamental human rights for all persons and groups within each country.

From this perspective, the protection of human rights, whether as fundamental constitutional rights or international norms, should therefore be seen as integral to the practical working of the present system of national politics and international relations, rather than simply the product of the moral impulse of so-called Western countries. Article 55 of the Charter of the United Nations, which is a treaty ratified by all Islamic countries, provides:

> With a view to the creation of conditions of stability and well-being which are necessary for peaceful and friendly relations among nations based on respect for the principle of equal rights and self-determination of peoples, the United Nations shall promote: ... (c) universal respect for, and observance of, human rights and fundamental freedoms for all without distinction as to race, sex, language or religion.

According to Article 56, 'All Members pledge themselves to take separate action and in co-operation with the Organization [UN] for the achievement of the purposes set forth in Article 55.' Despite nominal protests against this view of national politics and international relations in the name of cultural relativism or contextual specificity, all governments seek to either show their compliance with these requirements, or justify what they represent as a 'temporary' failure to comply. All peoples of the world, including Muslims everywhere, have no choice but to organize their internal affairs and vital international relations through this system.

The idea of human rights is also critical to the concept of the nation–state, in the European sense that has been universalized through colonialism. As experience has shown, the citizens of any state need not only domestic protection of their fundamental rights, but also international safeguards against the failure of their nation–state to provide sufficient protection. Indeed, as noted earlier, the protection of the internal right to self-determination of their citizens is a condition for respecting a state's claim to exclusive territorial jurisdiction.[15] Since Islamic fundamentalists have accepted the present nation–state system, and in fact seek to seize control of the state in order to use its powers to their own advantage, they are required to accept its limitation by constitutionalism at the national level, and international law for the sovereignty of their state to be accepted by others abroad. This system is certainly not working well for many societies for a variety of reasons, and may indeed be totally transformed or replaced in the future. But whether the objective is reform, transformation or replacement, it can only happen from within the system, over time.

Subject to the caveat that familiarity with a model tends to inhibit one's ability to imagine an alternative to it, I am convinced that the present system is sound in principle, credible in practice, and consistent with the right of all, including Islamic fundamentalists, to self-determination. People everywhere have always gathered into political and social institutions in order to protect their vital individual and communal interests. Over time, they have either consolidated specific forms of association that they find conducive for their purposes, or modified and adapted those forms of association if they did not work. Among the wide variety of such institutions known to different human societies, past and present, the nation–state model appears to suit conditions of life in this age of massive urbanization, industrialization and global international relations. This system is also flexible and open to change by the totality of the population of the state in question.

But this process can only work for one group if it works for all others. From the perspective of this chapter, for example, Muslim persons and groups can expect the system to work for them only if they are willing to contribute to its working for others. For the system to work for as many persons and groups as possible, there is need for normative and institutional resources that people can use in pressing their own claims, and/or in seeking remedy for any wrong done to them. This mediation of competing claims to self-determination can happen within the normative and institutional resources of constitutionalism and human rights.

Conclusion

The analysis and proposal made in this chapter may appear to concede the underlying rationale of the 'end of history' or 'the clash of civilizations' theses, namely, the superiority of liberal conceptions of the state and society, or the inevitability of clash among the world's major cultural systems. This is not true, in my view, because capitalist liberalism is not the only valid and viable philosophy of the state, and a clash of civilizations thesis assumes too much uniformity within Western as well as non-Western cultures. I reject the first thesis as imperialistic and hegemonic, and the second as an invitation to mutual hostility and destruction. But I am not concerned here with refuting these misguided theories, though there are obviously good reasons for doing that. Rather, my purpose is to encourage Islamic fundamentalists to re-define and pursue their objectives within the framework of constructive interdependence precisely in order to successfully resist hegemonic elements in the present liberal paradigm, without sliding into a destructive clash with non-Islamic civilizations.

According to the approach proposed in this chapter, the present, admittedly Western, liberal paradigm should be seen as the product of past experiences of all human societies, and remain completely open to their perspectives today. In other words, Islamic fundamentalists cannot be expected to accept the limitations of global interdependence unless they are also allowed to contribute to its construction. Conversely, since the nature and future direction of the nation–state anywhere in the world today are the product of the contributions of all its citizens, Islamic fundamentalists have as much a right as other citizens to make that contribution from their perspective. As already emphasized, however, that can only be with due regard to the rights of others to make their contributions from their respective perspectives. In other words, Islamic fundamentalists must concede equal rights to all others, men and women alike, because that is a prerequisite condition for their own claim to equal rights. But as the preceding section has shown, Islamic fundamentalists would need to transform their ideology and practice if they are to pursue their equal rights to self-determination.

For Islamic fundamentalists, I suggest, such transformation needs to occur at a theological level before it can materialize among their communities, but the specific context of each community is also integral to the possibilities of theological change. Regarding the first requirement, theological transformation is necessary because of the inherently religious rationale of fundamentalist perspectives. But given the role of human agency in the interpretation and application of Islamic sacred sources, as emphasized earlier, the methodology and outcome of any possible theological transformation need to remain relevant and viable in the material circumstances of each community. If it is to have realistic prospects of success, a proposed methodology must be understood and accepted by a community, and believed to present a credible response to the needs of its members for peace, stability, development and protection of human dignity. In other words, the necessary transformation of the ideology and practice of Islamic fundamentalists must reflect the synergy between the theological dimension and material conditions of all Islamic communities around the world today.

Subject to the need for deeply contextual analysis for each movement, I believe that a clear appreciation of the role of both internal and external actors and factors is necessary for the transformation of Islamic fundamentalist movements in general. At the internal level, a religious community is unlikely to engage in self-critical reflection and theological innovation if it perceives that to constitute a serious threat to its collective identity and security. Such perceptions, in turn, may emerge from a combination of internal and external factors. For example, internal factors include the lack of social and political tolerance of dissent, without which there is no room for self-critical reflection and theological innovation, while Western colonialism and post-colonial domination of Islamic societies are commonly perceived as an external threat to collective identity and security of these societies.

These two types of factors can also be seen as the internal and external dimensions of the proposed framework of constructive interdependence. Agents of internal transformation are insiders who are responding to their own concerns as well as to pressure from outside. In the case of Sudan, briefly discussed above, internal concerns include the needs of the country as a whole for peace, political stability, development and the protection of human dignity of all its population. External pressures include the opposition activities of the NDA, and SPLA in particular, as well as the costs of increasing isolation at the international level. All these concerns must be addressed by the NIF, as well as by their opponents at home and abroad.

In conclusion, I am not suggesting that Islamic fundamentalist movements will succeed in achieving the proposed transformation. Rather, I am arguing that they must achieve this transformation if their claim to being a legitimate and sustainable expression of the right of Muslim peoples to self-determination is to be taken seriously. I also wish to emphasize that my analysis does not assume Islamic fundamentalists to be either all-powerful and invisible or helpless victims of external actors. Indeed, my aim includes acknowledging that they do have a choice for action themselves. In the final analysis, social movements, including Islamic fundamentalists, can vindicate their claim to represent the right of their communities to self-determination by learning to exercise that right within its legitimate normative and pragmatic limitations. Failure to do so will be tantamount to conceding the imperialist hegemony of 'end of history' or mutual destruction of 'clash of civilizations'.

Notes

1 Reference here is to these claims as presented, respectively, by Francis Fukuyama, *The End of History and the Last Man*, New York: Free Press, 1992; and Samuel P. Huntington, *The Clash of Civilizations and the Remaking of World Order*, New York: Simon and Schuster, 1996.

2 On the origins, sources and development of *Shari'a*, see Abdullahi Ahmed An-Na'im, *Toward an Islamic Reformation: Civil Liberties, Human Rights and International Law*, Syracuse: Syracuse University Press, 1990, Chapter 2.

3 The following outline of the basic profile of an 'ideal' model of Islamic fundamentalism is drawn from Richard Mitchell, *The Society of the Muslim Brothers*, London: Oxford University Press, 1969; Johannes J.G. Jansen, *The Neglected Duty: The Creed of Sadat's Assassins and Islamic Resurgence in the Middle East*, New York: Macmillan, 1986; Rifa'at Sayyed Ahmed, *The Armed Prophet: The Rejectionists*, London: Riad al-Rayyes Books, 1991a; Rifa'at Sayyed Ahmed, *The Armed Prophet: The Revolutionaries*, London: Riad al-Rayyes Books, 1991b; and Sadik J. Al-Azm, 'Islamic fundamentalism reconsidered: a critical outline of problems, ideas and approaches', Part I, in *South Asia Bulletin*, vol. 13, nos 1 and 2, 1993, pp. 93–121, and Part II, in *South Asia Bulletin*, vol. 14, no. 1, 1994, pp. 73–98.

4 See, for example, Olivier Roy, *The Failure of Political Islam*, Cambridge, MA: Harvard University Press, 1994.

5 For an overview of this history see, generally, Ira M. Lapidus, *A History of Islamic Societies*, Cambridge: Cambridge University Press, 1988.

6 The following brief review is based on I.M. Lewis, *Islam in Tropical Africa*, 2nd edn, Bloomington: Indiana University Press, 1980; and J.S. Trimingham, *The Influence of Islam upon Africa*, 2nd edn, Harlow: Longman, 1980.

7 Joseph Schacht, *Origins of Muhammadan Jurisprudence*, Oxford: Oxford University Press, 1959, p. 84; S. Vesey-Fitzgerald, 'Nature and sources of the *Shari'a*', in Majid Khadduri and Herbert Liebesny (eds) *Law in the Middle East*, Washington, DC: Middle East Institute, 1955, pp. 85–112, at p. 91.

8 See, generally, James Piscatori, *Islam in a World of Nation States*, Cambridge: Cambridge University Press, 1986.

9 The Declaration on Principles of International Law Concerning Friendly Relations and Co-operation among States in Accordance with the Charter of the United Nations, GA Res. 2625 (XXV), 24 October 1970 (my emphasis). For elaboration and analysis of these issues see, for example, Martti Koskenniemi, 'National self-determination today: problems of legal theory and practice', *International and Comparative Law Quarterly*, vol. 43, 1994, p. 241.

10 Alan Buchanan, 'Self-determination, secession and the rule of law', in Robert McKim and J. McMahan (eds) *The Morality of Nationalism*, New York: Oxford University Press, 1997.

11 Frederic Kirgis, Jr, 'The degrees of self-determination in the United Nations era', *American Journal of International Law*, vol. 88, 1994, p. 306.

12 See An-Na'im, *Toward an Islamic Reformation*, Chapter 4, on the nature and scope of discrimination against the non-Muslim population of a country ruled by traditional formulations of *Shari'a*, as advocated by Islamic fundamentalists.

13 The following overview of the recent history of Sudan is drawn from the following sources: Muddathir Abd al-Rahim, *Imperialism and Nationalism in the Sudan*, Oxford: Clarendon Press, 1969; Mansour Khalid, *The Government They Deserve: The Role of the Elite in Sudan's Political Evolution*, London: Kegan Paul International, 1990; Matin W. Daly and Ahmad Alawad Sikainga (eds) *Civil War in the Sudan*, London: British Academic Press, 1993; and Francis M. Deng, *War of Visions: Conflict of Identities in the Sudan*, Washington, DC: The Brookings Institution, 1995. For the most recent developments, see *Horn of Africa Bulletin*, published every second month by the Life and Peace Institute, Uppsala, Sweden.

14 Abdullahi A. An-Na'im and Francis Deng, 'Self determination and unity: the case of Sudan', *Law and Society*, vol. 18, 1997, pp. 199–223.

15 Buchanan, 'Self-determination', p. 301.

Select bibliography

Al-Azm, Sadik J., 'Islamic fundamentalism reconsidered: a critical outline of problems, ideas and approaches', Part I, in *South Asia Bulletin*, vol. 13, nos 1 and 2, 1993, pp. 93–121, and Part II, in *South Asia Bulletin*, vol. 14, no. 1, 1994, pp. 73–98.

Jansen, Johannes J.G., *The Neglected Duty: The Creed of Sadat's Assassins and Islamic Resurgence in the Middle East*, New York: Macmillan, 1986.

Lapidus, Ira M., *A History of Islamic Societies*, Cambridge: Cambridge University Press, 1988.

Roy, Olivier, *The Failure of Political Islam*, Cambridge, MA: Harvard University Press, 1994.

Sayyed Ahmed, Rifa'at, *The Armed Prophet: The Rejectionists*, London: Riad al-Rayyes Books, 1991a.

Sayyed Ahmed, Rifa'at, *The Armed Prophet: The Revolutionaries*, London: Riad al-Rayyes Books, 1991b.

3

STRATEGIES FOR PUBLIC PARTICIPATION

Women and Islamic fundamentalism in Malaysia

Sharifah Zaleha binti Syed Hassan

The occurrence of Islamic fundamentalism in the 1970s was undeniably a significant event in the history of Malaysia. The phenomenon, popularly referred to as *dakwah*,[1] coincided with changes in the economic and political spheres that the country was experiencing as it tried to institutionalize industrial capitalism and representative democracy. The breakdown of the traditional family, the demands of urban living, racial disunity and continued dependence on the West caused certain segments of the Malay intelligentsia to reassess the relevance of their traditional beliefs, worldviews and identity in the modern context. Some chose to self-reflect through nationalism and multiculturalism, while others resourced Islamic teachings, fundamentals and philosophy for inspiration and guidelines on how to organize for religious and social reforms. Operating through loosely structured congregational groups and movements, the latter group called on Muslims to rediscover the Islamic past and its rich cultural and intellectual heritage believed to have the answers to all social ills and problems. Muslims, the religious activists claimed, needed to empower themselves with religious knowledge, spread the Islamic message and demonstrate their Muslimness by leading a lifestyle in accordance with the *Shari'a*. So, Islamic fundamentalism in Malaysia was, and still is, a cultural ideology that advocates a rediscovery of the Islamic past as well as empowerment projects with strong religious and ethnic components. The Islamic past is important in the fundamentalist projects as a focus of their emphatic messages against the West and its 'agents', as well as a frame of reference to rebuild Malaysian society along Islamic lines.

As elsewhere in the Muslim world, the 'woman question' featured significantly in the Islamization projects of the religious fundamentalists. Fundamentalists' discourses on the nature, status, role and images of women had produced polemics on 'veiling' and modes of integrating women in development. Unlike in Algeria, Afghanistan and Bangladesh, where the 'woman question' was discussed in relation to the nationalist struggles aimed at achieving political independence and modernizing society, in Malaysia it was raised against the backdrop of Malay resistance to continued cultural dominance of the West and was aimed at asserting an Islamic identity. When Islamic fundamentalism started to unfold in the 1970s, Malaysia had already achieved independence and the way was already paved for women to enter the workforce and participate in politics. So in the Malaysian case, Islamic fundamentalism implicated women, in particular Malay women, by showing them that they were vulnerable to external influences, easily preyed upon and exploited in the name of development and modernization. Religious fundamentalists addressed the 'woman question' with a view to redefining women's behaviour and their appearance and determining the range of activities within and outside the domestic sphere that were deemed appropriate for them.

This chapter focuses on Islamic fundamentalism and its effects on Muslim women in Malaysia. It has three aims: one, to show the role that the 'woman question' plays in the discourses and programmes of the religious fundamentalists; two, to show how Islamic fundamentalism influences women's strategies in public participation; and three, to discuss the extent to which Islamic fundamentalism affects the civil liberties of Muslim women in present-day Malaysia.

Modernization in Malaysia: an overview

Malaysia, a federation of thirteen states, came into being in 1963. It encompasses the Malay Peninsula,[2] which has eleven states and the two states of Sabah and Sarawak located on the island of Borneo. A variety of ethnic and religious groups make up Malaysia's population which now stands at approximately 20 million. The most politically and culturally dominant ethnic group in the country is the Malays. Found mainly in the Malay Peninsula and having inhabited the country for a few thousand years, the Malays are classified as *bumiputra*, meaning 'sons of the soil', alongside other indigenous groups such as the Iban, Kadazan, Melanau, Orang Asli, Bidayuh, Bajau and Bugis. Today the Malays make up about 56 per cent of the total population of Malaysia, followed by the immigrant groups including the Chinese (33 per cent) and the Indians (10.2 per cent). With very few exceptions, all Malays are adherents of Islam. So intertwined are religion and ethnicity among the Malays that being a Muslim in Malaysia is synonymous with being a Malay. The non-Malays, on the other hand, subscribe to a variety of religious faiths, such as Christianity, Buddhism, Hinduism, Taoism, Sikhism, Islam and indigenous religions. Unlike the Malays, religion is not an important identity marker among non-Malays.

Before becoming British colonies in the nineteenth century, the Malaysian states were organized into ruler-centred societies and egalitarian tribal units. In the Malay Peninsula especially, there were several Malay Sultanates, whose rulers saw in Islam a source of legitimacy for their roles as heads of state and guardians of Islamic and customary laws (*adat*). When the British took control of these states, they made the local rulers abrogate most of their political power to the British officers or 'Residents'. The British then introduced a civil administration and legal system that was separate from the Islamic legal system, thereby separating religion from the state. In the economic realm, the British systematically exploited the country's natural resources to develop tin and rubber industries and created urban centres to serve as service centres for the working of these resources. Chinese and Indians were brought in to work in these indus-tries. They started to migrate in huge numbers into what was then called British Malaya in the middle of the nineteenth century.

Colonialism no doubt stimulated modernization but it had negative consequences for ethnic relations in the country. Due to the British 'divide and rule' policy, colonialism led to a division of labour along ethnic lines, with the Malays in agriculture and civil service, the Chinese as miners and urban entrepreneurs, and the Indians as plantation workers. Over time, gross inequities in terms of income and services developed among the Malays and non-Malays, in particular the Chinese. This was because, left to tend rice fields in the villages, the Malays had no access to schools, salaried jobs, business opportunities and other services which were avail-able in the town areas. The people who could access these services were the Chinese, Arabs, Indian Muslims and members of the Malay aristocrats who resided in the towns.

After the Second World War and as Malaysia (then called Malaya) moved towards independence, pluralism and the relationship between Islam and Malay national identity were hotly debated as Malay leaders struggled to ensure continued political dominance in the face of the non-Malay presence. Independence came to the eleven states in the Malay Peninsula in 1957.[3] These states formed a monarchy with a federal struc-ture of government, bicameral legislature and a sovereign elected on a rotating basis from among the nine Sultans.[4] The new nation, then called

Malaya, had its own constitution, some provisions of which unambiguously favoured the Malays. The Malaysian constitution, for example, acknowledged Malay as the national language of the country and Islam as its official religion and forbade non-Muslims from proselytizing among Muslims.

The major task for the Alliance Party[5] which ruled Malaya after independence was to integrate the different ethnic groups and the interests of the dominant political forces in the country. It was an uphill struggle for the Malaysian leadership since the democratization of the political process allowed political parties to play up communal issues. The privileged status of the Malays continued to be disputed and racial tension, which was running high because of communal politics, culminated in the racial riot on 13 May 1969. On the economic scene, Malaysia continued the pattern of industrial production initiated by the British in that it exported commodities such as rubber, tin, oil palm and timber, imported consumer goods and built factories. Compared to other Third World countries at that time, Malaysia's economic development was quite impressive; for example, in 1965 the country registered a 5 per cent growth rate. However, many of the capitalist-based development projects that were implemented were not very successful in reducing the economic gap between the rural and urban areas. Since this problem could be socially and politically destabilizing, the Malaysian government launched the New Economic Policy (NEP) in 1971. The aim of the NEP was to create a viable Malay middle class and to ensure 30 per cent Malay participation in employment. Towards this end, the government mounted efforts to create new growth centres and industrial parks and to develop the existing educational system, so as to provide opportunities for Malays to have access to education and jobs in the agricultural, manufacturing and service sectors of the country. The desired Malay middle class did materialize. Today most of its members live in the urban areas and, in terms of occupation, belong to the professional, technical, administrative, managerial, clerical, service and retail categories.[6]

Women, development and modernization

Modernity and modernization in Malaysia were introduced by, and implemented through, capitalist enterprises that were developed by the British. During colonial times, industrial capitalism produced conditions under which the local population had little choice but to engage in work for wages. Since then capitalism has proved to be a source of inspiration for Malaysia to design economic development projects aimed at achieving social transformation and overcoming the retrogressive effects of certain traditional practices and institutions. Thus in Malaysia, modernization goes hand in hand with economic capitalist development, causing changes in the family structures, political system, gender relations and value orientation of the people. How Malay women experienced modernization and were impacted by the process prior to the rise of Islamic fundamentalism will be described below.

Traditionally Malay women lived in closely-knit communities in villages that thrived on *padi* cultivation and fishing. They worked on *padi* fields alongside the men during planting and harvesting time, wove mats and cloth and undertook petty trading selling fruit, vegetables and foodstuffs. Local customs and Islamic law did not prevent them from owning and inheriting property, which in those days took the form of land, ornaments, houses, domestic utensils and weapons. Society's norms required that women linked up with male kinsmen, such as their fathers, brothers and uncles, who negotiated marriages and other domestic necessities of life on their behalf. Such arrangements sanctioned cultural constructs of women as housewives and mothers, while the ideal woman was someone with great potential for domesticity. There was division of labour along gender lines in traditional Malay society, but it was not obvious. The activities that were considered becoming for women were cooking, washing, sewing, caring for the young and the aged and managing household finances, whereas work such as felling trees, fishing, ploughing and hunting were deemed fit for men. In such a situation, domesticity was so highly valued that a Malay woman was believed to acquire social standing when she got married. This was because through marriage, a woman could demonstrate her capability not just to cook, care and manage the household but also be depended upon by others. She became an adult and a mature person through marriage.

The modernization measures of the British impacted on Malay women in no small way. The British model of development not only divided work in the agricultural and industrial sectors along ethnic lines but favoured men against women as members of the workforce. So women had no access to the many job opportunities in the rubber estates, tin mines, firms and government offices. Women in general, and Malay women in particular, could not work in the rubber estates or the tin mines which became the domain of the Indians and Chinese respectively. Nor could they secure white-collar jobs as government servants or office personnel because they did not have the required formal education. Only a small number of Malay peasant women became integrated into early industrial capitalism and they comprised the family members of those peasant men who grew cash crops such as coconut and coffee for local markets and for export. These women helped their husbands or male kinsmen in the farms but were not paid. For these women, modernization meant working longer hours at devalued household work that brought little or no money at all.

For Malay women of aristocratic background, modernization meant something else. Unlike the peasant women who were integrated into the capitalist system through the cash crop economy, aristocratic women experienced capitalism through education. Many of these women attended vernacular, English and Arabic schools[7] that were built by the British and the local elite in or around the towns where they lived. However, only very few of them worked after leaving schools. Many left school before completing their education in order to marry. For many parents at that time, schools were places that provided their daughters with basic literacy and skills in cooking and sewing to help them become effective housewives. Modernization for this category of women meant learning skills that could be put to use only in the private sphere. In short, society did not see any need for women to be educated beyond basic literacy. If they were absorbed into the workforce, it was to become teachers, clerks and social welfare officers. However, the number of women who had outside employment was so small that their contribution to the economy was negligible.

It appears that changes in the economic landscape of Malaya and growing urbanization in colonial times resulted in renegotiation of the sexual division of labour in the family and community with negative consequences for women's position in society. Previously Malay men and women had cooperated in the domestic and public realms, attending to the needs of the family and community, but modernization based on the colonial model undermined this arrangement. Modernization made a clear distinction between the domestic and public realms on the basis of the type of work that men and women did. Since Malay men were engaged in cash-crop agriculture and salaried work as government servants, these came to be viewed as the activities most appropriate for men. The women's domain, on the other hand, centred around activities that were economically and socially undervalued, such as the production of food and crafts. As a result, irrespective of their class background, Malay women became economically dependent on men. This reinforced the belief that because of mental and physical differences between them, it was more appropriate for men to assume public roles and for women the domestic ones.

Nevertheless, the impact of modernization on the small group of Malay women who had been exposed to formal education had somewhat different political ramifications. In the late 1920s, preceding the struggle for independence, some women teachers ventured into the political sphere.

They joined Malay-based political associations that were committed to help Malays advance in political, social and economic fields and foster higher education among Malays. The women members of these associations, operating through such associations as the Selangor Malay Union and the Union of Johore (Malay) Women Teachers, initiated discussions on the backwardness of Malay women and clamoured for the establishment of teachers' training institutes to ensure a steady supply of teachers in the country.[8]

Women's activism became more obvious after the Second World War and in the anti-colonial struggle. Political parties such as the Malay Nationalist Party (MNP), the United Malays National Organisation (UMNO) and the Pan-Malayan Islamic Party (renamed the Islamic Party of Malaysia or *Parti Islam SeMalaysia* or PAS), to name a few, needed women's support for their cause. So each incorporated into its party structure a women's section or 'wing'. Thus the MNP had the Progressive Malay Women's Corps, UMNO the *Kaum Ibu* UMNO (later renamed *Wanita* UMNO), and PAS the *Dewan Muslimat*. During the struggle for independence and to be in line with party policies, these women's political auxiliaries focused on issues of patriotism, Malay unity and loyalty, even though they were conscious of the need to address issues of sexual inequality arising from the structure of social relations between men and women in the respective parties.

Thus, on the eve of independence, Malay women were not about to flood the country's labour force. Most of them were still confined to the private realm, and job opportunities for them in the public sector also grew very slowly. In the political field, Malay women were visible, but as canvassers and voters, not as party leaders. Although political parties granted Malay women public participation, they denied them equality in terms of decision-making.

After Malaysia achieved independence in 1957, development measures were aimed at rectifying the inequities in terms of services, income and employment opportunities between the rural and urban areas that the implementation of British colonial policy had generated. Towards this end, the Malaysian government intensified rural modernization by building roads, schools and clinics, improving the transport system, constructing canals for irrigation, introducing modern farm technologies, expanding credit facilities and relocating landless villagers on new tracts of land that had been cleared for the planting of rubber and palm oil. At the same time that the agricultural sector was being modernized, the government opened up new growth centres on land previously covered by jungle to become the sites of factories and modern housing. In the area of education, academic programmes that focused on science, management, communications, medicine and architecture were incorporated into the existing school and university curricula.

In the Malaysian government's vision of development, women and men, irrespective of ethnic origin, were targeted to receive formal education up to the tertiary level and be absorbed into the public and private sectors. The response from the Malays towards the policy on national development was very encouraging. This was evident from the increase in the number of Malay girls who enrolled in secondary schools and who became income-earners, working in the agricultural sector and in the government. Increases in the literacy rate also caused many rural women to migrate to the cities, especially to Kuala Lumpur and Petaling Jaya, in search of higher education and salaried jobs. By 1970, women in general made up about 37.2 per cent of Malaysia's labour force and about half of them were Malay women.[9] Although a majority were found in the agricultural sector, those in the public sector worked in a variety of occupations as teachers, government officials, academics, clerks and secretaries.

The pattern of change described above without doubt contributed to the greater visibility of women in the public sphere of the major towns in Malaysia. There, women were generally educated, income earners and economically quite independent from men. These women accommodated a Western lifestyle, combining Western attire with traditional ones. They were also proficient in English, moderately activist and quite work-oriented. In local parlance, these women were called 'wanita moden', meaning 'modern women'. They contrasted drastically with rural women who were portrayed as old-fashioned, conservative and backward. So just before Islamic fundamentalism unfolded in the country in the 1970s, there was a growing polarity between 'modern' and 'traditional' lifestyles, representing two different subcultures, the 'alien' and the 'home-grown' women.

Islamic fundamentalism and the woman question

The rise of Islamic fundamentalism

In Malaysia, there have been two waves of Islamic fundamentalism. The first wave occurred in the 1920s when the country was still a British colony. During that time, awed and perturbed by Western science, modern technology and rationalism, religious reformers emerged calling on the Malays to purify Islam of indigenous accretions and to reject traditionalist interpretations of Islam so they could empathize with the West.[10] The

Kaum Muda's[11] or religious modernists', call for reforms resulted in the establishment of the previously mentioned Arabic schools and the ascendancy of orthodox Islam. The second wave of Islamic fundamentalism, also known as the *dakwah* phenomenon, started in the 1970s, about fifteen years after Malaysia achieved independence and was slowly being transformed by the processes of industrialization, urbanization and democratization. Although the two waves of Islamic fundamentalism differed in terms of genesis and impact on society, their occurrence clearly shows the crucial role that Islam plays in Malaysia as an organizing force capable of mobilizing Muslims to support or protest against the existing religious authority and the state.

In Malaysia, Islamic fundamentalist movements did not arise in villages but in the cities, namely Kuala Lumpur and Petaling Jaya, where Islamic networks of mosques, religious schools and religious bureaucracy were underdeveloped. Furthermore, all the religious activists were Malays, thereby qualifying it as an ethno-religious phenomenon. Islamic fundamentalism too did not occur suddenly or was explosive in nature. It gradually unfolded in the cities and then spread into the wider sectors of Malaysian society.

The early signs of rising religious consciousness were manifested in the behaviour of individual men and women who, for example, began to avoid food items believed to contain substances forbidden (*haram*) in Islam, such as gelatine. Some refused to buy chicken meat and beef that were sold in the markets for fear that the animals had not been slaughtered in accordance with Islamic prescriptions. A few started to gather friends and neighbours to form study circles (*usrah*) and informal congregational organizations (*jemaah*) that were structured around self-declared religious teachers (*ustaz*) to fathom the *Qur'an* and Islamic religious sciences so as to enhance their religiosity. Out of some of these religious groups, Islamic movements (*gerakan dakwah*) emerged to propose social and religious reforms and to openly challenge the status quo of Malay-based political parties and the existing religious authority as controllers of Islamic solidarity in the country. Three major ones that made quite an impact on the Malaysian religious scene were the now defunct *Jemaah Darul Arqam* or *Al Arqam*[12] in short, the *Jemaah Tabligh*, and the Muslim Youth Movement of Malaysia (*Angkatan Belia Islam Malaysia* or ABIM). The leaders and members of these movements were university students and members of the burgeoning Malay middle class. A majority of them were rural migrants who had recently moved to Kuala Lumpur and Petaling Jaya and who had little or no knowledge at all of the Islamic religious sciences. The fundamentalists did not engage the state in theological discourses when arguing for reforms but instead made personal and psychological appeals to the general public to be aware of the deleterious consequences of Western-inspired modernization for their personal and collective Islamic identities.

Several factors combined to prompt the fundamentalists to mobilize for political action around Islam. One of them was exposure to events taking place in countries such as Algeria, Sudan, India and Pakistan where religious renewal had already taken place. The other was the change in the material conditions in which Malays were living as a result of intensified industrialization and urbanization in the first decade after Malaysia had achieved independence. As stated above, previously rural settlers, many Malays were now drawn through migration to Kuala Lumpur and Petaling Jaya, to acquire education and jobs. These culturally displaced Malays could not invoke kinship bonds to regulate their social and religious affairs and to manage the incipient stress and strains of urban living. In the absence of kin network, the *usrah* group and *jemaah* became the alternative bases for urban dwellers to cooperate with one another. Other factors contributing to the rise of Islamic fundamentalism were increasing ethnic polarization, the high incidence of rural poverty, and an apprehension about the leadership style of Malaysia's first Prime Minister, Tunku Abdul Rahman Putra Al Haj which tended to favour non-Malay interests over the Malays. All these factors coalesced to cause some segments of the urban-based Malay middle class to seek solace in Islam and to formulate solutions to help Malays come to terms with the post-independence economic and political situation.

To the fundamentalists operating through Islamic movements, there were several issues which were pressing and needed to be addressed. These were the legitimacy of foreign ideologies as bases on which to develop Malaysian society, the role of the state as the sole definer of Islamic orthodoxy, the relevance of the simple equation between Islam and Malayness and the efficacy of political parties as an instrument of protest. The fundamentalists did not offer one but several ways of resolving these issues. The *Al Arqam* movement, founded in 1968 by a religious teacher named Ashaari Muhammed, called for a restoration of the classical Islamic society that existed during Prophet Mohammed's time. Being restorationist and revivalist in nature, the *Al Arqam* urged Muslims to repent, abandon their existing lifestyles and relocate themselves in Islamic villages (*kampung Islam*) or communes. The *Jemaah Tabligh* originated in India and had been in existence in Malaysia since 1950. Using the influence of *dakwah* ideology, the *Jemaah Tabligh* re-entered the Malaysian religious scene as an Islamic movement. An all-male religious organization, it called on Muslim men to form loosely structured groups to spread the Islamic message in and outside Malaysia. The main concern of the *Jemaah Tabligh* was to enhance moral solidarity among Muslims. As for the ABIM, which was formed in 1971 and originated as a student organization, it strongly believed that the problems faced by the Muslims could be solved through a gradual transformation of Malaysian society from a secular to an Islamic one. The movement focused on remoulding individual Muslims through education (*tarbiyah*) and mission work (*dakwah*) so they could become God-conscious (*bertaqwa)*, dynamic and critical individuals capable of instituting further change in society.

Although the above fundamentalist movements differed from one another in terms of history, goals and organizational structures, they were similar in four important respects. First, their arguments for religious reforms proceeded from a criticism of the West, Western economic and intellectual dominance and secularism. Concerning the West, Anwar Ibrahim, the former Deputy Prime Minister of Malaysia, when he was leading the ABIM, said that through colonialism, the West had distanced the people from Islam in the name of modernism and emancipation.[13] In a similar vein, the *Al Arqam* movement criticized Western-rooted approaches to rural development in Malaysia for introducing alien concepts and altering existing worldviews and lifestyles in ways that deviated from the Islamic ideals.[14] Second, all three fundamentalist movements agreed that as a prerequisite for participating in religious renewal, Muslims should view Islam as a comprehensive way of life (*ad din*) and a total system (*nizam*), not just as a set of abstract beliefs and laws to be memorized. Third, they also agreed that all proposals for religious reforms should draw inspiration from the *Qur'an*, *Sunna* of Prophet Muhammed and Islamic theological sources. Thus at the heart of Islamic fundamentalism in Malaysia was a rediscovery of the Islamic cultural and intellectual heritage envisioned as a long and gradual process which entailed a rejection of Western civilization, the development of Islamic neighbourhoods, social order, state or nation, and the forging of a self-conscious Islamic collective identity. A key activity in the process that the fundamentalists identified as crucial for the transformation to take place was *dakwah*. *Dakwah* means to 'invite one to Islam'. In the context of religious renewal in Malaysia, it was about enlightening people about Islam and intensifying the Muslims' own commitment to Islam. Underlying the fundamentalists' concern with *dakwah* was the assumption that in Malaysia insufficient efforts had been made by the established religious authority to spread the Islamic message to Muslims and non-Muslims alike and to educate the general public about Islam and its role in society. Hence, the need for lay people to actively participate in *dakwah*.

The Malaysian government, in particular UMNO, viewed the Islamic movements with some degree of apprehension but made no attempt to suppress them. It adopted an accommodating attitude towards *dakwah* and tried to coordinate the missionizing activities of the fundamentalists through a newly established body, the *Dakwah* Foundation of Malaysia. UMNO, which had cut for itself the image of a modern and secular party, attempted to strike a chord with them by paying more attention to Islam. Being in power, the party established new Islamic institutions such as the Islamic Bank and the International Islamic University of Malaysia, restructured mosque administration, incorporated a *dakwah* unit in the religious bureaucracy of every state and upgraded the status of the *Shari'a* courts to that of the civil courts. UMNO's political opponent, the PAS, which had been clear right from the beginning of its desire to Islamize Malaysian society, endorsed the fundamentalists' call for reforms. However, it was not until 1982 that the party readjusted its political strategies to reflect its fundamentalist posture. One of the things the party did to this effect was to declare that it would not put forward women as electoral candidates because a *hadith* said that a community led by a woman would not succeed.[15] By the mid-1980s, apart from the three *dakwah* organizations mentioned above, political parties, individual *ulamak* and independent preachers (*pendakwah bebas*) were helping to spread fundamentalist ideology into the wider sectors of Malaysian society thereby influencing members of the general public to organize for religious and political activism through a variety of community and national level projects with the common aim to Islamize society. These developments clearly show that Islamic fundamentalism in Malaysia was not a passing phenomenon. It is here to stay and its power is manifested in different forms and levels of Malaysian society.

The woman question

The theme of gender or 'the woman question' featured quite prominently in the fundamentalists' discourses, especially in the ABIM and the *Al Arqam*. Both organizations discussed the matter in relation to the issues of morality and cultural authenticity that continued adherence to Western-derived ideologies and practices raised. The *Al Arqam* movement pointed out that in giving women freedom, the West rendered them defenceless and easy prey to unscrupulous males. Caught in such a situation, they became identity-less and morally loose. Muslim women, the *Al Arqam* said, should be protected against lewdness and promiscuity through the bond of marriage. The ABIM did not consider emancipation of women as undesirable or problematic. It noted that in Malaysia women had the tendency to abandon an Islamic lifestyle in favour of a secular one primarily because society did not help define their identity in Islamic terms. Therefore women must be re-educated about their true nature, their potential and the substantial role that they could play in society and development.

Two major concerns were underlying the fundamentalist discourses on the link between women's freedom and moral degradation. The first was the concern for a proper understanding of the nature and place of women in society according to the universal truth of Islam. Here the major assumption was that mankind had needs to procreate, which should be fulfilled within marriage and through family institutions. The relationships between spouses and the rights of women prescribed in Islam stemmed from a recognition that men and women were different physically, mentally and emotionally. The rights accorded to women in Islam respected their true nature, such as women's need for motherhood, the ethereal character of their feelings and the nobility of their manners. This being the case, the fundamentalists argued that women's rights in Islam were not 'empty rights' as experienced by Western women but rights acquired with true spiritual fulfilment. These rights included the right to education, to work, to participate in public life and to acquire, use and inherit property. In fact, these rights are better provided for in Islam because they are granted in a way that truly appreciates the nature of women.

The second matter that proved of great concern to the fundamentalists was the ongoing cultural onslaught by the West and its 'agents' on the Muslim world. By Western 'agents', the fundamentalists meant those Westernized intellectuals whose model of development had been informed by ideologies such as socialism, communism and nationalism. To return to the 'woman question', the fundamentalists saw 'modern' and 'Westernized' women, who mingled freely with men, wore revealing clothes and valued absolute independence, as cultural betrayers and victims of runaway consumerism. As embodiments of social ills, these women could easily undermine family values that were essential to forge unity among members of the *umma*. So campaigns would have to be mounted against 'Westernized women' not because of who they were but what they stood for.

Strategies for public participation

In fact, the 'woman question' formed part of a broader discourse on ethno-religious identity, development, modernization, and cultural integrity that the religious fundamentalists carried on. The language of egalitarianism and democracy, used by the fundamentalists to argue for women's position and rights in Islam, was not towards the creation of a just and equitable society but towards denouncing the West as a politico-cultural entity. This being the case, the role of the 'woman question' was merely to justify the reconstruction of Islamic womanhood.

In Malaysia, this process basically involved enlightening women about their nature and true purpose in life and projecting an image of a woman who was non-passive, socially engaged and politically sensitive, just as the Prophet Mohammed's wives Khadijah, Aisyah and Zainab. Implicit in this project of identity reconstruction were two assumptions: one, that women were quite ignorant of the religious demands of Islam and two, that, being 'weak' and naïve about life's vagaries, women had to be protected (*dilindungi*). 'Protection' in the Malay culture does not imply control of women by men. It is more about safeguarding and defending women from various dangers and any untoward event. Nevertheless, the desire to re-educate and protect women justified the religious activists, male and female, to draw on Islamic teachings for ideas on how to recast Malay women in the Islamic mould and to lay down the strategies for them to be involved in society. They did this with respect to three matters: the personal appearance of women, women's public roles and religious activism.

Personal appearance

When it first emerged in the 1970s, Islamic fundamentalism was quite pre-occupied with the personal appearance of Muslim women and their dress form. Both were discussed in relation to the concept of female *aurat* and issues of morality and cultural authenticity. Malays understood *aurat* to mean parts of the body that must be concealed in order to avoid shame (*malu*) and preserve modesty. In Malaysia, male religious activists linked *aurat* to moral laxity and the absence of modesty demonstrated by Western women as well as those 'modern' women described earlier. They therefore appealed to Muslim women to cover their *aurat* which in this case included the hair and all parts of the female body. This act of 'covering one's *aurat*' is referred to as *bertudung*. '*Tudung*' in the Malay language means 'a lid' or 'a cover'. To *bertudung* means to don the headscarf. The latter is usually a head-covering resembling a nun's wimple that reached down to the woman's shoulder or slightly below the waist. The headscarf is usually worn over the two-piece loose fitting traditional Malay dress called *baju jurung* or a long-sleeved gown of Middle Eastern origin called *jubah*. So *bertudung* in Malaysia is like 'veiling' in Iran. It is a dress form which in the context of religious renewal served as a powerful image and symbol of Islamic identity carrying messages of decency, modesty, virtue and piety. In addition, *bertudung* reflected a symbolic dissociation from Western cultural milieu. Its function was to enhance cultural uniformity and to promote a serious Islamic image for religious activism.

In the 1970s, voluntary 'veiling'[16] occurred among those women who joined the Islamic movements mentioned earlier, in particular the *Al Arqam* and ABIM, which, though structured around and led by men, gave women a substantial role in religious activism. These were women who were born in the mid-1940s and whose formative years coincided with a society over which the spirit of colonialism and Western modernity was slowly losing its grip. These women were entering the urban milieu of Kuala Lumpur and Petaling Jaya, which was dominated by the Chinese and still culturally unconsolidated. In the two cities, Malay women who had benefited from colonial modernization projects to become secretaries, teachers, clerks, government officials and university instructors were few. These women too did not develop extensive social networks nor stood out as the desired model of womanhood for young rural migrants. In this context, the fundamentalists' call for Muslims to 'return to the roots' and 'to come to their senses' (*insaf*) was especially powerful because of its promise for salvation and capacity to link these women to the more transnational Islamic community or the *umma*.

The number of Malay women who took to 'veiling' in the 1970s was relatively small compared to those who did not. They were referred to as the *dakwah* people (*orang-orang dakwah*) and stood out against mainstream culture because of their attire, puritanical stance and 'holier-than-thou' image. Starting in the 1980s, 'veiling' became more widespread as more Malay women in the urban and rural areas faithfully observed the Islamic dress code. This process could be attributed to two factors. The first was the entry into Malaysian society of more young and educated women who had undergone tertiary education in the late 1970s at home and abroad and who, unlike the earlier generation, had not experienced colonialism at all. These were the beneficiaries of Malaysia's New Economic Policy. They had been socialized into taking pride in their own race and culture and into competing with the non-Malays. When they were students, these women rallied around Islam and had come to see in the religion clear and unambiguous rules that could and should be upheld. So starting in the early 1980s, it was the members of this cohort who voluntarily took to the veil.

The other factor was the role of the government and political parties, more specifically UMNO and PAS, in the spread of fundamentalist ideology to the wider sectors of Malaysian society. As indicated earlier, although both parties did not necessarily agree with the reform agenda and strategies of the *Al Arqam*, ABIM and *Jemaah Tabligh*, they were not inimical to religious activists' call for women to demonstrate their Muslimness by donning the *tudung*. In fact, PAS and UMNO deployed their own *ulamak* and preachers to impress upon the general public the importance of observing the Islamic dress code. As a result, more women, irrespective of class and social background, took to 'veiling'. Some did it because of personal religious conviction and others for fear of being thought irreligious, secular and culturally aberrant. There might be pressure subtly applied on Malay women to undertake 'veiling', but the strong desire to conform which characterized Malay culture also accounted for widespread 'veiling' among urban and Malay women in the 1980s.

Today in Malaysia, 'veiling' is no longer something exceptional or extraordinary as it was in the 1970s. Nor is it a form of male oppression of women. 'Veiling' is a form of 'critical consciousness arising out of freedom of choice'[17] which Malay women have enjoyed all along. In the 1970s, there was a close relationship between 'veiling' and a woman's religious inclination and political interest. During that time, 'veiled' women generally were rural migrants and religious activists who were affiliated to either the *Al Arqam* or ABIM. Nowadays, 'veiling' does not provide a guide to the educational qualification, social status, religious inclination or political interests of Malay women. There is also no relationship between a woman's attire and her desire to pursue a public or professional career. There are 'veiled' women who are highly educated, do not work but are very active in politics. Then there are 'veiled' women who are lowly educated but are income-earners. There are also women who don the headscarves in the workplace but do not put them on when they go out after office hours.

Women's public role

As pointed out earlier, when Islamic fundamentalism first occurred, the number of Malay women who had entered Malaysia's workforce had increased considerably. Although the fundamentalists discussed at length women's public roles, they did not call for women to withdraw from the public sphere. What they did do was to urge the Muslim public to identify the types of activities that were appropriate for women. In their scheme of things, all three fundamentalist organizations agreed that women should be involved in child-bearing, child-rearing and other domestic labour. However, on the question of whether or not women should take up outside employment, the fundamentalists had differing views. The *Jemaah*

Tabligh was silent on the matter. Its silence and the fact that it was an all-male organization might be interpreted to mean that it disapproved of women working. The *Al Arqam* and ABIM had no qualms about women developing their potential through education and for work but insisted that they should not hold occupations that would promote sinful activities or put them in danger. These jobs ranged from selling lottery tickets to serving in the casino and night clubs, which from the fundamentalists' point of view should be avoided at all cost.

On the issue of women's involvement in society, the ABIM was positive about women taking up outside employment and balancing it with domestic work. The *Al Arqam* movement, on the other hand, preferred Muslim women to leave mainstream society and contribute their labour and skills to help develop and sustain the Islamic villages of which they formed a part and the *Al Arqam* movement as a whole. This was in line with the movement's main goal to produce a counter-culture in the form of the Islamic classical society. So women in the *Al Arqam* villages normally fulfilled their traditional roles as wives, mothers and co-wives. Those who possessed the required skills undertook female-oriented vocations such as nursing, teaching, producing clothes and foodstuffs such as cakes, noodles, *catch-up* and vegetables.

It must be pointed out here that, although Islamic fundamentalism triggered some reflection on the issue of women and domesticity, there was no coercive measure whatsoever taken by the fundamentalists or their supporters to make Muslim women stay at home. The question of whether or not women should work and become income-earners remains merely rhetorical. The decision to work or not to work is left to individual Malay women and their immediate families. Often, the decision on the part of a woman to resign from a post to concentrate on her family is based more on practical needs than on religious conviction. Furthermore, there is a steady increase in the number of Malay girls attending schools and universities. In the workforce, more Malay women have risen to positions of authority as managers, senior executives, professors, directors of companies, banks and research institutes. All this goes to show that despite the fundamentalists' reservations about Muslim women giving priority to outside employment, Malay women are equipping themselves with the necessary skills to help them become income-earners and are consciously translating their potential as career women.

Religious activism

Prior to the occurrence of *dakwah*, Malay women could engage in participatory action through political parties and voluntary associations. In the religious realm, they were totally excluded as positions as *imam* and preachers were reserved solely for religious scholars (*ulamak*), all of whom were men. Islamic fundamentalism now produced religious movements which were determined to bring Islam back to the centre stage of public life, to keep it alive and dynamic. To achieve this, they intended to intensify Islamic mission work, or *dakwah Islamiyah*, which was thought to be waning. With the exception of *Jemaah Tabligh*, the other *dakwah* movements were prepared to involve women in religious and social activities to help promote the Islamization cause.

As with the Islamic message of 'veiling', the fundamentalists' call for religious activism in the name of *dakwah* had great psychological and personal appeals to two strata of women. The first was the previously mentioned culturally displaced educated women of rural origin who were born in the mid-1940s and who were sceptical of the virtues of Western modernity. The second category comprised of women who were the products of Malaysia's NEP and who had received tertiary education in the 1970s and mid-1980s in Malaysia or abroad, where religious renewal had earlier taken place. The pattern of religious activism of these two strata of women in religious activism differed somewhat. For those women in the first stratum, participatory action in the realm of religion was possible if they joined the ABIM or *Al Arqam*, since these were the only bodies at that time which served as social contexts within which women could learn how to missionize. However, religious activism for these women took different forms, depending on the organization with which they were affiliated. The women who joined the *Al Arqam* movement did not appear in public to proselytize since that task was assigned to the male members. For the *Al Arqam* women, religious activism involved a constant struggle to purify themselves from Western accretions, to develop the inner strength to enable them to make material and emotional sacrifices for the sake of Islam and the *Al Arqam* movement, to exercise self-control to bring to fruition the ideal Islamic society envisioned by the founder and leader of the movement. In their own minds, and of the men who dominated the movement, religious activism was an externalization of a calm and peaceful *jihad* (legitimate rebellion). *Al Arqam* women accomplished this by fulfilling their roles as wives, mothers and co-wives, contributing their legal, medical, literary and accounting skills to the upkeep of *Al Arqam*'s commercial enterprises, running sewing and craft shops, canteens, food-processing and book publishing, and accompanying their husbands on *dakwah* missions within and outside Malaysia.

The women who joined the ABIM became socially engaged through a variety of activities. For a nominal fee, they could affiliate with HELWA (an acronym for *Hal Ehwal Wanita* or Women's Affairs), the women section of the ABIM. At the height of its popularity,[18] the ABIM had about 5,000 female members distributed all over the country. However, the women who were religiously active in the ABIM were those in the upper echelon of the movement. Mostly professionals, these women helped plan and implement short- and long-term programmes that focused on religious education, Arabic literacy, charity work, religious conversion and rehabilitation of new converts. HELWA leaders and ordinary members carried out these religious consciousness-raising programmes through a variety of activities. They organized *Qur'an* study groups, conducted numerous seminars and conferences to discuss women's issues in development, gave informed addresses (*ceramah*) on social and religious issues, contributed articles on religion and society in the local newspapers, magazines and academic journals and participated in training programmes aimed at inducing confidence and motivation among Muslim youths.

Towards the end of the 1980s, the ABIM and *Al Arqam* were no longer the only organizations that provided the opportunities for women to be involved in religious activism. Political parties, individual *ulamak*, independent preachers (*pendakwah bebas*) and populist imams were also actively involved in the religious intensification now carried out in the name of 'Islamization', no longer '*dakwah*'. This time religious activism was less about denouncing the West as with making Malay Muslim virtues serve the modern and civil needs of the citizenry, empowering men and women with various branches of Islamic religious knowledge, including Islamic mysticism, and encouraging greater reflection as well as debate on matters of common concerns such as social injustice, corruption and nepotism to name a few. So among the Malay urban dwellers, who made up 45.6 per cent of the total urban population in 1990,[19] numerous social and religious groups emerged that were centred around mosques and communal prayer houses (*surau*), as well as local level, Islam-oriented, non-governmental organizations with which men and women could affiliate for activist purposes.

For the religiously active members of the second stratum of Malay women – the products of the NEP – the ABIM and *Al Arqam* were less attractive contexts compared to the local religious groups and associations for engaging in participatory action. By 1990, both the ABIM and *Al Arqam* had lost their lustre as authentic Islamic movements. In the case of the *Al Arqam* movement, many unsavoury stories circulated about the exploitation of its female members. As for the ABIM, the movement was said to be too elitist and leaning heavily towards the government. We do not know for certain to what extent changes in the images of the ABIM and *Al Arqam* prevented the second stratum of women from joining these movements. But the new thinking was that local social and religious groups could do an equally good job at Islamizing society as the national level religious organizations. Besides, being organized around *surau* or mosques, these associations have become integral features of urban community life and therefore are easier for women to identify with.

There is a dearth of information about these community-based social and religious groups. Their differences in terms of structural organization, membership and roles notwithstanding, these groups without doubt provided alternative contexts to the national level religious organizations for Malay women to organize for religious activism. The religiously inclined women in present-day Malaysia normally affiliate officially or unofficially to the parent organization, which could be a local non-governmental organization or the committee responsible for planning and implementing religious and social activities in the local mosque or *surau*. Sometimes working together with the male members of the organization or on their own, these women mobilize female preachers to hold religious classes and talks (*ceramah*) to discuss Islamic doctrinal matters as well as current issues that concern women. Among the issues discussed are women and health, quality time between spouses, domestic violence, women's rights in Islam, juvenile delinquency and polygamy.

The range of issues and problems that capture the imagination of women activists in the present era evidently has a lot to do with the effects of the postcolonial development model, which aimed at firmly locking Malaysia into the world capitalist system and transforming the country into a developed country by 2020. Looking at their activities and their concerns with the issues mentioned above, one thing becomes obvious. Women religious activists are facing new challenges on how to balance the need to assert Islamic womanhood, reaffirm the progressive elements of Islamic culture with respect to the woman question, and create a democratic and just society safe for women. In the process, a new consciousness is quietly but certainly evolving. At the moment, this consciousness is most evident among members of *Wanita* JIM, the women section of a new *dakwah* organization called *Jemaah Islah Malaysia* (JIM). JIM is an offshoot of the ABIM and came into being in 1990. Its women section, *Wanita* JIM, was formed three years later, in 1993. What is striking about *Wanita* JIM is its outright claim that its members are 'fundamentalists *and* contemporary' (*fundamental dan kontemporari*). This is to say that *Wanita* JIM is proud to be called 'fundamentalists' and try to show that 'fundamentalists' are not retrogressive, but very much current and in touch with modern times. Contrary to a widely held assumption that fundamentalist women are passive followers of Islamic fundamentalism, *Wanita* JIM actually played an active role in articulating a new model of Islamic women in Malaysia. If, previously, fundamentalist women were portrayed as puritanical, reactionary and exclusivist, the 'fundamentalist and contemporary' Muslim woman's image, on the other hand, is puritanical, proactive and inclusivist.

In line with the policy of its parent organization, *Wanita* JIM dedicates itself to creating Islamic neighbourhoods in the urban and rural settings. Appearing quite recently on the Malaysian religious and political scenes and being extremely sensitive to the rapid changes in technology and human development occasioned by economic globalism, *Wanita* JIM addressed the Islamization issue by focusing on religious education, training of women in areas of information communication technology (ICT), family management and family counselling and promotion of women rights. So towards this end, the active members of *Wanita* JIM set up help centres for women, organize religious talks and seminars, conduct courses to improve computer literacy among women and develop women leadership skills. In 1997, *Wanita* JIM started to network with other women organizations such as the National Council of Women's Organizations and the Women Lawyers Association, so it could make an input into the discussion on women and gender issues at the national level. So far, *Wanita* JIM has participated in, and contributed to, the formulation of a new document presented to the government, called the 'Women Agenda For Change'.

Wanita JIM therefore can be considered a reform-minded Islamist feminist group.[20] Although guided by the policy of its parent organization, in this case JIM, at the heart of *Wanita* JIM is the desire to improve the status and moral well-being of Muslim women. Its gender sensitization projects are not so much about oppression and marginalization of women as about ensuring that women gain the respect already recognized for their roles as mothers, daughters and employees. Undeniably *Wanita* JIM has an important public role to play. However, its potential for success among women in the rural and urban areas, young and old, its impact on the 'woman question' in Islam and the challenges that it brings to the feminist discourse on gender rights have yet to be explored. Although members of *Wanita* JIM meet regularly to discuss Islamic philosophy and teachings, there is no one among them who tries to offer a radically different understanding of Islam, its law and women rights in Islam. Like other fundamentalist groups, *Wanita* JIM believes that unfettered rights for women in Islam have no place in the Islamic belief system and that another view is surely wrong. However, the group is exploring possibilities for dialogue with secular feminists on gender inequality. It may meet with difficulties and setbacks because of its own political naïveté and the biases against and apprehensions about religious fundamentalists being conservative, rigid and chauvinistic which certain feminist groups in the country may still entertain.

Growing feminist consciousness is also discernible among leaders of *Dewan Muslimat*. As pointed out earlier in this chapter, since it was penetrated by fundamentalist forces in 1982, PAS has made a stand to stop women from standing as candidates in the elections. The *Dewan Muslimat* leaders, comprised of highly educated women, recently presented a concept paper to party leadership arguing for women party members to take part in the elections. The party's spiritual leader Datuk Nik Aziz Nik Mat relented by saying that 'We [PAS] will select women candidates to vie for parliamentary seats in the next general elections.'[21] Although it is hard to tell whether or not that PAS leader would follow through his promise, it is obvious that members of *Dewan Muslimat* too are trying to push for change in PAS. Looking at their background, it is clear that the leaders of *Dewan Muslimat* are those women who have adhered to the model of Islamic womanhood that the fundamentalists attempted to construct in the initial phase of Islamic fundamentalism. Paradoxically, these women have utilized 'veiling' and other religious pursuits required of them to gain a respected Islamic identity to their own political advantage. They argue against the men who dominate PAS that women's public role should no longer be construed as a source of moral disorder, considering that Islamic neighbourhoods and communities have materialized in the country. These women are therefore a force to reckon with in PAS and whom men do not find easy to control and subdue. Though still occupying subordinate status in their respective organizations, these women feel empowered and confident and, as in the case of *Wanita* JIM, are prepared to address secular feminists' concerns over issues of oppression, gender discrimination and gender inequality, using the Islamic perspective.

Conclusion

In Malaysia the Islamic fundamentalism that unfolded in the 1970s has been, and still is, an important religio-political activity involving to a large extent the Malay population. Its original aims were to rebuild

Malay–Muslim identity and link it to the Islamic past in the hope of enhancing confidence among Malays to help them face the numerous challenges of economic globalism. Islamic fundamentalism had, and still has, the wide backing of Muslims from all walks of life and manifests itself in different forms and at different levels of society. Following on this, the Malaysian government has come to recognize that there are several versions or models of Islam in the country, as reflected in the use of such terms as 'liberal Muslims', 'extremist Muslims', 'progressive Muslims' and mostly recently 'fundamentalist and contemporary Muslims'.

Unlike certain fundamentalist groups in countries such as Egypt, Algeria and Palestine that are militant in nature, fundamentalist groups in Malaysia do not deploy Islamic resources in the service of violence and racial disharmony. Islamic fundamentalism does evoke a strong sense of separateness between Malays and non-Malays, but does not cause a breakdown of positive social values and social institutions in the country. Partly because of government support and partly because of high economic growth, Islamic fundamentalism stimulates institution-building activities in the areas of education, charity work and community development.

Following social change triggered by Islamic fundamentalism, the fate of Muslim women in Malaysia has not been negatively affected. Islamic fundamentalism does not erode the civil liberties of Muslim women. Muslim women can work, exercise their rights to employment on the basis of their merits and vote. It is in the field of politics that fundamentalist ideology has been used to curtail women's involvement in decision-making. But then again, this is not widespread and is confined only to the Islamic Party of Malaysia (PAS). In maintaining that it will not field women candidates in the elections, the party may not consciously think that women can have any input in civil liberty. However, that stance can stop women from accessing opportunities to participate in decision-making processes at the national level. In Malaysia, women's participation in the process is crucial, considering that women are more sensitive to the practical and strategic needs of women. Furthermore, culturally speaking, it is considered more appropriate for women to articulate women and gender issues than for men to do so.

On the question of women's rights, Islamic fundamentalism in Malaysia did not trigger a paradigm shift to allow Muslims to recognize those rights as human rights. They hold on tightly to the belief that unencumbered gender equality has no place within the Islamic belief system. The new generation of Muslim women, who have earned a respected Islamic identity and who, by asserting themselves through political parties and NGOs, also subscribe to this view. However, in order to secure a greater role in the public sphere, these women are prepared to negotiate with the male leadership in their respective organizations using the framework of Islam.

The condition and fate of women in Malaysia have not been, and still are not, critical compared to other Muslim countries so as to merit the attention of human rights organizations. Islamic fundamentalism certainly has not changed the situation. In fact, there has not been any record of bad treatment of Muslim women on the basis of religious conviction. Also fundamentalist forces in Malaysia have adopted a non-confrontational *modus operandi* which makes it possible for concerned parties to negotiate with them. This *modus operandi* is a feature of Malay culture and tradition which generally favours negotiations to open conflict.

Notes

1 '*Dakwah*' means 'to invite one' to Islam but in the 1970s it had a threatening tone because, when articulated by religious activists, the term denoted criticism against indifference shown by the state and society towards Islam.

2 For some time, the Malay Peninsula was referred to as West Malaysia while Sabah and Sarawak were called East Malaysia. Since reservations were raised with regard to the use of the terms 'East' and 'West', because they implied separateness, the Malay Peninsula is now referred to as Peninsular Malaysia, while the states of Sabah and Sarawak retain their names.

3 The British relinquished their control over Sabah and Sarawak in 1963. The two states together with Singapore joined Malaya in 1963 to form the Federation of Malaysia. Singapore, however, seceded from Malaysia in 1965.

4 In Malaysia, the states that have Sultans are unofficially classified as 'royal states', to distinguish them from those states that do not have Sultans. The nine royal states are Perlis, Kedah, Kelantan, Terengganu, Pahang, Perak, Johor, Negri Sembilan and Selangor. The non-royal states comprise Sabah and Sarawak and two states in Peninsular Malaysia, Penang and Melaka. In each of the non-royal states, the head of the Islamic religion is the governor. The Malaysian sovereign, referred to as the *Yang Di Pertuan Agong*, is chosen from among the nine Sultans. He serves as the *Yang Di Pertuan Agong* for a period of five years.

5 The Alliance was made up of three communal parties, the United Malays National Organization (UMNO), the Malayan Chinese Association (MCA) and the Malayan Indian Congress (MIC). These parties, together with several others, later formed the National Front or *Barisan Nasional* (BN), the ruling party in Malaysia now.

6 Abdul Rahman Embong, 'Malaysian middle classes: some preliminary observations', *Jurnal Antropologi dan Sosiologi*, vol. 22, 1995, pp. 31–54.

7 Arabic schools were actually modern religious schools. These schools differed from traditional religious learning centres called *pondok*, in that Arabic schools taught students not just Islamic theological sciences but also secular subjects such as geography, history and mathematics.

WOMEN AND ISLAMIC FUNDAMENTALISM

8 Virginia H. Dancz, *Women and Party Politics in Peninsular Malaysia*, Singapore: Oxford University Press, 1987, p. 24.
9 Rahmah Ismail and Zaini Mahbar (eds), *Wanita dan Pekerjaan*, Bangi: Penerbit Universiti Klebangsaan Malaysia, 1996, p. 25.
10 William R. Roff, *The Origins of Malay Nationalism*, New Haven, CT: Yale University Press, 1967.
11 '*Kaum Muda*' means 'the young group'. Their opponents, the religious traditionalists, were called the '*Kaum Tua*' meaning 'the old group'.
12 The *Al Arqam* movement was banned in August 1994 because as the movement expanded in size and popularity, its leader, Ashaari Muhammad, started to impart messianic messages about the coming of the *Mahdi* (Hidden Imam). In a book and through talks, the leader of the *Al Arqam* movement claimed that his former teacher had not died but would one day return as Imam *Mahdi*. Later, Ashaari claimed that he had a dialogue with Prophet Muhammad in the Kaabah in Mekah and that he was the young man from the Prophet's tribe who was to herald the coming of the *Mahdi*. These claims were not acceptable to orthodox Islam and according to Islamic law as enforced in Malaysia, Ashaari was found guilty of spreading deviationist teachings. This decision was arrived at by the National Council of Islamic Religion which issued a legal ruling (*fatwa*) to that effect.
13 Anwar Ibrahim, *Jelaskan Wadah Perbaru Tekad: Pesanan Buat Generasi Muda*, Kuala Lumpur: ABIM, 1975.
14 Muhammad Syukri Salleh, *An Islamic Approach to Rural Development: The Arqam Way*, London: ASOIB International, 1992, p. 48.
15 Dancz, *Women and Party Politics*, p. 221.
16 For purposes of discussion, I use the term 'veiling' to refer to the adoption of the Islamic dress code or to *bertudung*.
17 Judith Nagata, 'Modern Malay women and the message of the veil', in Wazir Jahan Karim (ed.) '*Male' and 'Female' in Developing Southeast Asia*, Oxford: Berg Publishers, 1995, p. 111.
18 ABIM was a very influential organization in the 1970s, but when its third president, Anwar Ibrahim, left the organization in 1982 to join Dr Mahathir Mohammad's administration and UMNO, ABIM popularity as a non-partisan organization declined. See Muhammad Kamal Gassan, 'The response of Muslim youth organizations to political change: HMI in Indonesia and ABIM in Malaysia', in William R. Roff (ed.) *Islam and the Political Economy of Meaning*, London and Sydney: Croom Helm, 1987, p. 183.
19 Mohd. Yusuf Kassim, 'Perkembangan ekonomi selepas 1970', in Hairi Abdullah (ed.) *Titian Warna: Sejarah Pembangunan dan Perubahan Citra Kuala Lumpur*, Kuala Lumpur: Penerbitan Sejarah, 1995, p. 120.
20 Compare Azza M. Karam, *Women, Islamisms and the State: Contemporary Feminism in Egypt*, London: Macmillan Press, 1998.
21 *Kuala Lumpur Star*, 6 February 2001, p. 4.

Select bibliography

Dancz, Virginia H., *Women and Party Politics in Peninsular Malaysia*, Singapore: Oxford University Press, 1987.

Moghadam, Valentine M. (ed.) *Gender and National Identity: Women and Politics in Muslim Societies*, London: Zed Books, 1994.

Muzaffar, Chandra, *Islamic Resurgence in Malaysia*, Petaling Jaya: Pelanduk Publications, 1987.

Nagata, Judith, 'Modern Malay women and the message of the veil', in Wazir Jahan Karim (ed.) *'Male' and 'Female' in Developing Southeast Asia*, Oxford: Berg Publishers, 1995, pp. 101–20.

Rashila Ramli, 'Democratisation in Malaysia: toward gender parity in political participation', in *Akademika*, vol. 53, 1998, pp. 61–76.

4

'RENEW OUR DAYS AS OF OLD'

Religious fundamentalism and social change in the modern Jewish state

Alice Shalvi

The old shall be renewed and the new shall be sanctified.
(Rabbi Abraham Isaac Kook, Chief Rabbi of Palestine,
1921–35)

The development of Jewish law

Judaism is a religion based on the implementation in everyday life of moral and ethical principles, the essence of which is first summarized in the Ten Commandments believed to have been given to the Children of Israel at Mount Sinai by God, acting through his intermediary, Moses. These commandments, formulated as imperatives of commission and prohibition, are supposed to find practical expression through the strict observance of the priestly code of 613 biblical commandments predicated on the *Pentateuch*, which expand upon and explicate the *Decalogue*.

The biblical commandments have, in their turn, been further expanded, explicated, interpreted and debated over the past 2,500 years by successive generations of sages, whose decisions and dictates are presented in the Oral Law (*halakhah*) first codified in the *Mishnah* by Yehuda Ha-Nasi in the second century CE; again in the *Talmud*, which was composed between the second and sixth centuries; once more by Moses Maimonides in the twelfth century; and finally in the sixteenth century by Joseph Caro in the *Shulkhan Arukh*, which is currently considered the principal codificatory receptacle of *halakhah*.

A study of the codificatory trend in Jewish law reveals the interesting historical phenomenon of a recurring revival of activity at intervals of 100 to 200 years. However, for the past 400 years or so there has appeared no further generally recognized or authoritative code that embraces the entire field of Oral Law. Furthermore, for over 200 years the entire code has ceased to be universally accepted by all members of the Jewish faith (or people, as it may now be more appropriate to refer to them).

This change is primarily due to the 'enlightenment' of the late eighteenth century, which increased secularization and weakened traditional *Talmud* study, and to the emancipation of the Jews which occurred in Europe at about the same time. Between them, these two developments radically changed the face of Jewish society, for with the emancipation occurred an abrogation of Jewish organizational (and, gradually, also judicial) autonomy, which led to the division of that society into traditional and non-traditional elements, as well as religiously observant and secular.

The process of rabbinical reinterpretation continues to the present day, conducted by hundreds – even thousands – of rabbis worldwide, wherever Jewish communities exist. But these rabbis are now sectorized within different 'denominations' or 'streams' of Judaism and enjoy varying degrees of authority beyond (or even within) their respective affiliations. The major non-Orthodox streams are Reform Judaism, which has almost completely abandoned *halakhic* authority, and Conservative Judaism, which is based on *halakhah*, but stresses the importance of its reinterpretation in the light of changing social norms.

Rabbis of the various streams do not necessarily agree with or valorize each other. Indeed, the *responsa* and edicts of Conservative and Reform rabbis and the practices of their respective adherents are fiercely criticized and rejected by the Orthodox and Ultra-orthodox (*haredi*) streams, who question the authenticity and deny the very legitimacy of the newer streams.

Concurrently with the development and reinterpretation of Jewish law, there occurred a development of *minhag* or custom, which, over time, attained a status approaching that of law and is considered by many to be equally binding. In fact, many Jews, whether religiously observant or non-observant, would be hard put to it to identify what is law and what is custom, so much has the latter attained an aura of compulsion. The same is true, though to a somewhat lesser extent, of *masoret*, tradition, which, however, lacks all the binding elements of both *halakhah* and *minhag*.

Fundamentalist or 'classical' Orthodox tradition

Contemporary Jewish fundamentalism (like religious fundamentalism in general) may be defined as a fidelity, often rigid, to religious tradition, ideology or sacred text and the literal (or extremely strict) interpretation of such text.

The tradition which governs Jewish fundamentalist thought and practice is, above all, androcentric and patriarchal, drawing a clear distinction
between male and female, traceable to that found in the opening chapter
of Genesis, which, among other things, narrates the creation of humankind: 'Male and female created He them.'

In this respect, Judaism is no different from other religions. What one
legal authority has identified as 'a core feature of religious fundamentalism', namely 'the vigorous political promotion, and legal reinforcement of
gender roles whose explicit intent entails the subordination of women',
exists also in Judaism.[1]

The gender-based distinction finds expression in a wide variety of elements in Jewish theology and religious practice, beginning with the very
language both of the biblical text and of the liturgy which developed only
much later. In Hebrew, which is a gender-inflected language lacking the
neuter form, the deity is masculine as, in the standard liturgy, is the person
addressing Him, the 'I' of prayer. Thus, for example, the individual who,
in the biblical citation which is part of the daily prayer, is bidden to 'love
the Lord thy God' is male. Even the tenth commandment, in referring to
'thy neighbour' posits both a male subject and a male correlative in the
neighbourly relationship. Hence the injunction is not to covet one's neighbour's 'wife', rather than his or her 'spouse'.

Jewish theology is similarly androcentric. The command which (literally) 'embodies' the unique relationship between God and the Jewish
people finds physical expression in the circumcision of every male child at
the age of eight days. While Jewish prayer, as recited by both men and
women, refers to 'Thy covenant which Thou hast sealed in our flesh',
Jewish women (perhaps fortunately, given the horrors of female genital
mutilation) do not bear that seal.[2]

The covenant was initially entered into with Abraham and reconfirmed
with the successive patriarchs, Isaac and Jacob. Though Jacob had a
daughter, Dinah, the tribes of Israel derived only from his twelve sons.
Significantly, the only part of the Genesis narrative in which Dinah figures
as a protagonist deals with her abduction by Hamor, son of Shehem, and
the subsequent bloody avenging of the stain on the family honour by her
brothers, Shimon and Levi. Throughout the entire episode Dinah is objectified, silent, her voice unheard and unrecorded. The verb which recurs
most frequently with reference to her is 'to take', an action performed on
her by both her abductors and her brothers.

Traditional Jewish ritual is also androcentric. The two most significant
events in the life of a Jewish male are his circumcision and his *bar-mitzva* –
the 'coming of age' on his thirteenth birthday – which makes him

responsible for his own actions, imposes on him the practice of the commandments and makes him eligible for inclusion in the quorum of ten adult males, which is a prerequisite both for the recitation of some of Judaism's most central and sacred prayers (including the mourners' *Kaddish*) and for the reading of the Law from a *Torah* scroll, which occurs on Mondays, Thursdays and the Sabbath.

Women are not eligible for inclusion in the prayer quorum. They are also exempt from fulfilling some of the commandments, most specifically those which are time-bound (that is, have to be performed at specific times of the day or the year). In this respect, women are categorized in Jewish law together with male minors and Canaanite slaves – a significant grouping!

Not only have Jewish women not enjoyed equal status in synagogue and other ritual; they have also been denied the type and degree of Jewish education traditionally deemed essential for Jewish males, whose ideal occupation, in the opinion of traditionalists, is the study of the Law (that is, the *Talmud*). Forbidden entry into the house of study (*Beit Midrash*) and the *Yeshiva* (Talmudic seminary), Jewish women (with only a very few exceptions) have until recently lacked the knowledge required in order to be actively involved in the interpretation of *halakhah*. Needless to say, this means that they cannot be recognized or ordained as rabbinical authorities.

Women's traditional role and social status

The traditional roles of the Jewish woman, once again predicated on the earliest chapters of Genesis, are those of wife ('helpmate'), mother and home-maker, roles performed in the private, domestic domain that is itself considered a bastion of Jewish life and practice. The family and the domestic venue exemplify ideals to which Jewish women are to aspire.

In legal terms, a Jewish woman is subject to the authority of a male relative, first as daughter and later as wife. Indeed, the Jewish marriage ceremony is an act of symbolic purchase (though no money needs to change hands) in which the bride becomes her husband's property, while he undertakes to provide for all her needs, including sexual satisfaction. The Hebrew word for 'husband' is 'owner'. A woman can be released from marriage only if her husband, of his free will and being of sound mind, places in her willingly outstretched hands a *get* or bill of divorcement. There have never been, nor are there at present, any women on the three-member panels of rabbinical judges which authorize (but cannot finalize) the granting of a divorce. In Israel, the rabbinical courts have sole jurisdiction over personal law and there is no option of civil marriage or civil divorce for any citizen, irrespective of the religion of which they are officially registered as members.[3]

While excluded from any role in public prayer – an exclusion which, in Orthodox circles, has been extended to all public roles in society – Jewish adult women are obligated to three commandments which are incumbent only upon them, all of which are predicated on their being married homemakers. These are, respectively, *ner*, the kindling of lights which ushers in the Sabbath and the Holy days; *niddah*, the physical apartness or separation between husband and wife during and immediately after menstruation – a separation which must continue until there is no further sign of menstrual blood and the woman has purified herself by immersion in a ritual bath (*mikveh*); and *halah*, the setting aside and burning of a portion of the bread dough in commemoration of the Temple sacrificial rites.

The overriding quality desired in the traditional Jewish woman – and the one most frequently adduced by religious authorities as a justification for her exclusion from the public arena – is modesty. Woman's voice is decried by fundamentalists as an 'abomination', as is woman's hair, while other parts of her body are considered inducive to lascivious thoughts in men. Thus Orthodoxy demands that married women cover their hair (or, in some extremely fundamentalist communities, shave their heads upon marriage prior to covering their baldness with a kerchief); that unmarried women and girls keep their hair neatly braided and never 'dishevelled' (the latter being a sign of wantonness and even prostitution); that all females wear long-sleeved garments and stockings at all seasons and that their clothing never reveal the contours of their bodies. There is, however, no demand to conceal the face, though cosmetics are frowned upon.

While Judaism has no practice comparable to *purdah* (the seclusion of Muslim and Hindu Indian women from public observation), in Orthodox circles women are customarily expected to stay away from the company of men, even when the latter congregate in a private home. At all times they are expected to speak softly, avoid boisterous behaviour of any kind, and above all never to raise their voices in song except when there is no possibility whatever of their being heard by man. According to *halakhah* a man and woman (other than a married couple) may not be alone together in a closed room. Marriages are frequently arranged by the parents or acquaintances of the couple; courtship is brief and there are (albeit increasingly infrequent) cases in which the bride and groom first meet only days before the wedding and are never alone together until after the ceremony. At Orthodox weddings, men and women do not mingle, there is no mixed dancing and, when space allows, the sexes celebrate in separate rooms.

Ultra-orthodox men will not shake hands with women, nor sit beside them, even in public vehicles.

In the synagogue, Orthodox women are concealed behind a *mehizah*, a dividing screen designed to make them invisible to the eyes of male worshippers. Frequently, they are relegated to an upper room or gallery where, in many cases, they are not only not seen, but are also prevented from seeing (or, in some cases, even from hearing) what is going on in the course of the service.

The traditional role of *materfamilias* which Jewish women are expected to fill has in recent years, especially in Israel, become a kind of 'maternal imperative', the motto of which seems to be 'the more, the better'. Ultra-orthodox women pride themselves on bearing as many as fourteen or fifteen children; in this they are comparable to earlier generations of women, a major difference being that now the children survive, creating an enormous burden in terms of time and money.

Fundamentalist rabbis forbid the use of contraception and cessation of pregnancy, sometimes even in cases where medical opinion has indicated that pregnancy might prove physically incapacitating or even fatal to the mother. Recently the Israeli media reported cases in which such rabbis provided fertility pills to childless women or to those who were having problems in becoming pregnant once more after having borne 'too few' children. Paradoxically, the rabbinical edict in such cases goes counter to *halakhah*, which permits and even prescribes abortion if the mother's life is at risk and which at all times, even during labour or delivery, gives the mother's life precedence over that of the unborn child.

The trauma of the Holocaust and the loss of six million Jewish lives has cast such a profound shadow over contemporary Jewish society that it is comparatively easy to induce guilt in any woman who fails to do her utmost to replace the lost generation. In Israel, the threat of being outnumbered by the hostile surrounding countries or by the indigenous Arab population provides another impetus. Needless to say, multiple births and the consequent duties of mothering also serve to keep women securely confined to their households.

Despite this confinement, Orthodox – and particularly Ultra-orthodox – women continue the long-established tradition of women being income-earners, often even the primary income-earners in the family, in order to enable their husbands to engage in full-time *Torah* study – an occupation which is considered the fulfilment of the most important of all commandments, since it teaches one to obey the other commandments. Whereas in the past it was often difficult to combine or reconcile income-earning with the demands of modesty and separation of the sexes, modern technology has facilitated such a combination; women can and do use telephones, facsimile machines, computers and other electronic devices in order to work from home. Not only can working hours then be flexible and consistent with the demands of family, but – paradoxically – the degree of technical knowledge and skills required has resulted in women being far better educated than their menfolk, whose studies are still confined primarily, even solely, to ancient texts whose contemporary relevance is questionable. Nevertheless, these women would be the first to maintain that what they are doing is as naught in terms of spiritual or religious values compared to what their husbands are doing. Their pride is precisely in that they are enabling that study to take place undisturbed and uninterrupted by material concerns and the exigencies of everyday family responsibilities.

Winds of change

Enlightenment, emancipation, the steady ascendancy of the non-Orthodox movements, the 'liberation' of secular women (both Jewish and non-Jewish) – all of these, together with other aspects of modernity, have had a dual impact on Jewish orthopraxis and fundamentalism. On the one hand, modernity has weakened the Orthodox hold over the Jewish community. On the other, it has aroused a (not unexpected) absolutist intensification of the practices that distinguish the Orthodox, Ultra-orthodox and fundamentalist sectors from the rest of society, a reaction which expresses itself in ever more severe attacks on the various phenomena that characterize modernity.

Zionism and the establishment of an autonomous 'Jewish state' in 1948 constituted the major challenge to Orthodoxy in the twentieth century, engendering (perhaps inevitable) conflicts between religious tradition and modernity, between the determination to establish a democratic mode of government that promised equality of opportunity, reward and status to all its citizens, 'irrespective of race, creed or sex' (in the words of the Declaration of Independence), and the dictates of traditional Judaism.

The majority of the pioneers who came from Europe to reclaim the land of Israel were secularists who had quite deliberately shaken off the shackles of religion, together with other aspects of what they considered to be ghettoized, effete qualities of Diaspora life. Similarly, secular Jews today constitute the majority of Israeli citizens. However, there has always been – and remains – an overriding desire to maintain certain basic Jewish principles and practices which are considered fundamental to ensuring the Jewishness of the state – a state in which 20 per cent of the citizens are non-Jewish Muslim or Christian Arabs. Thus, Saturday is the official

Sabbath, or day of rest, and the Jewish calendar determines public holidays; Hebrew is the official language – revived as a living language after almost 2,000 years of serving as the language only of prayer and study; and observance of *kashrut* (dietary laws) marks all public institutions. Yet all this did not suffice for the Orthodox and, more especially, the Ultra-orthodox sectors of Israeli society, many of whom quite clearly favour the establishment of a quasi-theocracy in which Jewish law would take precedence over – or would at least infuse – legislation passed by a democratically elected parliament.

In order to exert maximal influence on the legislative process, various sectors within the religious community in Israel established political parties, which over time have significantly increased their representation in the *Knesset* (Israel's parliament), and exploited their growing electoral power by bringing pressure to bear on successive governments in order both to impede secularization and to increase the financial and material benefits extended to the Orthodox population.

The political platforms of these parties clearly aim at ensuring that Orthodox *halakhic* principles maximally determine such critical issues as 'Who is a Jew?',[4] Sabbath and Holy day observance, and personal status (in particular, marriage and divorce). Since 1977, the fundamentalist religious parties have gained so much power that whichever majority party seeks to set up a coalition government is left with little option but to surrender to at least some of the demands made by the religious parties on whose support it depends.

Perhaps the most remarkable increase in power has accrued to *Shas*, the most recently founded of the Orthodox parties, which combines religion and ethnicity, claiming to represent the socio-economically deprived sector of Israeli society, those who immigrated from the Arab states in the early 1950s and who are still in many respects discriminated against.

Like fundamentalist groups elsewhere (for example, the *Hamas* under the Palestinian Authority), *Shas* has won adherents by developing social and educational services which ease the burden of the poor, and they have done so by extorting subsidies and funding in return for their support of successive governments, irrespective of the political ideology of the ruling party.

Shas's educational institutions are sex-segregated from early childhood on and their curriculum is extremely narrow, focusing on religious studies that are taught from a strictly fundamentalist, non-critical point of view. Nevertheless, increasing numbers of moderately religious or even wholly non-observant families are availing themselves of these kindergartens and schools because they alone provide hot lunches, longer school days, and busing. Since poorer parents also tend to have more children, the proportion of young people attending *Shas* schools is constantly growing, with subsequent intellectually detrimental effects.

What is probably more damaging to the democratic mode of government to which Israel aspires is the fact that members of the *Knesset* from the religious parties never make a political decision without first consulting their respective 'spiritual leaders', rabbis who are, of course, not democratically elected. These leaders, it should be stated, are clearly guided by expediency and non-spiritual considerations.

Probably the most significant indication of religious control in Israel is the fact that there is no true separation of state and religion such as exists in most democratic regimes. The *Knesset* legislates some aspects of religious life and practice, such as Sabbath working hours, while supervision of the implementation of such legislation is in the hands of a state-appointed, state-salaried Chief Rabbinate, a Chief Rabbinical Council, local and regional religious councils and rabbinical courts, all of whose members are Orthodox males. Rabbinical courts have sole jurisdiction over personal status. Only state-recognized rabbis may officiate at weddings, if the marriage is to be officially recognized by the Ministry of the Interior (which itself has long been in the hands of representatives of one or other of the religious parties). None of the non-Orthodox streams of Judaism enjoys official status; a marriage service conducted by one of their rabbis must have an official representative of the local rabbinical council present to 'legitimize' it, or it will not be recognized as valid. While non-Orthodox conversions are similarly not recognized, a recent legislative amendment which implemented the recommendations of a government-appointed commission on this vexed topic brought about the establishment of a multi-denominational School for Conversion. Those wishing to convert may study with a rabbi of their choice – Orthodox, Conservative or Reform – but the subsequent examination, as well as the actual rabbinical court of conversion, are still exclusively Orthodox.

Lack of clarity regarding the power and the right of the state to coerce citizens into personal observance of *halakhah*, even when the latter is expressed in civil law, combines with individual and collective resistance to coercion to generate political and even physical opposition to the strict implementation of *halakhically* based laws.

Thus there has been strife regarding Sabbath shopping and operation of public places of entertainment on official days of rest. Hotels have had their *Kashrut* certification cancelled because they displayed a Christmas tree for the benefit of their Christian guests or held New Year's Eve celebrations in defiance of the fact that the Jewish New Year begins on *Rosh*

Ha-Shanah, which usually falls in September or October. There is no public transport on the Sabbath, but no prohibition on private traffic. However, certain roads in districts heavily populated by Orthodox Jews are closed to all traffic for twenty-five hours, from sundown on Friday. Disputes arise when these roads are main arteries, particularly when they lead to essential services, such as hospitals. On such roads there have been incidents of stoning of cars and other acts of violence perpetrated by the local residents, who resent the disturbance of their day of rest. Ironically, the throwing of stones is an act forbidden on the Sabbath, but this has not acted as a deterrent.

Far more wide-ranging an impact results from the Orthodox monopoly over personal status – a monopoly which ensures that there is neither freedom of, nor freedom from, religion in what purports to be a modern, democratic, pluralist state. There is neither civil marriage nor civil divorce in Israel.

Rabbinical law regarding marriage and divorce has already been discussed. On the whole, that law is in essence compassionate even though it is not egalitarian. Thus although a divorce becomes absolute only through an act voluntarily performed by both spouses, there are *halakhically* approved methods by which a recalcitrant husband (that is, one who refuses to grant the *get*) may be 'persuaded' to do so. These range from pre-nuptial agreements to annulment by the rabbinical courts. The latter is particularly relevant when the husband has absconded or is otherwise unavailable to deliver the bill of divorcement.

Although civil rights activists and particularly women's organizations have been actively engaged in attempting to persuade the Chief Rabbis to instruct the rabbinical courts to act in accordance with these *halakhically* approved remedies, there is no sign of imminent change in the attitudes or decisions of the courts. While the vast majority of recalcitrant husbands continue with impunity to harass or impose unlimited suffering on their wives rather than release them from the marriage bonds, women who similarly refuse to accept the *get* are designated 'rebels' whose husbands may then even be given permission to take a second wife, while they themselves remain undivorced and therefore neither eligible for any kind of financial support or sharing of property, nor able to marry another man.[5] Any children a non-divorced woman may bear in an extra-marital relationship will be considered *mamzerim* (bastards) and neither they nor their descendants for ten generations will be permitted to marry a Jew.

Women and religious fundamentalism

Since the establishment of the state in 1948, women have enjoyed equal civil rights and have benefited from a considerable amount of enlightened legislation and legal decisions extending their rights and privileges beyond those traditionally enjoyed in *halakhah* or in the practice of Jewish communities in the Diaspora.

Among the laws promulgated by the *Knesset* in 1951, the Education Law and the National Service Law both stipulated equality of the sexes, while later laws assured equal opportunity in employment, equal pay and pension rights, freedom from sexual harassment, and so on. In addition, Israeli women were early on accorded privileges, such as paid maternity leave, which are still not universally available to women elsewhere.

Nevertheless, as we have seen, autonomy and equality do not extend to areas where religious, rather than civil, law has supremacy. Furthermore, there remains the strong influence of *minhag*, or custom, especially in the Orthodox and Ultra-orthodox communities, which supersedes civil law in the eyes of their members.

Thus, for example, schools which are under the supervision of the state-religious branch of the Ministry of Education and, even more so, those which belong to the independent Ultra-orthodox network, do not offer their girl pupils the same kind or degree of Jewish studies that they consider mandatory for boys. Most of the state-religious schools have, over the past thirty years, become single-sex schools, as the Ultra-orthodox always were. Even those schools that have remained co-educational segregate the sexes in separate classes. The study of *Talmud*, considered *de rigueur* for boys, continues to be denied to girls, except in a very few private schools accredited by the state-religious system. No government-subsidized *yeshiva*-style institutions of higher Jewish education exist for women, though one such seminary recently won a case in the High Court of Appeals, which ordered the Ministry for Religious Affairs to grant it per capita funding comparable to that allocated to men's *yeshivas*.

With considerable difficulty and admirable determination, some Orthodox women have surmounted innumerable obstacles placed in their way by rabbinical authorities and have qualified as para-legal 'pleaders' permitted to appear before the rabbinical courts in divorce proceedings. In 1999, in an historic and unprecedented move, two women graduates of one of the women's seminaries were accorded the status of 'advisors' (but not *halakhic* 'decisors', as men are called) in the areas of dietary laws and family purity. Their status and legitimacy are being assured by the numbers of Orthodox women who consult them on these two issues and who will in all likelihood ultimately seek and abide by their opinions in other areas. Once again, as in civil societies all over the world at all times, the truth of the dictum 'Knowledge is Power' is being demonstrated. However, these women have no official status, nor do they receive payment of any kind from official sources.

In accordance with the Orthodox stress on modesty, attempts have been made to ban the employment of women in positions which bring them into contact with male clients, such as serving as postal clerks or bank tellers. While some banks have acceded to these demands in branches located in religious areas, the state-operated postal service has not. In at least one city with a large religious population, women are required to sit at the back of buses, or, on occasion, travel in segregated vehicles. Neighbourhoods populated primarily or even solely by the orthodoxly observant frequently prominently display notices warning women that they must comply with strict standards of what constitutes modest dress or risk being ousted or otherwise attacked. Indeed, women employees of the Ministry of Education, which is located on the border of one of Jerusalem's Orthodox quarters, have suffered verbal and physical attack for wearing short skirts or sleeveless dresses. Women who have sought to pray at the Western Wall in the Old City of Jerusalem (the sole relic of the Temple which was destroyed in 70 CE, one of Jewry's holiest sites), which is controlled by the Ministry for Religious Affairs, have been attacked and, in fact, forbidden to worship there wearing prayer shawls, raising their voices or reading from a *Torah* scroll. Their appeal to the High Court, first presented in 1989, has yet to be satisfactorily resolved.

In the Orthodox community, political power, like religious authority, is vested solely in men. Apart from the National Religious Party, which is the only truly Zionist of the religious parties and which was until recently comparatively moderate, none of the religious parties has ever fielded a woman candidate for election to the *Knesset*. Nevertheless, it is well known that in the Ultra-orthodox community the wives of the most politically powerful rabbis exert considerable influence behind the scenes.

Conclusion

All the above should make it clear that the modern State of Israel is a land of innumerable contradictions and paradoxes. On the one hand, it has universal suffrage and a democratically elected parliament, but within that legislature are represented parties that openly declare their desire to replace democratic rule with a theocracy in which Jewish law (*halakhah*) will take precedence. It is one of the few countries that have had a woman prime minister; yet until 1977 Ultra-orthodox rabbis forbade the women of their communities to vote. In Israel's Supreme Court, women currently number three out of a total of fifteen judges, yet there is not a single woman judge in the rabbinical court system. Israel has a law mandating universal conscription, yet religiously observant young women may request exemption on grounds of modesty. Furthermore, married women and mothers are exempted from military service, in accordance with the overruling importance placed on marriage and motherhood even among secular women. Israeli theatres, most of which are state- or city-subsidized, boast numerous outstanding women actors and there are equally numerous fine women singers in both classical and popular entertainment. Yet religiously observant girls and women perform only before all-female audiences, while no Ultra-orthodox male will attend a performance by females.

Emancipation, freedom and liberty are countered by reaction and repression. But there is undeniably a light at the end of the tunnel of fundamentalist oppression – a light kindled by women themselves. It is the light of learning and knowledge – for so many centuries the monopoly of Jewish males. Like their non-Jewish 'sisters', Jewish women have struggled against all odds to attain the scholarship that grants intellectual, and ultimately also social, authority. There are already an impressive number of women rabbis in the Reform and Conservative movements in Israel as in the Diaspora. In the opinion of many feminists, the time is not far away when there will also be Orthodox women whose *halakhic* authority will equal that of male rabbis, whatever title they may be accorded in place of 'rabbi'. Re-interpreting and re-visioning Jewish law and practice, collaborating with non-Orthodox women similarly concerned with the secure establishment of a democratic, pluralist, egalitarian civil society, they may well bring about a spiritual revolution which will enable a blending of Judaism with modernity such as will make an ineradicable, irreversible impact even on the currently far too conservative quasi-secular state of Israel.

Notes

1 Courtney W. Howland, 'The challenge of religious fundamentalism to the liberty and equality rights of women: an analysis under the United Nations Charter', *Columbia Journal of Transnational Law*, vol. 35, 1997, p. 271.
2 A modern revision of this prayer, introduced by the non-Orthodox denominations, refers to a less literal 'circumcision of the heart'.
3 Muslims and Christians come under the jurisdiction of the *Shari'a* or the ecclesiastical courts, respectively.

4   The Law of Return guarantees Jewish immigrants to Israel both citizenship and various rights and benefits not available to non-Jews. Since the Orthodox rabbinical establishment does not recognize the legitimacy of conversions performed by non-Orthodox rabbis, numerous immigrants who regarded themselves as Jews, because they or their forebears underwent such conversions, have been denied these rights and privileges.

5   Civil law forbids bigamy, but this obstacle has been overcome by the rabbinical authorities, who cite the supremacy of *halakhah* over civil law. Jewish law permits taking a second wife if the first is unable or unwilling to accept a *get*. It is an indication of the gender-based discrimination practised by the rabbinical courts that annually some 15–20 men receive rabbinical permission to take a second wife, while in the first 50 years of statehood fewer than 20 men were coerced into granting the *get* by threat of imprisonment.

Select bibliography

Adler, Rachel, *Engendering Judaism*, Philadelphia: Jewish Publication Society, 1998.

Biale, Rachel, *Women and Jewish Law: An Exploration of Women's Issues in Halakhic Sources*, New York: Schocken, 1984.

Halpern, Micah D. and Chana, Safrai, *Jewish Legal Writings by Women*, Jerusalem: Urim Publications, 1998.

Hauptman, Judith, *Rereading the Rabbis*, Oxford: Westview Press, 1998.

Howland, Courtney W., 'The challenge of religious fundamentalism to the liberty and equality rights of women: an analysis under the United Nations Charter', *Columbia Journal of Transnational Law*, vol. 35, 1997, p. 271.

Plaskow, Judith, *Standing again at Sinai*, San Francisco: Harper & Row, 1990.

5

RE-AWAKENING A SLEEPING GIANT

Christian fundamentalists in late twentieth-century US society

Nancy T. Ammerman

It is perhaps not surprising that most social scientists were caught off guard by the resurgence of fundamentalism in the late twentieth century. Social science was born in the West in the midst of the nineteenth-century transition from traditional agrarian societies to 'modern' industrialized ones. Many of the earliest sociologists were preoccupied with explaining not only how and why this transition was taking place, but also how society might be expected to hang together under new modern circumstances. All of the early theorists in sociology were interested in explaining what would likely happen to religion under conditions of modernity, and most expected drastic changes. One of the earliest, August Comte, simply posited that sociology would take the place of theology and philosophy as the 'queen of the sciences' and therefore be the new explanation for all human conditions.[1] Somewhat similarly, Karl Marx hoped that when workers were able to act on their own behalf, as full participants in the creation of the social order in which they lived, they would no longer need the veil of mystification and false comfort provided by religion.[2]

Max Weber, on the other hand, was convinced that religion – specifically Calvinist Protestantism – had been instrumental in making the modern transition possible.[3] But he was equally convinced that religion would not survive its own creation, that the world would become an 'iron cage' dominated by the logics of technology and the market, not by sacred ritual or divine command. A rational ordering of the world and means–end logic would so outperform the alternatives in accomplishing human goals that mystical and supernatural powers would simply wither from sight.[4]

Durkheim's vision was somewhat different. He was not so convinced that the world would become the sort of disenchanted realm Weber envisioned. Just as aboriginal groups needed the 'collective effervescence' of ritual and the power of the totem in establishing identity and norms for the group, so modern people would need some functional equivalent.[5] Eventually, he hoped, primitive and nationalist forms of religion would be replaced by a 'cult of humanity', where the idea of the sacred worth of the individual would bind the world's people together into one grand universal whole.[6] Traditional religious institutions would disappear, but something like religious ideas and functions might remain.

The theme throughout the work of these early social theorists was that the modern social order would displace traditional religion. If it remained, it would be in humanitarian, universalistic and disenchanted forms. In the 1960s, Peter Berger added one more possibility to the list of options for religion in the modern world. Since it could no longer be an overarching 'sacred canopy' for a whole society, he hypothesized, it could retreat to sheltering enclaves. By fortifying its boundaries, it could survive by resisting the onslaught of disenchantment and ambiguity.[7]

In the 1960s and well into the 1970s, religion in the United States appeared to conform rather nicely to this analysis. On the left, visible liberal Protestants were becoming increasingly universalistic, humanitarian and disenchanted – demythologizing the Bible and de-emphasizing dogma in favour of social activism. On the right, conservative Christians seemed content to live within their enclaves. And in the influential corridors of power, well-educated elites assumed that Weber had been right – science, technology and rational planning would slowly do away with the need for religion. Even if the vast majority of the US population remained deeply religious, for many of those in power the account of the world offered by secularization theories made sense. Their own lives had followed such a trajectory from traditional faith to rational scepticism, and they assumed that the rest of the world would naturally follow the same path.[8]

Neither precedent nor social theory had prepared for the political revival of fundamentalism in the late 1970s in the United States. When Jerry Falwell and a small group of pastors announced, in 1979, the founding of the Moral Majority, a religiously conservative political movement, people were shocked. Even if religion had been a vital ingredient in the Civil Rights movement of the 1960s, this was a different phenomenon. Civil Rights at least fit into a progressivist reading of history. A return to traditional values did not.

Others in the United States were shocked because talk about Christianity, morality and politics seemed to them an offensive mix of elements that were properly kept at arm's length from each other. The US Constitution's First Amendment seemed to many to prohibit religious people from bringing their faith into the political arena. A quarter century of court rulings had established a growing sense in US culture that religion, even if a vital element in individual private lives, simply did not belong in any aspect of public life, especially politics. For a group of preachers to call on citizens – as Christians – to try to bring public policy into line with traditionalist religious values seemed vaguely threatening to many. That sense of threat was heightened by the co-incidence of the Moral Majority's founding with the Iranian revolution. To many in the United States, a comparison between Khomeini and Falwell was natural.

In the years that followed, scientists and commentators struggled to catch up with reality. Just where had these traditionalist Christians come from, what did they want, and why did they suddenly emerge at this point in history? Many remembered an earlier time, in the 1920s, when 'fundamentalists' had been a visible factor in religious and secular politics, but even respected historians of American religion had pronounced that fundamentalist movement dead after its public defeat in the 1925 Scopes 'monkey' trial.[9] Historians had simply paid no attention to what had happened to conservative Christians in the half century since.

The seeds of mobilization

One of the first problems to be overcome in understanding the re-emergence of Christian fundamentalism as a political and cultural force in the United States was precisely this historical misconception. Fundamentalism had by no means disappeared after 1925. It had taken a lower public profile, but it had poured enormous energy into building its own institutions.[10] The basic social unit in which fundamentalism exists is the congregation. Sometimes these units are only a little larger than extended families, but whether it is 50 who gather or 5,000, fundamentalist congregations seek to provide the sort of nurture and emotional support that make them very powerful social units. Here people without extended families find both fictive kin and actual partners. Here people who live in vast urban areas create a 'village' of neighbours who celebrate births and deaths with them. It is no accident that believers so often refer to each other as 'brother' and 'sister', for the relationships they build in the congregation are often family-like in their intensity. From shared meals to shared projects to match-making, the congregation performs the rituals and functions of the traditional community.

But in the United States, in the period between 1925 and 1975, fundamentalists did much more than build congregations.[11] They also created schools and colleges, radio stations and publishing houses, book stores and television programs, mission agencies and youth camps. Most of this activity took place outside denominational bounds, since many fundamentalists had given up on the ability of denominations to stay orthodox. Many congregations had given up on denominationalism entirely and declared themselves independent. Others gave up on their own specific denomination and formed a new one. Even if congregations retained their traditional denominational allegiance, they increasingly aligned themselves with a growing network of independent agencies. Their Sunday school classes used curriculum from one of the new publishers. Their children enrolled in new youth programmes like AWANA,[12] and their older youth joined Youth for Christ or Navigators. There were dozens of Bible colleges to choose from, and every church supported a group of missionaries scattered throughout the world.

Meanwhile, working-class fundamentalists of the 1930s and 1940s had given birth to a generation of middle-class children. The people inside fundamentalism simply had more money to give to their churches, money that helped to fuel the institutional boom.[13] Theirs may have been a 'sheltering canopy' or an enclave culture, but it was a very large canopy and a very vigorous culture.

Among the most critical of the entrepreneurial work done by fundamentalists during this period was their investment in broadcast media. They were among the first to move into the world of radio, with programmes like the 'Old Fashioned Revival Hour' and the 'Radio Bible Class'. When television came along, they were equally eager to use its potential to reach new audiences with the gospel.[14] They were far from reluctant users of these modern technologies, and their eagerness is all the more remarkable for the financial commitment it required. For almost all of this period, the Federal Communications Commission required publicly licensed stations to devote some of their airtime – without charge – to 'public service' programming. Stations routinely took that to mean, at least in part, religious programming, and they provided free air time to churches and religious figures. But those chosen for free time were almost never the revival preachers and fundamentalists. Instead, they were the more moderate and liberal members of the Federal (later National) Council of Churches. As a result, fundamentalists who wanted to be on the air had to develop their own production companies, stations and funding sources. The ironic result was that when the Federal Communications Commission began allowing stations to count paid time towards their public service quota, liberal programmes that had been spoiled by free airtime dropped out of sight, and fundamentalist programmes dominated the airwaves.[15]

Part of the story of fundamentalism's resurgence in the late 1970s, then, is simply a story of available resources. This was a movement that had been building up its infrastructure for half a century and was ready to flex its muscles in a bigger arena. The other part of the story, however, has to do with the state of the arena itself. The 1960s and 1970s were times of great upheaval and change in US society. Norms of all sorts were being transformed, from the most public questions about the authority of a government to wage war, to questions of civil society, such as how people of different races would participate in public life, to questions as intimate as gender roles and sexual norms. No one could escape the sense that the world was changing in sometimes bewildering ways.

Into this caldron, the US Supreme Court handed down two key decisions, a decade apart, that helped to mobilize a new conservative Christian political movement. In 1963, the justices ruled that state-sponsored religious activities in public schools were a violation of the First Amendment prohibition on the 'establishment' of religion. For many people, to this day, this ruling meant that a godless government had kicked God out of the schools at the same time that evolution and birth control were welcomed in. Over the next decade and half, the evidence mounted in the minds of fundamentalists that the nation was being run by people positively hostile to their beliefs and determined to stamp out all vestiges of traditional religion in the coming generations.[16] There was a growing sense that if 'God's people' did not stand up for their principles, the nation might forever be lost. With the 1963 decision having unsettled many conservatives, the 1973 decision legalizing abortion brought them out of hiding and began to create the political agendas and alliances of the next three decades.

If the culture as a whole was in some disarray, that seemed doubly true in the South. Just as the Northern United States and Canada had experienced industrialization, urbanization and immigration in the last quarter of the nineteenth century, so the southeastern United States was experiencing those same forces a century later. Alongside radical change in racial norms, Southerners found themselves in a world they hardly recognized. The beliefs taken for granted in their small traditional communities had to be defended, if they were to survive in this new world.[17] Southerners joined concerned people throughout the country wondering where the nation's moral anchors would be found.[18]

This situation of disrupted tradition is indeed typical of the contexts in which fundamentalist movements arise. Fundamentalisms originate and thrive in times and places of basic cultural change, especially the change we call modernization. These changes involve both social structural shifts (such as urbanization) and/or ethnic and national transitions (including Westernized 'development' and colonialism). But more importantly, they involve changes in how people think about the world. Fundamentalists identify in these changes a variety of challenges to the presuppositions of their faith. The changes proceeding from the Enlightenment, for instance, have created basic challenges to the notion of revealed truth. Enlightenment people expect to discover knowledge through systematic, rational methods, not through mysterious revelations or traditional sacred authority. In addition, traditional faith is challenged by the ever-increasing reality of pluralism. Throughout much of human history, people simply could not avoid being a part of the religious tradition of their community. Today there are fewer and fewer places where such consensus exists. Faith must justify and defend itself, learning to explain and get along with other faiths.

But the modern situation has also posed a challenge to the definition of who Americans are as a people. Communities defined by land, family, tradition, language and religion have been replaced by the modern secular nation–state. A common language and secular law presume to mediate among the various groups and traditions that find themselves subject to the state's definition of territory and identity. In most instances, the power of religion has been limited, usually to a 'private' sphere.

Given these disruptions, sacred traditions cannot be assumed. They are neither our primary source of knowledge about the world, nor our guide in every area of life, nor the single set of practices at the centre of whole communities. Modern science, modern specialization, modern pluralism and the modern state have disrupted traditional life. Fundamentalisms are one response to that disruption.

The fundamentalist message

The new movement conservative religious activists created in the United States came at just such a time of disruption, but it built on both the organizational infrastructure and the ideas that had been nurtured during fifty years of relative obscurity. For Protestant Christians in the United States, those ideas came out of their evangelical and fundamentalist history.[19] As evangelicals, they emphasized the power of God to produce transformation in individual lives and the obligation of believers to proclaim that message. This emphasis on individual transformation has always made them distrustful of any claim that social structures or government programmes can engender either good or evil. Whatever the social environment, it is the individual person who must turn to God, be saved, and live a righteous life.

The guidelines for living that righteous life are found, according to evangelicals, in the Bible. Its unchanging truth contains everything we really need to know about the world and how to live in it. Evangelicals differ on exactly how the Bible is to be interpreted. Those closest to their early twentieth-century heritage insist on 'inerrancy'. Here the notion is usually that the 'plain truth' of the scripture is what we are to take it to mean. That is, the Bible means what it says. This is usually coupled with a belief that these words of scripture are timeless and were given to humankind by God himself, not subject to the whims of human authorship and historical contingency. Not all evangelicals are unwilling to engage in debates over the meaning and history of the biblical text; but all of them share a sense that the Bible is a reliable and trustworthy guide to life. The value of any social policy or piece of legislation can be judged by the degree to which it conforms to biblical injunctions.

Individual salvation and biblical authority remain at the heart of how newly-mobilized Christian conservatives think, but other ideas from their fundamentalist heritage have been significantly modified. During those fifty years of relative quiet, fundamentalists emphasized the importance of organizational and personal purity. The only sure route to orthodoxy was to avoid entanglements with others who might introduce heretical practices. Fundamentalists emphasized what they called 'separation'. They kept their churches independent, and they taught their members to avoid relationships and organizations that might tempt them into sin.[20] Compromise was not a good word, but it was a word they would have to learn once they entered the political arena. The genius of Jerry Falwell was to teach this group of separatists that they could cooperate with heretics if those heretics shared their concern for moral change in American politics and society.

The other traditional belief that underwent a transformation as conservative Christians entered politics was their emphasis on the imminent 'any day' return of Christ. Since the nineteenth century, people interested in biblical prophecy had held conferences and published charts showing how the 'End Times' were near. Those charts were based on 'dispensational premillennialism', a way of viewing human history that posited various religious eras defined by the mode of salvation (the Mosaic Law or the Christian Church, for example) available to those who lived in them. The events of a seemingly chaotic world were then charted as precursors to the 'Rapture', when all true believers would be swept up to heaven. Such notions were not especially encouraging of activity aimed at transforming this doomed world.

But in the 1980s, leaders such as Jerry Falwell and Pat Robertson began to tell this story in a new way, speaking not just of the approaching End, but also of what God can do 'in the meantime', 'while He tarries'. Such rhetoric created, as Harding argues, new ways to envision oneself and one's world.[21] To name themselves the 'Moral Majority' and to claim this time before the End as a time for God to work miracles opened up a space in the story for political action in the world.

These particular religious beliefs, then, provided the ideological grounding for the movement that arose in the 1970s and 1980s in the United States. These beliefs – evangelism, inerrancy, the Rapture and the like – were the distinctive dogma that had characterized a segment of American Protestantism for more than half a century and that now were carried forward and sometimes modified in new circumstances.

Fundamentalist story and rhetoric

As much as fundamentalism is a set of strict doctrines that emerged out of a particular religious tradition, more broadly it can be viewed as a set of rhetorical strategies that characterize a whole family of movements that may come from very different religious traditions. They share in common enough of what Martin Marty called 'family resemblances' to cast them into the same category.

They engage, first of all, in a rhetoric of tradition in the face of a changing or modernizing situation. Fundamentalisms claim as their goal the restoration of some former state of purity or orthodoxy, usually invoking a scriptural text. However, their position in a changed cultural setting necessitates both selective retrieval from the formerly dominant tradition and ideological innovation based on that tradition. They leave some things behind and adopt other new things that seem especially suited to the times, all the while talking as if they are claiming older tradition's whole cloth. Geertz aptly describes a contrast between 'being held by' and 'holding' beliefs.[22] In relatively stable cultural settings 'orthodoxy' is simply part of the assumed understanding shared by members of a society; one is 'held by' beliefs. In disrupted societies, the same beliefs become conscious and ideological; they must be 'held' and selectively retrieved from a contested history. This characteristic distinguishes fundamentalist movements from mere revivals.

Second, theirs is a rhetoric of clear boundaries. Fundamentalists think they have the truth and think that others should accept and live by that truth. This has several important corollaries. There are clear lines of social demarcation between believers and non-believers. These lines are likely to be both ideological and behavioural, with the fundamentalist group emphasizing certain styles of dress, speech and the like, that highlight their distinctive and traditionalist identity. But they are also clear about their opponents' identities. They highlight some aspect of the outside world as the root cause for cultural/religious decline and declare that enemy anathema.

These rhetorics, however, could be found in revival movements and sectarian groups that want nothing more than to bring their own flock into line. What distinguishes an activist fundamentalist movement from these is its rhetoric of transformation. They are willing to pursue change from the current state of affairs to some other. That change is sometimes anticipated in future divine action, as in millennialism or messianism, where the deity will bring about a break in history, recreating the longed-for ideal state. But not all millennial or messianic movements are fundamentalist. Africa is today awash in millennial movements, for instance.[23] Various messianic figures or promised millennial visions offer dramatic transformation of the economic, political and physical chaos suffered by many on that continent. While many of these borrow from Christian evangelical traditions, they represent something distinctly different from the traditionalist transformation of a fundamentalist movement. When fundamentalists use millennial rhetoric, its roots are in a widely shared text, rather than a new revelation.

Among the transformations sought by fundamentalist movements are also the individual transformation of conversion. By membership in the movement, individuals participate in the ideal state in anticipation of its actual establishment. But the real activists anticipate that change will come as a result of the concerted efforts of the movement's actions in the here and now. By their own divinely aided actions, members create the change they seek.

The change they seek is a restoration of a godly centre for their society. Theirs is a story about collective transformation, about who Americans are – and have been – as a people. We hear this in US fundamentalists' vision of America returning to godly ways, their talk about the Christian intentions of the Founding Fathers, picturing the American Constitution as a sacred document, and the like. It is also present in the rhetoric of the Italian Catholic movement *Communione e Liberazioni*, which organizes to re-establish the Roman Catholic Church at the political, economic and cultural centre of Italian society.[24]

The collective 'history' practised by fundamentalists places God at the centre. They act as if divine action is fully explanatory of human events – as much in the affairs of nations as in those of persons and families and churches, and as much today as yesterday or tomorrow.[25] They are likely, in fact, to collapse history into future, likening what happened to Jesus to what they experience today, or seeing what is expected to happen after the Rapture in what they watch on the news. Both history and future can be glimpsed in the present, and both demand action.

What we see in the United States and in other fundamentalist movements, then, is a sacred story, anchored in a sacred text that is about past and future but lays claim to the present. Having created a history that is premised on continuity between a past golden age and a future glorious triumph, their rhetoric about the present takes on transformative power, pressing the present towards conformity with those past/future visions. Their claims about 'tradition' are never merely about the past. They must retain enough of the elements in their culture's telling of its history to be plausible, but a mere call to the past would have no transformative power. Rather, in their linking of past to future, they claim the power of this future/past in the present.

Their vision of the future/past stands, of course, in opposition to the world as it now exists. They point to all the ills of US society – divorce rates, juvenile delinquency, pornography on the Internet, adultery in the White House – and they declare that God does not want us to live this way. If we turn to God, they promise, the United States will be healed of these ills. While some of the 'ills' they put on their list are matters of contention – homosexuality and abortion, for instance – many are matters about which many or most US citizens are concerned. Their claim that not all is well in their society is a claim that rings true to many. Their attempt is to offer a story that begins in a godly past, takes its cues from a sacred text, and leads – with the help of God's people today – towards a brighter, less troubled future.

Fundamentalist strategies of change

As we have already seen, Christian fundamentalism in the United States has been a movement built foremost on the strength of the alternative social structures it has constructed. For most of the twentieth century, its primary strategy for changing society was to create ways to escape that society. Congregations and families were buttressed by books, videos, movies, television and now Internet products designed with the conservative Christian in mind. From nursery school through elementary and high school and on to college or Bible Institute, the believer could be educated away from the harmful influences of secular culture. And with devices like the Christian Yellow Pages, believers could even conduct their business or look for a job where they would be surrounded by like-minded persons. This network of connections and business enterprise is not to be ignored. It is one of the responses of fundamentalists to the challenges of a culture they see as degenerate and alien.

The other response, of course, is to confront that culture in a variety of ways. The ambivalence of Christian conservatives towards direct efforts at social change is perhaps best seen in their strategies regarding education. By the late 1960s, many American fundamentalists had come to believe that public schools had become untenable for their children or for the Christian society of which believers dreamed. Schools had become too pluralistic, too committed to 'human rights', too secular. While one response was the rapidly growing 'Christian School' movement,[26] the other was an effort to take back the public schools. As the movement gained, during the 1970s, a broader understanding of its mission and power, it began to organize in support of a variety of changes in public education. Among the most visible on the national scene was a call for a Constitutional Amendment to allow prayer in schools, thus reversing the 1963 Supreme Court decision that had ruled public school religious exercises out of bounds. Various state legislatures attempted their own versions, but each was quickly declared unconstitutional.

By the end of the 1980s, one of the liveliest areas of fundamentalist political activism was largely invisible to the eyes of the national media. Hundreds of local parents were forming textbook review committees and getting elected to school boards. Visible activists in Texas and California were willing to organize pressure on publishers and testify at hearings. Success in those two huge textbook markets inevitably had effects throughout the nation.[27] Other parents inspected school libraries and objected to the teaching of sex education in their districts. Having begun to recognize the education of their children as something they were not willing to leave to an unbridled state, fundamentalists found themselves involved in political issues ranging from 'equal access' for after-hours student religious groups to tax-supported voucher systems that would allow 'parental choice' of private over public schools.

When the Moral Majority was formed in 1979, it took on the full range of political activities and issues, education simply one of them. Over the years, issues surrounding family life have always been central, with abortion and homosexuality the most visible and volatile. Activist fundamentalists have argued for the 'sanctity' of marriage and of foetal life as a cornerstone of any truly moral society.

Once provoked into action, fundamentalists have distributed information through newsletters, seminars, broadcast ministries and the Internet. They register voters and lobby Congress. And they have trained and encouraged conservatives in the fine art of running for office. No public office or bureaucratic position is too low; as political organizers, they realize that their crusade must begin from the ground up. Over the years, New Christian Right activists have learned how to play the political game. They are less likely to expect instant electoral success or legislative revolutions. They are also more willing to 'mainstream the message' saving the Bible-talk for insiders, emphasizing issues like schools and taxes for the broader electorate. Add this new pragmatism to their already impressive mobilization strategies (action alerts, phone trees, voter registration drives, training workshops) and increasing ability to share supporter lists across a wide network of conservative causes, and Christian conservatives can be a formidable political force.[28] They have convinced large numbers of new voters that involvement is important, and the high commitment of those voters sometimes outweighs their relatively small numbers.

The numerical strength of the movement has never been quite clear, however.[29] To the extent that they represent people of strictly fundamentalist religious beliefs, the constituency is clearly quite small. In at least some local elections, highly religious supporters have indeed seemed the only ones interested in Moral Majority candidates, and those candidates have lost.[30] To the extent that a moral coalition is being built, however, its size might be much larger. On some issues Moral Majoritarians do represent majority opinion, while on others they are a tiny minority. Sometimes their position represents the majority, even if their reasons for holding that position are far removed from the mainstream. Attempts to define and measure a coherent platform of issues held by any broad segment of the public have consistently had mixed results. In the heady early days of the movement, Falwell and other leaders (with ample help from news people) took generous credit for conservative political victories. In retrospect, such credit was probably misplaced.[31]

In part because they do enjoy relatively widespread support, Christian fundamentalists in the United States give no endorsement for violence as a strategy in their campaign to change society. No recognized leader in the movement has hinted that violence is a legitimate tool in the political process. In fact, most of the leaders are unwilling even to engage in civil disobedience, although they grudgingly say that such tactics may be alright for others.

That does not mean that there is no violence associated with this movement. On its fringes are a tiny minority of extremists who are willing to take up arms. Arguing, for instance, that the taking of life in defence of other lives is justified, a few have been willing to bomb abortion clinics and shoot the doctors who work there.[32] While the anti-abortion rhetoric of the movement as a whole helps to fuel these actions, the number of people who seek to stop abortion by violent means is very small.

Another very small contingent of potentially violent conservative Christians are the so-called 'militia' groups associated with the Christian Identity movement. Their ideology of racial purity and their rejection of federal governmental authority go well beyond what any mainstream fundamentalist leaders would advocate. In their reliance on scripture and their emphasis on tradition, they sound like other fundamentalists, but their racist interpretations of those scriptures shock even old-fashioned segregationists. Their sense of 'peoplehood' centres on the white race, not on the United States as a nation, and they are willing to defend themselves against the armed attacks they think they will have to face. It is a fragmented and scattered movement, but the actions carried out by people such as Timothy McVeigh (the Oklahoma City bombing of a federal building) and Benjamin Smith (the summer 1999 shootings of non-anglos in Illinois and Indiana) keep this small contingent of violent activists in the news.[33]

In addition to these Identity movements, there are also occasional sectarian Christian groups who find themselves at cross-purposes with the law. The United States has always been a hotbed for religious innovation, and conservative Christian ideas are occasionally spun off in some new direction that eventually entails violence. I know of no instance where such groups, usually led by ragtag prophets, have chosen violence as a preferred strategy of action. More commonly, their radical way of life, communal living, odd child-rearing customs and the like, put them at odds with their neighbours and with the families of their converts. In a few tragic cases, like Jonestown and Waco, those conflicts have escalated into full-scale violent confrontations.[34]

Forms of activism

Violent fringe movements, however, are genuinely small and rare in comparison with the relatively large body of US citizens who find various aspects of the conservative Christian agenda appealing. For a variety of reasons, this fundamentalist movement has taken the form of an organized political pressure group, not either a terrorist cell or a formal political party. Nor a political party because of the strong two-party tradition that forces both parties to appeal to a broader array of citizens than a strictly fundamentalist agenda would allow. Nor a terrorist group because the society is open enough to their agenda to allow relatively free range for legitimate organizing.

Perhaps the most hostile environment for the growth of fundamentalism is, as Wuthnow and Lawson point out, one in which the society is relatively homogeneous and stable, making for little in the way of cultural space for critique and diversity.[35] Where religious homogeneity is also tied to a strong or repressive state and to the dominant social classes in the society – as in some of Latin America – dissidence may be just under the surface, but it is quite unlikely to be expressed.[36] In contrast, where neither the state nor the society is hospitable to religiosity at all, fundamentalism is no more likely to grow than is any other form of faith. In contexts that are relatively hostile to their growth, fundamentalist movements – where they arise at all – are likely to emphasize the building of congregations and homes that can nurture and sustain the faithful, de-emphasizing any form of public activism.

The current situation

The 1980s were heady days of organizing and visibility for fundamentalists in the United States. The election of Ronald Reagan in 1980 marked the beginning of their acknowledged public influence. They weighed in on issues as wide-ranging as foreign policy and health care reform, in addition to pushing for increasing limits on access to abortion. With the end of the Cold War, however, fundamentalists lost one of their most potent symbols. When they wanted to point to where an unrepentant America might end up, communist lands had always provided a vivid threat. Their presence allowed fundamentalists to link their religious agenda (communists were godless, after all) with both domestic and international policy positions. Without the communist threat, it became much more difficult to identify the enemies against which 'God's people' must defend their nation. While 'Islamic terrorists' occasionally fill that role today, no single religious and ideological enemy has replaced communism.

Nor have their presumed friends always been effective at achieving fundamentalist goals. Even with Reagan in the White House, few things changed. The election of Bill Clinton was a major blow, and despite the Republican congressional triumph of 1994, activists recognized that they would have great difficulty achieving any of their legislative goals in the 1990s. George W. Bush is a much more sympathetic President, but it is not yet clear whether he will be any more effective in pushing fundamentalist-inspired legislation.

By the end of the decade, some key fundamentalist leaders were calling for a retreat from politics. Most prominently, Cal Thomas and Ed Dobson, both former Moral Majority insiders, published *Blinded by Might*, in which they argued that putting faith in politics was a bad idea. In part this is realism, they argue. 'Today very little that we set out to do has gotten done. In fact, the moral landscape of America has become worse.'[37] But in part it is a theological conclusion. Christians ultimately must trust God to change the world, not try to do it themselves, especially by amassing earthly weapons of money and votes. Thomas and Dobson are not sorry that the Moral Majority tried. They point to the way it has changed the national political agenda, convinced Christians to take their civic responsibilities seriously, and forced the nation to confront the question of how religious people can and should enter the political process. But they think conservative Christian energies are now better put into prayer and godly example, seeking to change by moral persuasion rather than political craftiness.

Not surprisingly, neither Jerry Falwell nor Pat Robertson are convinced by this argument. Robertson responds, 'What an affront to Christians who have been working tirelessly to restore godly leadership in America! This attitude reflects a creeping trend to completely remove critical moral issues from political dialogue.'[38] Falwell noted that he does not think 'religious conservatives have lost any of their power. I think they've lost their enthusiasm.' His response was to launch 'People of Faith 2000' in an effort to register 10 million new voters.[39] In these responses, ironically, both leaders have acknowledged a certain drift away from political organizing among their constituents.

At the same time that the break-up of the Soviet empire has deprived US fundamentalists of a political enemy, it has also provided them with an unprecedented opportunity to practise the form of activism with which they are most familiar – evangelism and missionary work. Dozens of American mission organizations are sending long- and short-term teams into Russia and its neighbours, aiming to begin literally thousands of new churches in the coming years. Again, the latent capacity in fundamentalist institutions has placed them in an advantageous position at this moment when new territory is being opened to missionary activity. All indications are that they are already achieving great success, with American-style mega-churches sprouting in suburbs around the world. Pat Robertson's own operation, CBN Worldreach, claims ministry activity in 158 countries.[40] In both Latin America and Africa, millions of converts are leaving the traditional religions of their countries to join evangelical and Pentecostal groups of all sorts.[41]

103

These far-flung outposts of US evangelicalism often look and sound very much like the home-grown version, with a similar message of repentance from society's ills. However, they differ from true fundamentalist movements in their break from their own society's religious traditions. In adopting significantly new religious ways, they lose the ability to claim to speak for the society's godly past. They simply cannot tell the sort of story US fundamentalists can about restoring the rightful place of evangelicals at the helm of society. In no other part of the world has evangelicalism ever enjoyed the cultural centrality that it can plausibly claim in US history. Like other new religious movements, however, these non-US evangelicals use religious ideas creatively, with fewer appeals to tradition and orthodoxy. This is seen most strikingly in the 'African Independent Churches' that freely mix elements from Christianity (often gleaned of late through the Internet) with practices from traditional African religions and sometimes dramatic new religious visions. But in more subtle ways, many Latin American evangelicals adapt the message to their own traditions, as well.[42] Where there are direct and ongoing ties between overseas converts and US organizations, there is clearly a possibility for US political agendas to be extended. But much of the evangelical growth overseas has shown a remarkable ability to shed the concerns of missionaries in favour of more indigenous attempts at social and personal transformation. Where US evangelicals are seen throughout the world, they should simply not be understood as 'fundamentalists'.

Policy dilemmas

The presence of visible and active Christian fundamentalist movements poses a number of challenges to non-fundamentalists who care about the public good. In the case of the Christian movements in the United States, those dilemmas have rarely been about how to prevent religious violence. That the vast majority of conservative religious groups are content to live peaceful lives – even if they dream of some future transformation of this world – is an important fact to remember. The most spectacular failure of US law enforcement in recent years – the raid on the Branch Davidians in Waco – happened when that basic premise was forgotten. When law enforcement fails to understand the nature of oppositional religious rhetoric, assuming that the apocalyptic scenes believers sometimes paint are their literal intentions, that misunderstanding can become a self-fulfilling prophecy.

Still, recent violent attacks by white supremacists, anti-abortion crusaders, and so-called Christian Identity adherents have chastened some mainstream activists whose rhetoric failed to be clear in condemning the use of violence. Violence by fringe elements in an oppositional movement is always a possibility, and every society is faced with the question of how to mobilize its resources so as to diminish lethal discontent and how to contain and prevent those who are tempted to step over the line.

A much more common dilemma posed by fundamentalist participation in politics is the question of how their explicitly religious positions ought to be treated in public debates. Liberal assumptions have been that public debates should be, by definition, conducted on universalist and secular terms. Fundamentalists have countered with the liberals' own rhetoric of tolerance and inclusion to argue for their right to participate as Christians in public life. Here they are joined by many other culture critics who note that 'universal' never really is all-inclusive, that supposedly neutral rules reflect the predispositions of some (powerful) members of the society more than others. A more genuinely pluralist notion of public life is therefore making new room for fundamentalist participation.[43] Those who wish to oppose fundamentalist arguments, on whatever grounds, are obligated to mobilize and argue against fundamentalist ideas, not against the fundamentalist right to present those ideas.

Much more difficult are the questions surrounding the specific beliefs and practices fundamentalists wish to see embraced by others, as well as those they seek to protect for themselves. In the former case, the political process largely governs decision-making. If fundamentalists can convince enough people to vote in certain ways, changes and prohibitions will be put in place. But in the latter case, it is the courts that will decide. When people engage in religiously grounded practices that would otherwise be barred by law, US society invokes the contending powers of the generalized law, on the one hand, and religious liberty on the other. When the practice is something as heinous as murdering infants, we have little difficulty deciding that the law outweighs religious liberty. When the practice is barring homosexuals from membership in a private organization, the argument is less clear. Around the world, when religious conservatives of all sorts engage in practices that offend liberal sensibilities (restrictive gender and sexual practices most commonly), there is a necessary public debate to be had about the point at which issues of human rights supersede religious liberty. This is a debate that is likely to be ongoing for many years to come and will be shaped by the particular relationships between religion and state that characterize each society.

In all these debates, we will do well, I think, to remember that fundamentalists tap a rich vein of social discontent. Their point is precisely that this world needs to be transformed. Most often, their oppositional rhetoric is seen as 'anti-modern', and at this moment their opposition to modernity has a strong resonance. They point to society's over-dependence on science, its tolerance of nearly anything and everything, its attempt to make sure that public life is stripped of private belief and virtue. And in many of these criticisms of modern Enlightenment society, fundamentalists have been joined in recent years by a variety of other culture critics, from feminists to liberation theologians.

For those who assume that modernity is moving us inexorably towards a better future, fundamentalism is seen as a reaction, threatening to drag us back into a benighted past. But there may be other ways to read the story. Susan Harding's re-reading of the Scopes trial offers, for instance, a different interpretation.[44] Then, as now, the cultural centre was in fact a contested arena. Just which forces properly represent the path towards the future? In that earlier time, neither 'side' (modernists or fundamentalists) could yet claim hegemony. Only after the drama of the Scopes trial were modernists able to achieve a rhetorical claim on the centre, so that they could tell the story as if they had 'won'. They could finally cast the fundamentalist as the 'other'. Today, it is not yet clear who will eventually be able to tell the story of this era as its winner, and who will be its 'other'.

Fundamentalists do not simply react when they invoke the past. They respond to real dilemmas faced by large numbers of people in the culture, and they create solutions to those dilemmas. They exercise cultural power by voicing a critique of modernity and by imagining a world that is different. Theirs is an active effort to construct the future, contesting the powers of those who claim the right to tell the culture's story. Their particular way of telling the story depends on reclaiming older texts and traditions. They place those traditions – and the ways of life their community constructs from them – into a contested cultural arena. They are, in most cases, unlikely to win clear dominance over the culture's centre. There are simply too many other voices contending for the right to reshape the narratives. But if we are to understand fundamentalism, we must understand that the contest in which they are engaged is not simply modernity (us) versus reactionaries (them). It is a contest in which we are all engaged.

Notes

1 Kenneth Thompson (ed.) *August Comte: The Foundation of Sociology*, London: Nelson, 1976.
2 Karl Marx, 'Contribution to a critique of Hegel's *Philosophy of Right*', in T.B. Bottomore (ed.) *Karl Marx: Early Writings*, New York: McGraw-Hill, 1963, pp. 43–59.
3 Max Weber, *The Protestant Ethic and the Spirit of Capitalism*, trans. Talcott Parsons, Boston: Beacon, 1905 [1958].
4 Max Weber, *The Theory of Social and Economic Organization*, trans. A.M. Henderson and Talcott Parsons, New York: Free Press, 1947.
5 Emile Durkheim, *The Elementary Forms of the Religious Life*, trans. Joseph Ward Swain, New York: Free Press, 1915.
6 Emile Durkheim, 'Individualism and the intellectuals', in W.S. Pickering (ed.) *Durkheim on Religion*, London: Routledge & Kegan Paul, 1975.
7 Peter L. Berger, 'From the crisis of religion to the crisis of secularity', in Mary Douglas and Steven Tipton (eds) *Religion and America*, Boston: Beacon, 1982, pp. 14–24; Peter L. Berger *The Sacred Canopy*, Garden City, New York: Anchor Doubleday, 1969.
8 I have presented a more extended version of this argument in 'Telling Congregational stories', *Review of Religious Research*, vol. 36, no. 1, June 1994, pp. 289–301.
9 In the 1920s, the state of Tennessee passed a law prohibiting the teaching of evolution in its public schools. Science teacher John Scopes challenged the law, and he was defended by prominent lawyer Clarence Darrow against equally prominent prosecutor William Jennings Bryan. Darrow lost the case, but so humiliated Bryan (who died a few days later) that fundamentalism and its anti-evolution crusade were thoroughly discredited.
10 Important remedies to this historical oversight are found in Joel A. Carpenter, *Revive Us Again: The Reawakening of American Fundamentalism*, New York: Oxford University Press, 1997; and George Marsden, *Reforming Fundamentalism: Fuller Seminary and the New Evangelicalism*, Grand Rapids, MI: Eerdmans, 1987.
11 A more detailed discussion of this period can be found in Nancy T. Ammerman, 'North American Protestant Fundamentalism', in Martin E. Marty and R. Scott Appleby (eds) *Fundamentalisms Observed*, Chicago: University of Chicago Press, 1991.
12 The acronym stands for 'Approved Workmen Are Not Ashamed' and is a reference to a verse from the New Testament book of *II Timothy*. This programme is organized like Boy Scouts or Girl Guides, but around religious activities rather than physical or civic ones.
13 W.D. Sapp makes this point about Southern Baptist growth in 'Southern Baptist responses to the American economy, 1900–1980', *Baptist History and Heritage*, vol. 16, 1981, pp. 3–11.
14 Razell Frankl, *Televangelism: The Marketing of Popular Religion*, Carbondale, IL: Southern Illinois University Press, 1987.
15 Jeffrey K. Hadden, 'Religious broadcasting and the mobilization of the New Christian Right', *Journal for the Scientific Study of Religion*, vol. 26, no. 1, 1987, pp. 1–24.

16 This view is supported by Richard J. Neuhaus in *The Naked Public Square*, Grand Rapids, MI: Eerdmans, 1984, and in several essays included in Neuhaus and Michael Cromartie's *Piety and Politics: Evangelicals and Fundamentalists Confront the World*, Washington, DC: Ethics and Public Policy Center, 1987.

17 Nancy T. Ammerman, 'The New South and the new Baptists', *Christian Century*, vol. 103, no. 17, 14 May 1986, pp. 486–8.

18 This upheaval in the South was critical to the growth of a successful fundamentalist movement in the region's largest denomination, the Southern Baptist Convention. See Nancy Tatom Ammerman, *Baptist Battles: Social Change and Religious Conflict in the Southern Baptist Convention*, New Brunswick, NJ: Rutgers University Press, 1990.

19 For a more extended discussion of Fundamentalist history and ideas, see George M. Marsden, *Fundamentalism and American Culture*, New York: Oxford University Press, 1980.

20 For a description of such a separatist church, see Nancy Tatom Ammerman, *Bible Believers: Fundamentalists in the Modern World*, New Brunswick, NJ: Rutgers University Press, 1987.

21 Susan Harding, 'The politics of apocalyptic language in the Moral Majority movement', in Martin E. Marty and R. Scott Appleby (eds) *Accounting for Fundamentalisms*, Chicago: University of Chicago Press, 1994.

22 Clifford Geertz, *Islam Observed*, Chicago: University of Chicago Press, 1968.

23 On African millennial movements, see Jean Comaroff, *Body of Power, Spirit of Resistance*, Chicago: University of Chicago Press, 1985, and Karen E. Fields, *Revival and Rebellion in Colonial Central Africa*, Princeton, NJ: Princeton University Press, 1985.

24 Dario Zadra, '*Communione e Liberazione*: A fundamentalist idea of power', in Marty and Appleby, *Accounting for Fundamentalisms*.

25 For a discussion of fundamentalist rhetoric, especially their reading of history and future, see Harding, 'The politics of apocalyptic language'.

26 Alan Peshkin, *God's Choice*, Chicago: University of Chicago Press, 1986; Susan Rose, *Keeping Them Out of the Hands of Satan*, New York: Routledge, 1988.

27 Susan Rose, 'The impact of fundamentalism on education', in Martin E. Marty and R. Scott Appleby (eds) *Fundamentalisms and Society*, Chicago: University of Chicago Press, 1993, pp. 452–89.

28 Mark J. Rozell and Clyde Wilcox, *Second Coming: The New Christian Right in Virginia Politics*, Baltimore: Johns Hopkins University Press, 1996.

29 Attempts to assess that strength include S. Rothenberg and F. Newport, *The Evangelical Voter*, Washington, DC: The Institute for Government and Politics, 1984; J. Simpson, 'Support for the Moral Majority and its sociomoral platform', in David Bromley and Anson Shupe (eds) *New Christian Politics*, Macon: Mercer University Press, 1984, pp. 65–8; S. Johnson and J. Tamney, 'The Christian Right and the 1984 presidential election', *Review of Religious Research*, vol. 27, no. 2, 1985, pp. 124–33.

30 See, for example, S. Johnson and J. Tamney, 'Factors influencing vote for a Christian Right candidate', paper presented to the Society for the Scientific Study of Religion, Louisville, Kentucky, 1985, and J. Guth, 'The GOP and the

Christian Right: the case of Pat Robertson's campaign contributors', paper presented to the meetings of the Midwest Political Science Association, in Chicago, Illinois, 1987.

31 Jeffery K. Hadden makes this point in 'Televangelism and the future of American politics', in Bromley and Shupe, *New Christian Politics*, pp. 151–68. Estimates of strength varied widely from exaggerations immediately following the 1980 election to a series of debunking studies, including S. Johnson and J. Tamney, 'The Christian Right and the 1980 presidential election', *Journal for the Scientific Study of Religion*, vol. 21, no. 2, 1982, pp. 123–31; and J. Guth, 'Southern Baptist clergy: vanguard of the Christian Right?', in Robert Liebman and Robert Wuthnow (eds) *The New Christian Right*, New York: Aldine, 1983, pp. 118–32. However, by 1984, the assessment changed again to account for the organizational strength that accrued to the movement over time. Johnson and Tamney, 'Christian Right and the 1984 presidential election'; and J. Guth, 'Political activism among a religious elite: Southern Baptist ministers in the 1984 election', paper presented at Society for the Scientific Study of Religion, Savannah, Georgia, USA, 1985, were no longer debunking.

32 The Associated Press provides a summary of eight abortion-related violent incidents in the period between 1993 and 1998. See http://cgi.cnn.com/US/ 9810/24/abortion.violence.

33 Christian Identity ideology and its links to various recent violent incidents are described in Jeff Stein, 'Christian Identity is for pantywaists', *Salon News*, 12 August 1999. Available at http://www.salon.com/news/feature/1999/08/11/ christian_identity.

34 A good overview of the Waco case can be found in Stuart A. Wright (ed.) *Armageddon in Waco: Critical Perspectives on the Branch Davidian Conflict*, Chicago: University of Chicago Press, 1995.

35 Robert Wuthnow and Matthew Lawson, 'Sources of Christian fundamentalism in the United States', in Marty and Appleby, *Accounting for Fundamentalisms*.

36 David Stoll makes this point about the break-up of Catholic hegemony in 'Jesus is Lord of Guatemala: evangelical reform in a death squad State', in Marty and Appleby, *Accounting for Fundamentalisms*. See also David Martin, *Tongues of Fire: The Explosion of Protestantism in Latin America*, Oxford: Basil Blackwell, 1990, p. 59.

37 Cal Thomas and Ed Dobson, *Blinded by Might: Can the Religious Right save America?*, Grand Rapids, MI: Zondervan, 1999, p. 23.

38 Pat Robertson, 'A message from the President', Christian Coalition website, http://cc.org/countdown/letter.html.

39 Laura Meckler, 'Falwell announces voter drive', *Associated Press*, 15 April 2000.

40 'CBN WorldReach: Bringing hope to a world in need', http://www.cbnworldreach.org/highlights1999.htm.

41 Christian Smith and Joshua Prokopy argue that Latin America is undergoing a genuine pluralization of religions, with evangelicals challenging Catholics, and both being joined by various syncretic new movements and other world religions. See their edited volume, *Latin American Religion in Motion*, New York: Routledge, 1999.

42 See especially Tod D. Swanson, 'Refusing to drink with the mountains: traditional Indian meanings in evangelical testimonies', and Stoll, 'Jesus is Lord of Guatemala', both in Marty and Appleby, *Accounting for Fundamentalisms*.
43 Making this argument from very different positions are Stephen L. Carter, *The Culture of Disbelief*, New York: Basic Books, 1993, and Jose Casanova, *Public Religions in the Modern World*, Chicago: University of Chicago Press, 1994.
44 See Susan Harding, 'Observing the observers', in Nancy T. Ammerman (ed.) *Southern Baptists Observed: Multiple Perspectives on a Changing Denomination*, Knoxville, TN: University of Tennessee Press, 1993.

Select bibliography

Ammerman, Nancy Tatom, *Bible Believers: Fundamentalists in the Modern World*, New Brunswick, NJ: Rutgers University Press, 1987.

Bendroth, Margaret Lamberts, *Fundamentalism and Gender: 1875 to the Present*, New Haven, CT: Yale University Press, 1994.

Brouwer, Steve, Gifford, Paul and Rose, Susan D., *Exporting the American Gospel: Global Christian Fundamentalism*, New York: Routledge, 1996.

Carpenter, Joel A., *Revive Us Again: The Reawakening of American Fundamentalism*, New York: Oxford University Press, 1997.

Harding, Susan Friend, *The Book of Jerry Falwell: Fundamentalist Language and Politics*, Princeton, NJ: Princeton University Press, 2000.

Lawrence, Bruce, *Defenders of God*, San Francisco: Harper & Row, 1989.

Marsden, George M., *Fundamentalism and American Culture*, New York: Oxford University Press, 1980.

Marty, Martin E. and Appleby, R. Scott (eds), *Fundamentalisms Observed*, Chicago: University of Chicago Press, 1991.

Marty, Martin E. and Appleby, R. Scott, *Accounting for Fundamentalisms*, Chicago: University of Chicago Press, 1994.

Riesebrodt, Martin, *Pious Passion: The Emergence of Modern Fundamentalism in the United States and Iran*, trans. Don Reneau, Berkeley, CA: University of California Press, 1993.

6

PATHWAYS OF FUNDAMENTALIZATION

The peculiar case of Mormonism[1]

Walter E.A. van Beek

Fundamentalist movements, despite their apparent variety (as exemplified in this volume), share some clear characteristics. First, their theology is text oriented without critical scholarship;[2] fundamentalists claim that scripture is infallible; shun revisionism in interpretation;[3] and use a selective literalism in order to preserve the notion of an inerrant scripture. They believe that the authority of the text transcends translation problems, just as it supersedes the processes of history and the constraints of culture. Sometimes, the sacred text ought not to be translated (as in the case of Islam), or the quality of translation is judged on the transparency of the resulting text. Often doctrine and trust in the interpreter's faith are important arguments in the evaluation of translations.[4] The interpretation of scripture is an arena for authority, as in principle scripture is accessible for everyone; theological anarchy is kept at bay by a clear structure of authority, in order to solve the question whose interpretation is to prevail.

Socially, fundamentalists tend to model their social and economic life on the pristine congregations of original believers, in order to restore the old order of community.[5] Flights from the 'evils of the world' are common, in an *hijra*-exodus pattern[6] that can been seen in Islam, among the New England Puritans, the Afrikaner 'Great Trek', as well as among the Mormons, as we shall see. The building of a 'just society' starts from ideology but creates political strongholds, with virtual theocracies.

Culturally, fundamentalists focus on evil, control over sexuality, and involvement of the family inside a practical theocracy which combines hierarchy and equality. Finally, fundamentalism is never finished, but has an inherent need for continuous cleansing and redefinition of identity.

111

Such fundamentalist religions have mechanisms to revive themselves and should be seen as a continuous process of fundamentalization.

In this chapter, we shall look at one particular instance of Christianity, usually called Mormonism, in effect, the Church of Jesus Christ of Latter-Day Saints, and some of its derivatives. What processes of fundamentalization are discernible inside this major[7] but relatively new Christian tradition?[8]

Restoration of fundamentals: the LDS Church

The story of Mormonism has often been told.[9] The Church of Jesus Christ of Latter-Day Saints (henceforth LDS Church), as is its correct name,[10] stems from American soil and may be considered the most typically American of all Christian churches. The opening scene is in upstate New York, an area dubbed 'the Burned-over District' because of the many evangelization movements that have passed through it. The time is the early 1800s, when massive changes swept through the region. Conservative religious movements vied with itinerant preachers and budding quasi-religious Utopian movements, which tried to re-establish family values, defended small-scale local communities and attacked women's emancipation.

> Into this light came Joseph Smith, the 24 year old New York farmer, who founded a religion based on his translation of a set of golden plates delivered by an angel. The Book of Mormon, a record of God's dealings with the pre-Columbian ancestors of the American Indian, not only explained the Hebrew origins of the Indians, but established America as a chosen land destined to receive the fullness of the everlasting gospel. Written in King James English, Smith's translation sounded biblical, but its location and conceptual framework were American. The Book of Mormon gave America a sacred past and a millennial future. It became the keystone of a new American religion.[11]

At first, the fledgling church grew slowly. Officially founded in 1830 with six official members, it counted seventy adherents a year later when it moved to Kirtland, Ohio. Later, growth went faster, with new recruits from among former Methodists, Presbyterians, Baptists, Shakers and Millerites. After Kirtland, a secondary centre in Jackson County, Missouri, was designated as the new Zion, the ultimate place of the gathering of the Saints.

The first decade of the LDS Church was difficult; the Mormons operated on a communal basis, assuming a strong role in local economics and politics, which in due time generated conflicts with other groups. One obvious reason for tension was the Mormon religious doctrine, the claim of Joseph Smith to be a prophet of God, the new Scripture and the exclusive claim to revealed truth (though not uncommon in that part of America). Mormons were accused of land speculation, of improper banking, of aspiring to political offices, and of anti-slavery views. Yet, during these Ohio and Missouri years, a strong religious foundation was laid. Joseph wrote down and compiled his revelations, established a 'school of prophets', organized the church with twelve apostles, built a temple, organized a communal society and published a hymn book. In those years, Joseph and his close followers developed new conceptions of the Godhead; a radically different view of mankind's sacred history; an encompassing plan of salvation, as well as a new way of worship; a close-knit organization and a missionary system. In short, he laid the foundation for the new Christian tradition of Mormonism. Two specific aspects made the Mormon project quite unique, in their own words 'peculiar': communality and polygamy.

Economically, the Mormons criticized capitalism and individualism, their dominant environment. Early Mormonism emphasized cooperation, egalitarianism and provision for the needy: 'Its goals were common ownership of property and classlessness.'[12] In Ohio and in Missouri, and later in several Utah communities (by Brigham Young), the 'Law of Consecration' or the 'United Order' was implemented.[13] The idea was to combine communalism and private enterprise. Individuals or families 'consecrated' their property to the church, but retained use of it through the crucial principle of 'stewardship'. The bishop of the ward – a pivotal figure in these communities – held the deeds of the consecrated possessions as 'church common property'; his duty was to give out these properties as he saw fit in the form of stewardships, in order to have everyone earn their own living. Family organization was strictly preserved. The 'surplus' of each steward, i.e. *paterfamilias*, should be re-consecrated to help the needy, to gain additional stewardships and to 'build up the Kingdom of God': new chapels and ward houses or – very important – temples. This communal living was not a great success, though at least the Kirtland temple, the first of the church, was built by this kind of effort. In 1838 the Order was revoked by revelation,[14] and a 'lesser law' was installed: tithing. Henceforth all Mormons ought to pay one-tenth of their annual 'increase'.[15] This rule still applies.[16] Much later, when the LDS Church was firmly established in the Utah valley, Brigham Young, the second prophet, revived the communal ideals of Joseph and restarted the Order in the early 1870s. Though that experiment, too, proved of short duration and limited success, it exemplifies the spirit of communitarism pervading the early Mormon communities and settlements. The Missouri settlements in particular tried to implement the communitarian ideas of the United Order. These settlements were designated as gathering places for the Mormons when they were expelled from Ohio. However, public outcry against them prevented the Mormons from 'building the kingdom of God' in Missouri. They were driven out into Illinois.

On a swampy bank in the bend of the Mississippi river, Joseph found his next and major refuge. Though Missouri remained the land of Zion in the minds of the Saints, the city of Nauvoo became the actual centre and place of gathering. Joseph had wrested a generous charter from the Illinois legislature, so Nauvoo could become a virtual city-state.[17] It was in Nauvoo, meaning the 'beautiful', that the Mormons developed their version of the 'City on the Hill': a theocratic community where the Saints not only could dwell in peace, but also hold power. It was to be for a short period only – as most episodes in early Mormon history – but for the Mormons a crucial and glorious one. Nauvoo grew rapidly to 12,000 in 1844, making it the second largest city in Illinois, next to Chicago. The Mormons ruled their own city, administered their own justice, and sported their own militia: the Nauvoo Legion, with Joseph as military commander, in fact as Lieutenant General.[18] Here they built their Kingdom of God, including the emotional centre of Mormon-dom, the temple.

At Nauvoo the most characteristic element of Mormon theology came to the fore, polygamy.[19] Ideas and rumours about this 'Celestial Marriage' had been floating around for some time, but the final revelation[20] was dated 12 July 1843.[21] The revelation pointed to the polygynous practices of Old Testament patriarchs, defining them as the will of God and as a higher order of marriage. The new element was marriage for all eternity, as opposed to marriage 'until death do us part': marriages were to continue in heaven. Wives of a righteous man would find salvation and celestial glory with him through such marriages. In the celestial sphere, the man 'would administer a patriarchal "universe" surrounded by his wives, children, and family'.[22] Though sexual stereotypes of the dependent female and the sexually inexhaustible male mingled here with theology, the first and foremost reason for 'polygamy' (as it was called by outsiders) or 'plural marriage' (the internal definition) was religious. And it would remain religious. Persons 'sealed' (a specific and crucial term in Mormon theological discourse) under this law would 'come forth in the first resurrection and would inherit thrones, kingdoms, principalities, powers and dominion'.[23]

Marrying 'celestial wives' started secretly before 1843, but Joseph Smith and his followers had been denying the practice. This pattern of public denial while in practice following the so-called 'Principle' was to persist until the late 1880s. The reason for this duplicity was persecution. Though the Mormons were at first persecuted for other reasons, their Golden Bible (Book of Mormon), their economic and political power and their insouciance of their neighbours, polygamy became the rallying point of opposition. Within the Mormon ranks it also met with great initial resistance. Brigham Young, later to be the leading exponent of polygyny in Utah, stated: 'I was not desirous of shrinking from my duty, but it was the first time in my life that I desired the grave.'[24] Emma Hale, Joseph's wife, never acquiesced to the new law, and reportedly threw at least one of his celestial wives down the stairs of her home. Eventually, the practice of polygamy became the test of loyalty to Joseph, but before his death no more than thirty of the church's top leaders had reportedly engaged in plural marriages.[25]

External resistance grew stronger while internally the Mormons closed ranks. The communities around Nauvoo and the Illinois government were ill-disposed towards 'bigamy and idolatry', and violent persecution was rife. An assassination attempt on the Missouri governor was attributed by some to the Mormons, and for any mishap the Mormons became the scapegoat of the far West. Turmoil came to a head when Joseph Smith had a printing press destroyed in his own Nauvoo on which Mormon dissidents published a newspaper critical of his domination. After legal manoeuvring, Smith allowed himself to be caught to stand trial, again.[26] In the spring of 1844, Joseph and his brother Hyrum put themselves under the protection of the security forces in the Carthage jail. However, a group of armed men forcibly gained entry, apparently after the security forces had abandoned them, and killed the Mormon prophet and his brother.

Several candidates for the prophet's mantle vied for the highest office post in Mormonism, but eventually Brigham Young, the President of the Council of the Twelve Apostles, won and became the second president. His was not a dispensation of visions and angels, not a constant renewal of laws. He was the organizer, the statesman and colonizer. When tension mounted against Nauvoo, the Saints had to leave their cherished city, their pride and glory, the new temple, unfinished. Then 'Brother Brigham' led the Saints in their exodus to the new promised land. 'The final move to Utah passed beyond the frontier into an institutional vacuum, where a totally new social order had to be established for survival, but where it could at the same time enjoy uninhibited growth.'[27]

The story of this great trek, like every great exodus in history, has become the source of legends, myth, pride and a deeply ingrained pioneer identity. It was a leap into the unknown, far beyond the limits of what was then considered civilization. It was a genuine exodus, and the Mormons appropriated Israel's experience. An identification with the people of Israel was present from the start, but the voyage to the new Promised Land, with its authentic Salt Lake, sharpened the awareness of *Israel redivivus*. Of course, the river leading from Utah Lake to the Salt Lake was called Jordan River, and of course the landscape became dotted with biblical names. In this Latter-Day Israel, the Patriarchal Order was revived; in 1852 Brigham Young proclaimed the 'State of Deseret' to be a polygamous state. The guiding principle of this state was to be religion: an orderly, cooperative and unified society over which the Mormons would have complete control. The City on the Hill thus became a theocratic state.[28]

Now the Saints could build their 'Kingdom of God'. In practice this meant hard work: building an irrigation system; mining; farming; and producing every commodity needed for the isolated communities. Converts, who flocked to Utah, complained that church sermons said little about the glories of heaven, and far more about 'Irrigation ditches, always irrigation ditches.'[29] Mormon enterprises were of a mixed economic type, combining principles of cooperative and private ownership. The irrigation system was necessarily the largest cooperative project; but also stores and manufacturing industries based themselves on cooperative work. The LDS Church bore a large part of the responsibility for all cooperative efforts itself, thus laying the foundations of its later corporate empire.[30] The communal spirit, however, the ideals of consecration and the United Order, refused to die. During the 'Panic of 1873', Brigham Young revived the cherished idea of his predecessor, and created over one hundred United Orders in various communities and enterprises: cattle and sheep herding; grist mills; sawmills and some trading companies.[31] Orderville, the most successful, operated for ten years, but ultimately followed the other experiments which had folded more quickly.

Mormonism: a very peculiar fundamentalism

Mormonism, like any movement which defies the existing order, has 'a lot of history'. But is it fundamentalist? If so, what is the specific Mormon character of fundamentalism, bearing in mind the observation noted above that Mormonism is best approached as a new Christian tradition?[32]

First scriptural inerrancy, literalism, the attitude towards the text. While in Protestant fundamentalism this implies the Bible, and nothing else, in

Mormonism the status of the Bible is different. The Bible is important indeed; the text is taken literally (as far as possible) and is authoritative. Its interpretation certainly follows the lines of common-sense approach, with little room for 'higher criticism'. But there are major provisos at two levels. The first is the transmission of the text. The Mormons also believe that the Bible is incomplete and partially corrupted. Incomplete, because many elements (books, epistles, gospels) are missing; partially corrupted because of faulty translations by uninspired or unrighteous translators: 'We believe the Bible to be the word of God as far as it is translated correctly', one of the – authoritative – Articles of Faith states.[33] This is partly a technical problem: in the past, people have left things out or made mistakes. But it has also moral dimensions: unrighteousness, 'priestcraft' and other evils are believed to have corrupted the text. More 'fundamental' still is the concept of revelation and the production of new scripture. Joseph Smith, as a prophet, produced new scripture. Part of this consists of translations of (newly discovered) old texts, like the Book of Mormon (dealing with pre-Columbian American populations), and the Book of Abraham (a translation from Egyptian papyrus texts). The other part is revelation proper: 'Verily, thus saith the Lord' or 'The heavens were opened and we saw', either as so-called 'extraterrestrial revelation',[34] i.e. a voice or vision coming down from heaven, or as inspiration, like an inspired prayer or the Joseph Smith story. These new scriptures have the same authority as the Bible, maybe even more.

Here we seem to be far removed from conventional fundamentalism. This is anathema for the usual fundamentalists, not only questioning the purity of the text, but even producing 'scripture'! The Bible is not only imperfect but new 'bibles' will also continue to appear. If this is fundamentalism, it is indeed a rather peculiar one. Yet, without stretching the notion of fundamentalism to this 'production of Scripture' in Mormonism, it is not as alien as it seems. After all, purity is what both Mormons and fundamentalists aim for: pure text. The classic strategy is to define the received text as pure, the Mormon strategy was to purify it oneself. Joseph Smith, during the last years of his short life, engaged in an overall correction of the Bible, called *The Joseph Smith Translation of the Bible*.[35] His aim was to remove all 'imperfections' from the text, thus restoring it to pristine purity, and ensuring easy comprehension. This all hinges upon the question of what a text is and whence its authority. According to Mormonism (and fundamentalists) the basis of scripture is the Lord speaking to a prophet. Given the idea of a living prophet, this means in practice: scripture is a (the) prophet speaking. The new revelations stated this clearly: 'And whatsoever they shall speak when moved upon by the Holy Ghost shall be scripture, shall be the will of the Lord, shall be the mind of the Lord, shall be the voice of the Lord, and the power of God unto salvation.'[36] Brigham Young went one step further and, in his characteristic way, declared that 'all those books [scriptures] are nothing compared to the living oracles'.[37]

Back to the fundamentals implies, for Mormons, back to the prophet. If that is accepted, the same principles of literalness, inerrancy, non-critical acceptance and obedience hold as in the usual form of fundamentalism. The words of the 'living prophet' are treated in the same way as the time-honoured citations of the Bible. But an open scripture raises one crucial problem: one of containment. If each prophetic utterance could become scripture, chaos would ensue. Thus, how to contain production of scripture? In Mormon practice this is done in three ways. First, Joseph's revelations, though extensive, are limited in number. Some utterances are part of scripture; some are just speech; some (quite a lot) are hearsay. In order to be scripture, revelations have to be accepted. From early in Mormon history, the congregation made the final decision on the scriptural status of new revelations.

The second limitation is that new revelations have to conform with earlier ones. The notion of the 'unity of truth' is important here. Revealed truth cannot contradict other – earlier – revealed truths. In fact, most Mormons hold that scientific truths cannot do so either, in the long run. So, in practice, revelations tend to be in 'biblical language': often as explanations of earlier statements or as answers to specific questions, though the format does vary.

A third limitation is that, after the death of Joseph Smith, the canon did not remain as open as it was during his ministry. Few 'prophets' (now called 'presidents') added to the corpus. The last new revelation was in 1978.[38] In fact, Joseph is called 'The Prophet' and continues to hold a special place in this respect. Thus, in practice the canon is 'half-open' and major new doctrinal developments through contemporary revelation are not to be expected.

Of course, this raises the problem of authority, a crucial issue in Mormonism where the position of the prophet is absolutely essential. At the early beginnings of the church, Smith was repeatedly challenged as a prophet. After all, everyone has similar access to scripture and truth; so why not to revelation? Meeting those challenges head on, Smith managed to reserve the revelations to his person and in so doing gradually established a principle of positional revelation: someone could only receive valid revelations for and on behalf of his calling and stewardship: the president for the Church, the bishop for the ward, and a father for his family. So a considerable number of revelations address the issue of the authority for revelation, thus equating the revelation of authority with the authority of revelation.[39] Struggles for authority were not absent, though. After the death of Smith, Young assumed leadership; but some factions stayed behind under different authority. We shall come back to Mormon splinter groups later.

Translation is of prime importance in the concept of Mormon prophetism. The Bible is considered to be inadequately translated; but this notion is fading, as we shall see. The Book of Mormon, in contrast, is considered to be a perfect translation from the golden plates into (biblical) English. The same holds for the papyri that generated the Book of Abraham.[40] Translation is at the heart of scripture formation, as the word of God is considered clear and unequivocal, and translation is the means to communicate. As for Bible studies, the Mormons, on the one hand, have not embarked upon textual criticism, have taken their distance from all kinds of 'higher criticism', but are quite interested in the study of ancient scripture, on the other. For instance, they have a considerable interest in the Dead Sea scrolls, as both the communities of the Essenes and their texts bear more than a superficial resemblance to the Book of Mormon communities. The principal point is the idea that a perfect, pure and 'authorized' translation is possible, but then only by processes close to revelation.

Closer to fundamentalist positions is the Mormon notion of 'restoration'. The LDS Church defines itself as the church of Jesus Christ restored on earth on a definitely New Testament basis. Administrative positions in the church are considered similar to those in the Primitive Church: bishops, evangelists (defined as patriarchs), teachers, deacons, elders, etc. Most important of all, the authority ('keys') of the priesthood of Jesus Christ is, the Mormons claim, in their hands. Restoration discourse also refers back to Old Testament times. Mormons also call themselves Latter-Day Israel, a restored Israel. The people in the Book of Mormon were descendants of Israel (through the tribes of Ephraim and Manasse) and so are their offspring: the Amerindians. But also all believers are considered part of the tribes of Israel, usually Ephraim. The blessings Jacob bestowed on his (grand)sons[41] are considered the proper legacy of the church; each devout Mormon once in his or her life is bestowed with a patriarchal blessing,[42] which indicates to which 'tribe' one belongs, either by birth or by adoption, no distinction is made between those two. This repristinization was a dominant theme in the earlier phases of the church, especially during the westward trek. The new country was redefined in terms of the holy land, and with its salt lake it fitted well into the pattern. Missionizing meant searching for the 'seed of Ephraim', and the hymns sang about the glory and crowning of Ephraim.[43]

Both types of pristine discourse, the New Testament Church and Old Testament tribal discourse, however, were for the most part just discourse. The only instance where the Mormons tried to emulate New Testament conditions might have been the United Order, but that was seldom explained by referring to the Book of Acts. The revelations of Joseph were the source and origin of it, not the Bible. The Primitive Church was emulated only in authority, as the 'one and only true and living church upon the face of the earth'. Restoration of that church meant restoration of the priesthood. But for the rest, the authority of the past was needed to give the present a firm foundation in order to march into the future. The same holds even stronger, for the Old Testament discourse. Defining oneself as Israel implied a claim to a spiritual inheritance, and thus to collective authority, not a revival of tribal living.

But the discourse did one thing which is very characteristic of Mormonism: it tied the church to a land, to a territory, to a holy place. The Israel-discourse territorialized the church: Latter-Day Israel had to gather. When 'Zion' was assigned to be located in Jackson County, Missouri, the Saints claimed a birthright to that place (even if they had to buy it first).[44] Later Nauvoo, still later the Salt Lake Valley, became the gathering place of the Mormons. Thus, Mormon missionaries abroad – those days mainly in Europe – stressed emigration to Utah.[45] The territorial discourse is typical American; though Mormons are very interested in Israel and its holy places,[46] Zion (defined as a twin city of Jerusalem) is still in Jackson County,[47] and of course the Mormon trail, from Cumorah in the East, where Joseph Smith found the plates of the Book of Mormon, over Nauvoo to the intermountain West, has acquired some historic holiness. The Book of Mormon is also full of references to the 'land of inheritance', of course inheritance for the present-day Indians, in southern Mexico, the most probable site for the events of the Book of Mormon.

This territorialization fitted in well with the actual patterns of authority. Mormonism was a state. Though not intending to be sovereign – the holiness of the American subcontinent precluded that – a Mormon territory with a state run by Mormons was a logical consequence of this 'peculiar' type of fundamentalism. When state and church were eventually separated (to a degree at least), the church retained the level of organization needed to run a civil administration. An ordered Kingdom of God is one of Mormon-dom's hallmarks. Hierarchy is important, underscored by the identification of the authority of and the authority for revelation. As is usual in fundamentalist organizations, however, egalitarian tendencies manifest themselves as well. It is a lay church, without paid ministry, the various positions rotating among people who perform them part-time. Leaders arise out of the rank and file, and the theological positions and acumen of leaders and followers do not differ much.[48] As Leone aptly put it, Mormons have a 'do-it-yourself theology'.[49] Still, obedience sets limits to egalitarian notions. Formally, leaders have to be sustained by the vote of the saints, by 'common consent'. This could be interpreted as a check on authority, but in practice it is not. Voting against proposed leaders is rare, and usually will not induce changes. But notions of fundamental equality underneath the organizational structure are easy to discern. The combination of job rotation with positional charisma tries to combine both: people are in authority as long as they are in office, and then they have all the authority that belongs to the position. After a few years, they are released and someone else takes the mantle. Also, in Mormonism's most sacred place, the temple, equality is stressed throughout.

Finally, among our aspects of fundamentalism, there is control over sexuality, and a focus on the family. The Mormons of old, with their polygamy, were 'peculiar' indeed – in fact 'peculiar' was their favourite self-definition. Present-day Mormons are less peculiar, and second to none in stressing family values and family orientation. The sexual mores are the traditional Christian ones, with sexual intercourse limited to legal marriage. Infringement of these norms is not only frowned upon, but may lead to excommunication. The church treats 'sexual transgression' very seriously. This may seem to contradict the early polygamy days, but there, too, the marriage 'covenant' was dominant: a man could not have intercourse outside the covenant (though he could covenant with more wives, evidently).[50] Observers in the 1860s in Utah extensively commented on the 'puritan way' in which the Mormons contracted their plural marriages. Mark Twain – no admirer at all of the Mormons – with his usual hyperbole called anyone who married those 'ugly Mormon women' a saint, the more he married, the saintlier he surely must be.

Our provisional conclusion is that 'classic' Mormonism, if classified as fundamentalist, is a very 'peculiar' case indeed. Yet, it does have the potential for fundamentalism to develop. And the processes of fundamentalization, as we shall see, will centre on that most peculiar of all institutions, polygamy. The twentieth-century LDS Church tried to put a maximal cognitive distance between itself and polygamy. Though about half of the twentieth-century presidents either had practised polygamy or were reared in polygamous families, those who continued to practice it after the final end of the 'Principle' in 1910 were excommunicated. In the present-day LDS Church, no room for polygamy is left: the monogamous family is the only road towards salvation. How polygamy came to be the principal arena within the Church, and the motor of fundamentalization, is the second part of the story of the Saints.

Polygamy as a fundamentalist arena

From 1852, when polygamy was declared by Young to be the law in Deseret, the Utah theocracy was a polygamous enclave in the larger United States.[51] That, and its different economic and political premises, made it increasingly alien to the federal government. The cherished isolation was not to last. Not only did the westward movement of the USA catch up with them, the Utah Mormons tried to enter the Union also. This cost them a severe reduction of their territorial claims and appointment of 'gentile' (non-Mormon) officials. Coming at a time when the question of slavery dominated the political agenda, the Mormon 'kingdom in the West' became an embarrassment for US President Buchanan. For a variety of unclear reasons[52] he sent an expeditionary force against the theocracy. Young managed to avoid shedding blood, by a scorched earth tactic, moving tens of thousands of Mormons from their farmsteads. The US army marched unopposed into the Salt Lake valley, stayed on and became part of the Utah scene. The whole issue was soon forgotten in the Civil War that followed, and in 1861 the soldiers left: federal officials were installed, and Brigham Young remained the real power in Utah.

Though the military intervention proved futile, the brushes with the United States were to continue. The Mormons were in a quandary: they desperately wanted statehood inside the United States, not only because of political necessity (Young always realized that there was no future for a separate sovereign state of Deseret) but also by doctrine. The Mormons considered the United States to be a sacred country and the Constitution an inspired document. For the United States, the basic problem was the theocracy, and the *casus belli* they were offered was that uniquely Mormon institution of polygamy. So, in the years after the Civil War, a legal battle ensued over polygamy. The Mormons based themselves on the freedom of religion, claiming that for them polygamy was a religious prescription. The federal government countered that religious freedom could not legitimize infraction of other civil laws, such as the anti-bigamy Act. The battle took place in the court rooms, and gradually increased in scope and intensity.

The newspapers took up the challenge and a stream of anti-Mormon propaganda ensued,[53] focusing on the 'twin relics of barbarism: slavery and polygamy'. The two became almost identical for the budding feminist movement, when women from the East started to deplore the miserable life of their wretched sisters in the Mormon West: being a plural wife must be just like slavery. The reverse was true, however. Utah women were quite independent, all the more so when their (collective) husband was on church callings – or hiding – and they had to run the family business on their own, with their co-wives. Also, they were among the first to obtain the right to vote (1870). Nevertheless, the federal government gradually escalated the legal measures against polygamy in a series of 'acts': the Morrill Act (1962), the Poland Act (1878) and the Edmunds Act (1882); the latter stripped polygamists of most of their civic rights. As a consequence, during the 1870s and 1880s Utah became the scene of 'polygamy hunters', jailing practising polygamists, or 'cohabs' as they called them. A system of 'gentile' judges, juries and clerks was set up, and sentences were increased to three and a half years in prison.[54]

Since during the late 1860s most leaders had 'entered the Principle', a large portion of the Church leadership went 'underground' in a migrant life that took them every few days from Mormon house to farm barn, a weary cycle of travel, hardships and narrow escapes. Others sought refuge in Mexico, Canada and Hawaii, where the existing laws were not enforced as strictly. Church President John Taylor, Brigham Young's successor (a companion of Joseph Smith at the time of his death), died in 1887, on the underground trail. His case is important as he had been the staunchest defender of plural marriage against mounting opposition. When, after his death, more moderate judges gave more lenient sentences to polygamists who turned themselves in (six months in prison), Congress stepped up the persecution and passed in 1887 the Edmunds–Tucker Act. This added a collective threat to individual harassment: the Church as such would become illegal if it continued to preach and practice the 'Principle'.[55] Of course, the Mormons contested the constitutional correctness of this act, but it was upheld by the US Supreme Court: the seizure of Church property was to be legal.

That made for a hot summer in 1890, when the church leaders had to decide on the future course. The religious fire, not very surprisingly, was fuelled by chiliastic expectations;[56] at least some members seemed to have expected the return of Christ at that time.[57] Under extreme pressure, Church President Wilford Woodruff, realizing that he was 'under the necessity of acting for the temporal salvation of the church', on 25 September 1890 drew up a declaration that the church would comply with US laws and abstain from plural marriages henceforth. This document is called the 'Manifesto' and as such has become part of the Doctrine and Covenants. At the general conference of the church, 6 October 1890, the Manifesto was 'unanimously sustained' as 'authoritative and binding'.

This not only ended polygamy, officially, but also the theocratic nature of the Utah territory, and in 1896 Utah was granted statehood. In fact, the battle for the United States was not against polygamy as such, as one federal representative candidly explained:

> We care nothing for your polygamy. It's a good war-cry and serves our purposes by enlisting sympathy for our cause; but it is a mere bagatelle compared with other issues ... your unity, your political and commercial solidarity, and the obedience you tender to your spiritual leaders in temporal affairs.[58]

But even if polygamy was the 'war-cry' and a convenient angle for the opposition, for the LDS Church it was the issue, and would remain so for a long time.

The Manifesto, evidently, did not end polygamy at one stroke. Several reasons account for that. First, the Manifesto did not use the same scriptural language as other revelations: it was articulated as a resolution to submit to the laws of the land and an advice to all members 'to refrain from contracting any marriage forbidden by the law of the land', it stated no penalties, it did not define plural marriage as 'wrong'.[59] Also the other leaders at that time were not asked to sign, so many considered it a political document rather than a revelation.

Later additions stated that past marriages continued to be valid. So after the Manifesto plural families moved together instead of splitting up. The arm of the law grew weaker, and the drive against the polygamists stopped. The Mormon kingdom was brought down to earth, and that was it. Some of the ire was rekindled in later years when it became clear that the church leaders continued to 'seal' plural marriages in Canada and Mexico, in secret, while publicly denying it (an old ploy the LDS leadership had used in the Nauvoo days). In 1904 this came to a head when Reed Smoot, an apostle, ran for a US Senate seat. Though Smoot had but one wife, his president, Joseph F. Smith, was found to be a practising polygamist. After another Manifesto, Smoot was accepted, the first in a long line of Mormon Senators and Congressmen. The latter Manifesto stated, 'If any officer or member of the church shall assume to solemnize or enter into any such marriage he will be deemed in transgression against the church, and will be liable to be excommunicated therefrom.'[60] This still left the door open in Mexico and Canada, and no manifesto was couched in terms of a revelation. Only in 1907 did the LDS Church formally affirm the separation of Church and state in a definitive rejection of polygyny throughout the Church.

Towards a corporate empire: the main road of Mormon fundamentalization

During a struggle that lasted half a century, the LDS Church first developed the notion of polygamy from an inner-circle spiritual prerogative into a living arrangement and finally into the central tenet of Mormonism. 'A peculiar people' the Mormons liked, and still like, to call themselves, with polygamy as the hallmark of that peculiarity up until 1890. Probably, the battle-cry of the federals moved the LDS Church to more emotional investment in the Principle than it might otherwise have done. Like any value at the centre of a battle, this one also gathered an enormous emotional weight and theological backing. Now, if a central tenet is attacked, what ways are open to react? Several types of reaction are known. The first is the classic reaction of hardening one's positions: the values at stake have to be lived in another context and setting. The second one is explaining away the conflict, adjusting to the new situation; this implies rewriting history. The third is simply to forget about the conflict and move to business as usual. All three can be found in the Mormon case. The last one, implying the least amount of emotional investment, was the reaction of the federal government. The United States had made its point, Utah became a state like the others; the vestiges of polygamy would die out; business as usual.

That option was not open to those who had invested heavily in the lost position: they had to choose between rewriting the past or to harden their standpoint and seek an escape. Both, as we shall see, generate fundamentalism. So, for the church, a major cognitive rearrangement had to be made. As LeGrand Richards, an apostle at the end of the twentieth century, stated: 'Our main goal was to beat the polygamy issue', and with success, he thought. The LDS Church engaged on a trail of battling against polygamy. The very practice it had defended with all its might was now sufficient reason for excommunication. Throughout the years after 1907, the Church stressed monogamous marriage, the nuclear family, and family values coming very close to the majority of Christian denominations, with the difference that the religious overtones of marriage became ever stronger. The recent official declaration on the family is a continuation of that development.

The transformation from a theocracy into a denomination was neither voluntary nor easy, but, once adopted, the LDS Church followed that course with conviction and determination.[61] Several notions helped in this transformation. One was – and is – 'constancy in change', the idea that all changes have not fundamentally altered the Church. Though this is true in several ways, the transformation was massive indeed. Often dubbed 'Americanization', the Church transformed from an enemy of the government of the United States (but a fervent supporter of the US Constitution) into the ultimate patriots. Mormons entered the political scene, most as staunch Republicans, and Utah is now considered the most Republican of all American states.

Theologically this generated a process of fundamentalization. During the first phase of its development not only open scriptures, but also a more liberal and open interpretation were present in the LDS Church. In the middle of the twentieth century, however, a marked process of fundamentalization set in. Literal interpretation, the rejection of 'higher' criticism, obedience to the 'Brethren' (church leaders) and a growing unease with evolutionary theories mark that period.[62] One reason is the role of lay ministers, without theological training, as formulators of doctrine and interpretation. This may of course lead to a more social-type scripture interpretation as well, but the Mormon example demonstrates that lay leaders with fundamentalist leanings more easily find acceptance and thus authority, and build up a power base within a hierarchy. In a strong lay organization it is easier to defend a fundamentalist position and to discredit liberal opponents, than the reverse. Thus, in the last half of the twentieth century, some fundamentalist apostles have dominated church publications.[63] This particular process of fundamentalization was increased by institutional changes, the second reason. The leadership brought all church activities under their direct control. Crack-downs on individual academics and critics, interventions in survivalist groups at the far right of the political spectrum, and a streamlining of education materials were the tools to get the membership back in line. One important aspect was the rapid growth of the Church after the 1960s. From a Utah-based church, the LDS Church grew to an all-American denomination with considerable presence in Latin America and Europe; at the turn of the century the LDS Church had already become a global phenomenon with 11 million members, more than ten times the number in 1945.

Control was and still is deemed essential and with it the idea of stability-in-change of the Church. The 'struggle with assimilation'[64] resulted in the Church becoming definitely American within the mainstream of American values. But it had one more crucial consequence. The combination of a strong organization, routinization of charisma and the homogenization of fundamentalist leanings transformed the church into a corporation. Many writers have commented upon the 'Mormon corporate empire' for various reasons. First, its management techniques have a corporate flavour; not surprisingly seeing that many General Authorities (as the leadership elite is known inside the Church) are called to their leadership positions after a successful career in industry. The second reason is wealth. From its large holdings in Utah, the Church through both its incomes from tithes and its former investments, amassed a large capital. The total value is not disclosed any longer, but is estimated in the billions of dollars. A huge building programme and a vast missionary programme are financed by it, but deficit spending is frowned upon in the Church administration. Thus was the Mormon theocracy with its open scriptures transformed into a fundamentalist corporation.

The critical voice in Mormonism, and the liberal leanings in theology (the word is actually little used, it is 'doctrine') come from history. The professionals are historians, and more recently social scientists. Quite naturally, some mistrust exists between the fundamentalist institutional core and the intellectual fringe. If conflict happens – as has been the case – the institutional church usually wins hands down. With its scriptures well in place, the interpretation and its doctrinal structure clearly demarcated, based upon a – be it selective – literalism, the hierarchy is well established. Though the LDS Church values education highly, the 'critical disciplines' of history and other social sciences are not trusted. Nor are some of the 'harder' sciences. Evolution is still a sensitive issue. Officially the LDS Church has maintained a neutral stance towards it, the only official position is that it has no position. At the turn of the century apostles could and did still speak out in favour of it in a courageous attempt to integrate all truth, revealed and researched.[65] But these times have changed; the more fundamentalist officials have put a larger distance between them and ideas about the origin of humans. Still, there is no official position; but no longer apostles speak about 'the aeons of time the creation took'. The main LDS Church education manuals routinely portray the biblical chronology (say, Usher's) as a history of the world. The sacred history blends, thus, with secular history, one of the fundamentalist characteristics.

The Mormon fundamentalist corporation was to be highly successful. It is, like most fundamentalist organizations, modern and well adapted and offers a counter-culture to the current values of the world. Sexual liberation in the 'world' contrasts with rigorous sexual norms inside the Church, sometimes verging – at least for a European – on prudery. Abortion, divorce and broken homes are set against an ideal picture of eternal families; substance abuse against the abstinence from tobacco, coffee and tea; criminality against solemn covenants with the Lord. Institutional bonding is strong: members pay one-tenth of their income, give time and effort in church 'callings' in their spare time, filling the many slots in the local and regional organization. The 55,000 missionaries (usually young people who serve for two years) are paid for by their families. Temples are visited on weekdays and Sundays are filled with worship in chapels and meeting houses. Claims on time and resources usually are met willingly, and underscore for the members the intrinsic value of the LDS Church, thus substantiating its claim to unique truth and authority. This demanding religion generates deep commitment and a high degree of identification. O'Dea in his trail blazing study[66] used the notion of 'ethnic group'. From their doctrine and their history, the Mormons have developed the notion of a 'people', a 'peculiar' people if possible. 'Peculiar' first by polygamy; nowadays by dietary rules and commitment to Church life. Though the tribal discourse on the 'Latter-Day Israel' has abated in recent decennia, the ethnic idiom is apt. Also, for the non-American LDS, the label has been used.[67]

The process of corporate fundamentalization has, as Mauss pointed out, one irony and one problem. The irony is that Mormonism draws closer to those forms of Protestant fundamentalism that have been 'the most vocal and vituperative of the anti-Mormons'.[68] The problem is that the definition of 'being a Mormon' tends to become dichotomous: one is either in or out. Mauss rightly draws attention to the fact that any authoritative and fundamentalist message is open to disillusionment. Any anomaly in preaching, practice or behaviour can rupture the edifice of doctrine and belief. This is a general fundamentalist dilemma: if a literal interpretation is untenable, there is a crisis of faith. The authority of the organization reinforces the authority of the interpretation, and both grow dependent on each other. As a consequence, Mormonism lacks a denominational fringe where people can still define themselves as Mormons, even though they may well disbelieve one or more doctrinal tenets.[69]

Second-order 'fundamentalists': polygamy forever

So far we have been treating Mormonism as if it were one undivided whole. The dominance of the Church of Jesus Christ of Latter-Day Saints makes that easy, but it is only part of the picture. Mormonism has had its share of schisms, much more than the average LDS member would suppose,[70] ranging from minute – and sometimes now extinct – splinter groups to sizeable groups, and at least one viable church, the Reorganized Church of Jesus Christ of Latter-Day Saints (RLDS).[71] In principle, schisms in Mormonism occur for two reasons: the problem of authority, and the problem of adaptation or assimilation. Authority questions are at the origin of the RLDS Church. Joseph Smith had been 'generous' in his indication of possible successors; but after his unexpected death, a struggle over leadership ensued. Though Brigham Young more or less won that struggle and led the majority of the 'tribe' to the far West, a number of Saints did not follow him. After some time they organized a new church under the leadership of one of Joseph Smith's sons, Joseph Smith III, later to be followed by his lineal descendants. Numbering some 250,000, the RLDS Church is still centred in the Mid-West, owns a portion of Nauvoo, the Kirtland temple and the site where the 'central temple of Zion' had been projected, in Missouri. They did not cast their lot with the main body, and their pathway through theology would be quite different, as we shall see later.

The second main split occurred in Utah on the issue of polygyny.[72] When in 1886 John Taylor was in hiding from federal agents, he was guarded by several men. One of them, Lorin Woolley, recounted later that one morning Taylor told his guards he had been visited during the night by Joseph Smith and Jesus Christ 'who had instructed him to hold fast to the principle and practice of plural marriage, despite the growing pressure'. Taylor then 'set apart' several men, including Woolley, and authorized them to solemnize plural marriages and other rituals, and also to authorize others to do the same.[73] After the Manifesto, when the LDS Church had repudiated its stance on polygamy, some diehards – including the son of John Taylor – held fast to the Principle. In 1912, Lorin Woolley came out with his account of the 1886 visitation, and a number of people believed in his authority to do so. In 1929, when he was the only survivor of the group Taylor ordained in 1886, Woolley became the formal leader of what came to be called the 'fundamentalists'.[74] He conferred apostleship on a 'Council of Friends', most already excommunicated from the LDS Church because of their practice of polygamy.

Thus was founded the so-called 'fundamentalist movement'; their largest offspring is the 'Fundamentalist Church of Jesus Christ of Latter-Day Saints', also known as the Johnson–Jefferson group.[75] The movement has been split extensively.[76] Though their names[77] are reminiscent of African Independent Churches in Mormon idiom, in principle they should not be treated as independent churches because almost all recognize the LDS Church as the legitimate and true church of God. However, they aim to correct and revitalize the LDS Church, and they often refer to themselves also as the 'Johnson-group', the 'Aldred-group', etc., to stress their continued adherence to the LDS Church. This feeling is not reciprocated by the LDS Church: they are excommunicated. Including a wide array of tiny groups, the total number of present-day 'fundamentalists' is estimated between 20,000 and 25,000.[78] The number is growing, because of the high birth rate and some conversions:

> Harry, now in his 60's, had been away from home on a business trip for several days. After a long drive he arrived at the family compound and was greeted by an excited group of about 20 of his 65 children and two of his five wives. He and his children and wives greeted one another warmly, especially since it was the weekend of the monthly family reunion and meetings. Everyone was expected home that weekend, including Harry's 37 sons and 28 daughters and their families and more than 300 grandchildren and great-grandchildren.[79]

Three tenets underlie Mormon 'fundamentalism':[80] the idea that the LDS Church went astray, 'out of order', by abandoning the 'Principle'. This hinges upon the second notion that plural marriage is a divine revelation that still holds as a commandment today. Finally, the acceptance of an authority not recognized by the LDS Church. As usual in fundamentalism, authority is at the root of the movement. Though fundamentalists recognize a priesthood other than the LDS Church, for them LDS presidents still are prophets; even if led astray on the issue of polygamy, they are still 'mouthpieces of the Lord'. That rather awkward theological position, and the continuing discourse on the authority of the priesthood, resulted in a continuous tendency to fragment, occasionally with violent interaction between different 'polygamists'.

Life as a polygamist had not been easy in the first half of the twentieth century. The LDS Church, determined to rid itself of its polygamist image, excommunicated all members of the fundamentalist Church in 1935, and promoted harsher civic anti-cohabitation laws in Utah, leading to arrest and convictions of practising polygamists. In 1944 and 1953 raids were performed by the civic authorities on the fundamentalist Short Creek community, arresting over 50 men (and jailing 20) in the first, and the entire community of 400 (men, women and children) in the second raid. Women with their children were transported to foster homes, under the accusation of child neglect and abuse. Later they were allowed to return, but only after severe deprivation and suffering. The irony that the LDS Church approved raids on polygamists which they had in the past themselves suffered from, was not lost on most spectators. After the 1950s prosecutions abated, and a media silence on polygamy prevailed in the LDS Church. However, adherence to fundamentalist doctrine and participation in their services are often considered sufficient causes for excommunication by the LDS Church. Actual polygamy routinely leads to excom-munication, if found out.[81]

Recently, the legal basis for attacks on polygamy has been eroding. In Canada a court concluded that fundamentalist 'cohabitation' was a reli-gious matter and that a law banning it would violate religious freedom, as guaranteed in the Canadian Constitution. In the United States similar sounds have been heard, and the issue is no longer explosive. It is still sen-sitive, of course, and many fundamentalists would rather conceal their allegiance to the Principle than flaunt their many wives. But times are changing. A 1991 obituary in a Salt Lake City newspaper ran as follows: 'He was a father of a numerous posterity, consisting of 7 wives and 56 children. He has 340 grandchildren and 70 great-grandchildren.'[82] The burdens of prison sentences are considered assets: proofs of faith and commitment, and gradually the fundamentalists are coming out of the closet. Some of them have started speculating on the overturning of the Edmunds–Tucker Act.[83]

Though the focus of attention is, as always, polygamy, the fundamental-ist movement is much more than a rescue of polygamy. The LDS Church changed in many more instances than just the marriage law. The funda-mentalists see the pre-Manifesto way of life as the pristine Mormonism, and try to emulate that lifestyle, negating the Manifesto, which is for them indeed a 'disconfirming event that profoundly altered the character of Mor-monism'.[84] Polygamy was just one aspect, though up front. Other issues are communal living and the integration of religious and secular authority. Most fundamentalists live in communal settlements on and over the border with Arizona in Southern Utah, or in other desert locations.

Because of their rejection by mainstream Mormon society as well as by their own choice, polygamists look to each other for social, economic and moral support. Also, community living is seen as a value in itself, as in early Mormonism. Finally, the priesthood authority in fundamentalist communities demands loyalty, strict adherence to norms and allegiance to the leaders, all of which are easier in communal settings. So the fundamen-talists offer a cohesive and orderly community life, with clear-cut values and behavioural rules. Leadership is patriarchal, in the tradition of the prophet-leader (though he is not always called that), assisted by a council of elders who manage the ecclesiastical as well as temporal life of the members. Some groups also operate in an urban setting (i.e. Salt Lake City) and are less outspokenly patriarchal, but often have strong links with a rural community. In a few of these, the old United Order villages of the 1870 project are being revived and function with the help of urban co-fundamentalists.

The fundamentalist groups differ in the degree of what they call 'conservatism'. In some rural communities, especially the United fundamentalist church, women and girls wear nineteenth-century clothing: high-necked, long-sleeved dresses well below the knee, the same as the Mormon pioneers wore. Hairstyles (braids and buns) also point back to former times. The relations between the genders, too, are modelled on the old order of Utah, and in church services the admonitions of Brigham Young are often cited with approval. Urban groups are not so easy to distinguish. In fact, until recently they dressed themselves and behaved in order to blend in with their environment. If their style is still conservative, with an insistence on 'modesty', that does not raise an eyebrow in Utah.

Children are the main orientation of the communities. fundamentalist groups share a clear pro-natal attitude, again as in the pioneer days. The average number of children in polygynous households is about 5–6 per wife, as in nineteenth-century Utah. Men and women are proud of the number of offspring, as the glory of their 'covenants'. Though children may leave the communities or abandon the fundamentalist life, the majority stays in. Leaders and followers recognize that the best adaptation for fundamentalist living comes from being born into it. Yet, they do make some converts, usually among disgruntled mainstream Mormons. Being as small as they are, fundamentalist communities are characterized by a close endogamy, sisters marrying the same husband, and in one case two sisters, each with her own daughter (from different fathers), married the same husband, all four of them.

These large families are often under a considerable financial strain. In urban settings the presence of co-wives – in fundamentalist idiom 'sister-wives' – makes gainful employment outside the home possible for mothers with small children, thus solving the perennial women's problem of child-care and working at the same time. In rural areas women work at whatever job is available, but some financial stringency is normal. Women's work is not frowned upon, as it was the custom also in the olden days: the pioneer women from polygamous households were well known for running the family business between them. Problems between co-wives do occur, and some opt out of the communities or families. Divorce, as in the main LDS Church, is painful and cuts across 'covenant' doctrine; but it does happen.[85] Throughout, the fundamentalist way of living the 'Law of Celestial Marriage' closely resembles the 'Puritan way' in which the pioneer Mormons are reputed to have implemented their polygamy. It is not easy, it is a challenge not quickly entered into, but it is the will of the Lord. If not, it could best be 'carried out on a shovel'.[86]

Throughout, the lives of fundamentalists are coloured by their ambivalent and complex relationship with the LDS Church. As said, for most fundamentalists the LDS Church is still the true church, whether they have been excommunicated by it or have never even been members of it. They see themselves as a corrective movement, not a new tradition. Urban groups or the so-called independent fundamentalists may try to participate as much as possible in the regular Mormon wards. Teenagers in the urban area sometimes receive priesthood ordinations, a few even go on a mission for the LDS Church.[87] Cases are known where a fundamentalist teenager had saved money for his mission, but was refused by the LDS Church leaders because of his fundamentalist leanings.

The fundamentalists make converts as well, often not so much by virtue of polygamy – which is alien for most converts – but by the strict clarity of doctrine, and some specific doctrines preached by Brigham Young that are not considered scriptural by the LDS Church. But polygamy as such can have its appeal. Influx of these converts on the whole implies less focus on polygamy, and more on community and doctrine. So, in the end, even if the fundamentalist movement is in the eyes of the outsider, especially the LDS Church, inexorably tied up with polygamy, it is primarily a return to the old order, to the nineteenth century, to communities, to doctrinal clarity and to daring prophets.

In some instances, communal living, that old haunting ideal of equality, has generated a fundamentalist-type movement without polygamy. The 'Old Order Levites', or the 'Aaronic Order'[88] has sprung from the same source: a desire to be communal, and a longing for the old Utopian days. The 'Levites' are not a Mormon splinter group properly speaking; but they have been heavily influenced by Mormonism. They reside in the 'Mormon Corridor' and consist mostly of ex-Mormons. Their theology is full of Mormon discourse, though recently some evangelical influence has been noted (and sought for). They have found their own 'One Mighty and Strong', according to the promise of Doctrine and Covenants.[89] This expression runs through a lot of fundamentalist discourse: 'the one to set in order the house of God'. The LDS Church referred to a future bishop in Zion, Jackson County, at the coming of the Lord. Others believed in a second coming of Joseph Smith, or Indians from the South Mexican jungle. For the Levites it is Elias, the Old Testament prophet, as an angel.

The early Levites desired to set the Mormon church in order, following Maurice Glendenning as their prophet. Glendenning had received revelations and visitations from the angel Elias, and wrote his texts in a shorthand only he understood, called the Adamic language. He was born in Randolph, Kansas on 5 February 1891. At an early age he began to hear 'music and singing', later poems. In 1928 he moved to Salt Lake City, joined the LDS Church, and in 1930 received a revelation from 'Elias who should come in the last days'. Thus instructed, he started to preach on the restoration of the laws of consecration and stewardship. Gradually he drew followers to his preaching, many of whom had become dissatisfied during the Depression. When he temporarily moved to Los Angeles, his followers kept contact. In 1942 the Order of Levi was organized, and he returned to Utah. Until his death in 1969, he was considered the mouthpiece of the angel Elias, First High Priest of the Order.

After his death no new prophets came forward, and the movement is led by 'inspiration'. Most of the early members were Mormons, quite a few from cooperatives that resulted from the United Order villages. At present the Levites run a number of villages on the Utah–Nevada border, trying to create a 'Utopia in the desert'.[90] At least with some success they try to recapture something that modern LDS society has lost.

Conclusion: Mormon pathways of fundamentalization

The early Mormon theological position seemed the antithesis of fundamentalism: open scriptures which were continually added to, an open 'freewheeling' doctrine, the main authority vested not in text but in a man, and a large selectivity in reading the received texts. The image of Joseph Smith, sitting at his table with his scribe, the King James version of the Bible open, and 'correcting' the text verse by verse, is as far removed from any picture of fundamentalism as can be. However, in a deeper sense, the roots for fundamentalization were present. In Mormon thought, the institution of the 'prophet' as the 'mouthpiece of the Lord' lies at the basis of scripture, and 'open scripture' is simply the re-establishment of an old situation. Inerrancy is important, but not as the inerrancy of 'scribes', but of prophets. Literalism is there, but not as literalism of text – originally – but as literalism in reading and hearing prophetic interpretation of the received text. The emphasis on the written word is there, albeit – originally – as a secondary rendition of the spoken word.

So nineteenth-century Mormonism should not be immediately classified as a fundamentalist church, because that would be stretching the definition too far. At least it could be a very peculiar one, consistent with the favourite self-definition of the Mormons. But it does have some crucial elements of fundamentalism already present. Authority, for instance, is crucial in the Mormon situation, an aspect that tallies well with other instances of fundamentalism. Translation is important as an inspired action, producing an authoritative text. Discourse on the past is there, while adapting to the present and moving ahead in a new situation. In this respect they are among the legitimate progeny of the New England Puritans.[91]

The constitutional crisis in Mormonism – the conflict over theocracy fought on the issue of polygamy – triggered off a process of fundamentalization along two pathways. The first is the main LDS Church way. With the communal experiments a thing of the past, the separation of church and state was forced upon the Mormons and they circumvented that in their move towards a new type of institution, the fundamentalist corporative empire. Ongoing revelation – that horror of fundamentalism – was tamed through the equation of LDS Church position with the right to receive inspiration and revelation: the authority *for* revelation domesticated the authority *of* revelation.

The second signpost on this road is the closing of doctrine before the closing of the canon. At the turn of the century, the speculative thrust of the nineteenth century was contained by building a coherent system of doctrine.[92] Theophanies gave way to the 'Plan of Salvation', a system of coherent and rational doctrinal presuppositions. Henceforth, the doctrine was to be the judge of scripture, not the scripture the source of doctrine. Additions to scripture in the twentieth century were few and far between, and happened in those areas where scriptural grounding of doctrine was weak.[93] In fact, such a semi-open canon, combined with an authoritative voice, is an excellent instrument to adapt to new circumstances, while maintaining a tradition-oriented discourse. Literalness in interpretation grew, but in support of the dominant doctrine, which was possible through 'proof texting', i.e. selecting a set of favoured passages.

The third mark is an increasing self-sufficiency in providing background knowledge on biblical situations, in the impact of scientific findings and artistic renditions. In the first phase the Mormon leaders were eager to integrate 'all light and truth', reasoning from an inclusive definition of truth. All sources of truth were the same, so eventually all had to be integrated. Though this is still an important position, facts and 'truths' from outside have become suspect. Revealed truth has become a fortress under siege.

The key issue of the road to fundamentalization is of course sex. Mormon marriage was domesticated: experimental forms were forbidden and gradually faded away.[94] But the Puritan ideals of marriage and the traditional gender roles remained and spilled over into the monogamous family ideal. The same zest the LDS Church had shown for polygamy was now focused on monogamy. Lost, at least partly, is discourse on the past.[95] The institutional growth of the LDS Church and its definitive adaptation to modern society have dampened 'Israel restored' discourse in favour of 'Christ's church restored' discourse. Lost, obviously, is communal life and the drive towards repristinization. Gained, from another perspective, is a diversification-through-growth and the creation of a 'indigenous' academic tradition: albeit under corporate pressure and often disclaimed; but still with enough 'critical mass'.[96]

The second road to fundamentalization is the 'Fundamentalist movement', a 'second-order' fundamentalization. Here the reverse holds of the LDS Church. Not the corporation is the model, but the community. Repristinization is the goal here, and a peculiar one. However, the 'relevant other' in this movement is not the Primitive Church; it is the nineteenth-century Mormon village, which rejected the separation of church and state. From that same century the movement inherited polygamy as the major arena, as their peculiar way of fundamentalism. The canon is not closed, but remains open; and doctrine is important and 'deep': though not at all uniform in the various splinter groups. Here, discourse on the past is in full swing and has become dominant: Latter-Day Israel is fully present in the sermons. Sharing the same scriptures with the LDS Church, selective literalness, doctrine orientation and inerrancy of the sources prevail. Prudish sexual norms and the freezing of fashion tie in with the rejection of modernity.

Authority is the key word, as everywhere in Mormon-dom, and the principal fall-out with the LDS Church is about the authority to change. fundamentalists recognize the fundamental authority of the Mormon church, while denying it the right to change. In short, the fundamentalist movement has opted for precisely those aspects of fundamentalism that the LDS Church had renounced: communalism, repristinization and the peculiarity of polygamy.

Though not dealt with in the description, the road of the 'third party', the Reorganized Church of Jesus Christ of Latter-Day Saints, is instructive here. This church, organized originally around the Smith dynasty, has opted for a different pathway, namely that of total assimilation. Though it has retained open scripture (its *Doctrine and Covenants* is much larger than the *Doctrine and Covenants* of the LDS Church), it distanced itself completely from polygamy. Gradually this church changed the prophetic order (no longer any lineal inheritance), included women in the priesthood, and moved its doctrinal stances very close to mainstream Protestant positions. This is the trajectory of assimilation and protestantizing. A denomination is the result. It is as close to mainstream majority as possible. It is now in the process of changing its name to maximize the distance from its Mormon roots.

136

The final conclusion has to be about fundamentalism itself as a category. The first suggestion from the peculiarities of the Mormon case(s) is that fundamentalism is a process rather than a phenomenon. Theologically it is a direction of thought, a discourse and a strategy for validation rather than a doctrinal system or a finished theology. Fundamentalism is a proclivity for certain types of arguments, a type of reaction against the social environment, as well as a direction towards the future. Fundamentalism implies a continuous process of recurrent fundamentalization.

The second suggestion is that fundamentalism is ultimately about power. As a movement, and especially when embedded in institutions, it has a basic focus on power. Theologically, it appropriates the scriptural authority into its own organization, and Mormonism does that more efficiently than most other. Authority, legitimacy – in Mormon parlance, 'keys' – are the central concepts in a discourse and a practice that revolve around the power to interpret (and in Mormonism to produce) authoritative texts, and base institutional structures on that legitimacy.

The third issue is identity construction. Fundamentalization is a process of adaptation and assimilation, as a way to 'go with the times' and still retain identity. Its tradition-oriented discourse permits an ideology of 'constancy in change' despite massive transformations, both in its context as well as within the fundamentalist structures themselves.

Which leads to the final conclusion: in our rapidly changing world, fundamentalism is here to stay and recurrent fundamentalization to be expected.

Notes

1 I thank Dr P. Staples and Dr A. Mauss for their constructive criticism and corrections.
2 J. Barr, *Escaping from Fundamentalism*, London: SCM Press, 1984, p. 45 ff.
3 H.U.E. Thoden van Velzen and Walter E.A. van Beek, 'Purity: a greedy ideology', in Walter E.A. van Beek (ed.) *The Quest for Purity: Dynamics of Puritan Movements*, Berlin: Mouton/de Gruyter, 1988, p. 10.
4 Philip L. Barlow, *Mormons and the Bible: The Place of the Latter-Day Saints in American Religion*, Oxford: Oxford University Press, 1991, p. 171.
5 Marvin S. Hill, *The Quest for Refuge: The Mormon Flight from American Pluralism*, Salt Lake City: Signature Books, 1989.
6 Thoden van Velzen and van Beek, 'Purity', p. 22.
7 The LDS Church has 11 million members.
8 With Jan Shipps I consider the LDS Church as a new Christian tradition. Jan Shipps, *Mormonism: The Story of a New Religious Tradition*, Urbana, IL: University of Illinois Press, 1985.
9 Leonard J. Arrington and Davis Bitton, *The Mormon Experience: A History of the Latter-day Saints*, New York: Vintage Books, 1979; James B. Allen and

Glen M. Leonard, *The Story of the Latter-Day Saints*, 2nd edn, Salt Lake City: Deseret Book, 1992; Rex E. Cooper, *Promises Made to the Fathers: Mormon Covenant Organization*, Salt Lake City: University of Utah Press, 1990; Robert Gottlieb and Peter Wiley, *America's Saints: The Rise of Mormon Power*, New York: Putnam & Sons, 1984; Shipps, *Mormonism*.

10 Recently the LDS Church has become more insistent on its proper name: the Church of Jesus Christ of Latter-Day Saints. I shall still use the 'LDS Church' as a shorthand, and use 'Mormonism' to denote the religious movement started by Joseph Smith, from which the LDS Church plus some splinter groups, emerged. 'Mormons', then, are those inside the LDS Church as well as those of the Reorganized Church – see below – and the many splinters, including those of polygamous persuasion.

11 Richard S. van Wagoner, *Mormon Polygamy: A History*, Salt Lake City: Signature Books, 1986, p. 1.

12 M. Leone, *Roots of Modern Mormonism*, Cambridge, MA: Harvard University Press, 1979, p. 1.

13 The main source on the United Order is Leonard J. Arrington, Feramorz Fox and Dean L. May, *Building the City of God: Community and Cooperation among the Mormons*, Salt Lake City: Deseret Book, 1976.

14 *Doctrine and Covenants* (*D&C*) 108. *Doctrine and Covenants* is the compilation of revelations to Joseph Smith and some successors, that make up one of the four *Standard Works* (= Scripture) of the LDS Church.

15 *D&C* 119.

16 'Increase', a typically agricultural term, later came to be interpreted as 'income'.

17 In fact Nauvoo came closer to the Puritan ideal of a 'City on the Hill' than most Puritan settlements. See Cooper, *Promises Made to the Fathers*.

18 The only one in the United States Army, at that time.

19 Technically, polygyny, as one husband could marry more wives, not the reverse.

20 *D&C* 132.

21 Joseph Smith claimed that he had received the revelation long before committing it to writing and surely long before the majority of the Mormons knew about it.

22 Irwin Altman and Joseph Ginat, *Polygamous Families in Contemporary Society*, Cambridge: Cambridge University Press, 1996, p. 27.

23 Van Wagoner, *Mormon Polygamy*, p. 56.

24 Altman and Ginat, *Polygamous Families*, p. 28.

25 Ibid.

26 Joseph Smith had been tried several times before and had always been released. Arrington and Bitton, *Mormon Experience*, p. 165.

27 Leone, *Roots of Modern Mormonism*, p. 16.

28 The area was of course Indian territory, but sparsely inhabited. Mexico nominally owned the territory when the Saints arrived, only to become part of the USA after the Mexican war of 1849. The State of Deseret comprised all present-day Utah and Nevada, small sections of Oregon, Idaho, Wyoming, Colorado and New Mexico, major portions of Arizona, and even a small part of California. This claim was not accepted by the federal government which

created the Utah Territory (still considerably larger than the Utah of today). But the former 'Deseret' is still 'Mormon Country' or the 'Mormon Corridor'.

29 Leone, *Roots of Modern Mormonism*, p. 58.

30 A.D. Shupe and J. Heinerman, *Wealth and Power in American Zion*, New York: Mellon, 1992; D. Michael Quinn, *The Mormon Hierarchy: Origins of Power*, Salt Lake City: Signature Books, 1994.

31 Arrington, Fox and May, *Building the City of God*.

32 See note 8.

33 This proviso is not made for the Book of Mormon, also a – claimed – translation.

34 Jan A. Montsma, *De Exterritoriale Openbaring: The openbaringsopvatting achter de fundamentalistische schriftbeschouwing*, Amsterdam: Vrije Universiteit, 1985.

35 Robert J. Matthews, *'A Plainer Translation': Joseph Smith's Translation of the Bible: A History and Commentary*, Provo, UT: Brigham Young University Press, 1985.

36 *D&C* 68:4.

37 Barlow, *Mormons and the Bible*, pp. 92, 93.

38 'Official Declaration 2', in *D&C*, abolishing colour discrimination from the LDS Church.

39 Montsma, *De Exterritoriale Openbaring*, p. 58.

40 In the *Pearl of Great Price*, the last of the four *Standard Works*.

41 The Book of Genesis, ch. 24.

42 Douglas Davies, *The Mormon Culture of Salvation: Force, Grace and Glory*, Aldershot: Ashgate, 2000.

43 The internationalization of the LDS Church in the last decennia has made such a discourse increasingly awkward.

44 Evidently, this was one of the points of conflict with the other Missourians.

45 It no longer does. The injunction to migrate has been lifted in the twentieth century, especially after World War II. The notion of gathering has changed into gathering in the 'stakes of Zion', i.e. in all countries where the LDS Church is organized. In practice this means staying at home.

46 Brigham Young University has a branch on the Mount of Olives in Jerusalem.

47 It is now in downtown Kansas City.

48 A. Mauss, *The Angel and the Beehive: The Mormon Struggle with Assimilation*, Urbana, IL: University of Illinois Press, 1994.

49 Leone, *Roots of Modern Mormonism*, p. 102.

50 Recently, the LDS Church issued a 'Proclamation on the Family', as an official statement of the Church presidency, stressing again the sanctity of marriage and the family. This proclamation is couched in terms which render it almost on a par with a revelation. But the content was not new at all, so it remains a proclamation.

51 This description of the ups and downs of Utah polygamy is based upon Embry, *Mormon Polygamous Families: Life in the Principle*, Salt Lake City: University of Utah Press, 1987; Richard N. Ostling and Joan K. Ostling, *Mormon America: The Power and the Promise*, San Francisco: HarperCollins, 2000; Paul E. Reiman, *Plural Marriage Limited*, Salt Lake City: Bookcraft, 1974; van Wagoner, *Mormon Polygamy*.

52 Arrington and Bitton, *Mormon Experience*, p. 166.
53 Gary L. Bunker and David Bitton, *The Mormon Graphic Image, 1834–1914*, Salt Lake City: University of Utah Press, 1983.
54 Arrington and Bitton, *Mormon Experience*.
55 Van Wagoner, *Mormon Polygamy*.
56 Walter E.A. van Beek, 'Chiliasme als Identiteit: De Heiligen en hun aller Laatste Dagen', in L.G. Jansma and D. Hak (eds.) *Maar Nog is het Einde Niet: Chiliastische stromingen en bewegingen bij het aanbreken van een millennium*, Amsterdam: Amsterdam University Press, pp. 117–38; D. Erickson, *'As a Thief in the Night': The Mormon Quest for Millennial Deliverance*, Salt Lake City: Signature Books, 1998; G. Underwood, *The Millenarian World of Early Mormonism*, Urbana: University of Illinois Press, 1993.
57 There is some discussion about the intensity of the expectations, yet a number of various arguments of the Saints pointed at 1890–1. Yet, it should be borne in mind that the LDS Church never indulged in date setting for the *Parousia*. Underwood, *Millenarian World*.
58 Arrington and Bitton, *Mormon Experience*, p. 182.
59 Altman and Ginat, *Polygamous Families*, p. 37.
60 Van Wagoner, *Mormon Polygamy*, p. 168.
61 Studies on Mormonism as a corporate endeavour abound: Allen and Leonard, *Story of the Latter-Day Saints*; Gottlieb and Wiley, *America's Saints*; Ostling and Ostling, *Mormon America*; Quinn, *Mormon Hierarchy: Origins*; D. Michael Quinn, *The Mormon Hierarchy: Extensions of Power*, Salt Lake City: Signature Books, 1997.
62 Mauss, *Angel and Beehive*, pp. 160 ff.
63 Ibid., pp. 171 ff; Barlow, *Mormons and the Bible*, p. 91.
64 Mauss, *Angel and Beehive*, p. 4.
65 Such as B.H. Roberts, *The Truth, the Way, the Life: An Elementary Treatise on Theology*, 1928, J. Welch (ed.) Salt Lake City: Brigham Young University Studies, 1994.
66 T. O'Dea, *The Mormons*, Chicago: University of Chicago Press, 1957.
67 Walter E.A. van Beek, 'Ethnisation and accommodation: The Dutch Mormons in the twenty-first century', *Dialogue*, vol. 29, 1996, pp. 119–38.
68 Mauss, *Angel and Beehive*, p. 191.
69 Van Beek, 'Ethnisation and accommodation'.
70 The massive bibliography of James B. Allan, Ronald W. Walker and David J. Whittaker, *Studies in Mormon History, 1830–1997: An Indexed Bibliography*, Urbana, IL: University of Illinois Press, 2000, offers seven large and densely printed pages of references to schisms.
71 The RLDS in 2001 has opted for a new name in which the 'Mormon connection' is done away with: 'Community of Christ'. For the sake of clarity I shall still use RLDS in this chapter.
72 The description of the fundamentalist position is based upon Altman and Ginat, *Polygamous Families*; J. Max Anderson, *The Polygamy Story: Fiction and Fact*, Salt Lake City: Bookcraft, 1977; J. Max Anderson, 'Fundamentalists', in *Encyclopedia of Mormonism*, vol. 2, New York: Macmillan, pp. 531–2; Hans Baer, *Recreating Utopia in the Desert: A Sectarian Challenge to Modern Mormonism*, Albany, NY: State University of New York Press,

1988; Martin E. Marty and R. Scott Appleby (eds) *Fundamentalisms and Society: Reclaiming the Sciences, the Family, and Education*, Chicago: University of Chicago Press, 1993; D. Michael Quinn, 'Plural marriage and Mormon fundamentalism', *Dialogue*, vol. 31, 1998, pp. 1–68; Embry, *Mormon Polygamous Families*.

73 In Mormon parlance, the 'keys'.

74 Altman and Ginat, *Polygamous Families*, p. 44.

75 Quinn, 'Plural marriage', p. 14.

76 Baer, *Recreating Utopia*, p. 35.

77 Like the 'Apostolic United Brethren', the 'Latter-Day Church of Christ', the 'Church of the Firstborn', 'Church of Jesus Christ of Solemn Assembly', 'Church of the Firstborn of the Fullness of Times', 'Church of Christ, patriarchal'.

78 Because of the illegal situation and the emotion associated with polygamy in Utah, they are not easy to count.

79 Altman and Ginat, *Polygamous Families*, p. 1.

80 Quinn, 'Plural marriage', p. 10.

81 Sometimes the LDS Church tries to find out on its own, with teams spying on people gathered at fundamentalist homes, or trying to infiltrate fundamentalist circles. Ibid, p. 27.

82 Altman and Ginat, *Polygamous Families*, p. 59.

83 The highly publicized *Green* case, prosecuted and sentenced in 2001, seems to be atypical. Green divorced his five wives after marrying them, though still cohabiting with them and their twenty-nine children. Both his claims on social welfare and his tendency to aggressively seek publicity (also on the Internet), proved to be a bridge too far for the Utah law. Of course, the LDS Church does not recognize Green as a member, even if Green claims to be so.

84 Shipps, cited in Quinn, 'Plural marriage', p. 9.

85 The same held for Brigham Young, who performed close to 2,000 divorces during his presidency.

86 Embry, *Mormon Polygamous Families*, p. 46.

87 Quinn, 'Plural marriage', p. 29.

88 Baer, *Recreating Utopia*.

89 *D&C* 85:7: 'It shall come to pass that I, the Lord God, will send one mighty and strong to set order in the house of God.' This text is crucial for most fundamentalists.

90 Baer, *Recreating Utopia*.

91 Cooper, *Promises Made*; P. Staples, 'Patterns of Purification: The New England Puritans', in Van Beek, *Quest for Purity*, pp. 63–90.

92 Apostle James E. Talmage was instrumental in that, among others, during the early twentieth century.

93 Such as the racial issue. See *D&C* 137.

94 L. Foster, 'Sexuality and relationships in Shaker, Oneida, and Mormon communities', *Communities: A Journal of Cooperative Living*, vol. 82, 1994, pp. 53–6.

95 Marie Cornwall, Tim B. Heaton and Lawrence A. Young, *Contemporary Mormonism: Social Science Perspectives*, Urbana, IL: University of Illinois Press, 1994.

96 Mauss, *Angel and Beehive*.

Select bibliography

Allen, James B. and Leonard, Glen M., *The Story of the Latter-Day Saints*, 2nd edn, Salt Lake City: Deseret Book, 1992.

Altman, Irwin and Ginat, Joseph, *Polygamous Families in Contemporary Society*, Cambridge: Cambridge University Press, 1996.

Davies, Douglas, *The Mormon Culture of Salvation: Force, Grace and Glory*, Aldershot: Ashgate, 2000.

Embry, Jesse, *Mormon Polygamous Families: Life in the Principle*, Salt Lake City: University of Utah Press, 1987.

Mauss, Armand, *The Angel and the Beehive: The Mormon Struggle with Assimilation*, Urbana, IL: University of Illinois Press, 1994.

Shipps, Jan, *Mormonism: The Story of a New Religious Tradition*, Urbana, IL: University of Illinois Press, 1985.

7

THE MONK'S NEW ROBES
Buddhist fundamentalism and social change

H.L. Seneviratne

This chapter explores certain aspects of the rise of Buddhist fundament-alism in Sri Lanka by focusing in particular on the definition of a new role for the Buddhist monk.[1] The new type of Buddhist monk who emerged as a result of this new definition of the monastic role became a major carrier and role player in the ideology and activist project of Buddhist fundament-alism as defined below. Developments in Sri Lanka arising from this project provide us with one of the most telling exemplifications of the negative consequences of fundamentalism. These developments are the tragic culmination of cultural processes going back to the mid-nineteenth century when the island was grappling with the social changes arising from exposure to the Western world.

Fundamentalism: a definition

In conventional usage, the term 'fundamentalism' is derived from the historical and theological study of Christianity, and refers to the adherence to orthodox beliefs, such as the inerrancy of Scripture and the literal acceptance of the creeds as fundamentals of Protestant Christianity. In contrast to this sense, in which the term refers to specifically Christian phe-nomena, the term has recently come to designate *any* religious extremism involving intolerance of other beliefs, and a related attempt to claim for a specific group exclusivity and hegemony in a given polity. The origin of this usage goes back no further than the aftermath of the Arab–Israeli war of 1967. This period witnessed a resurgence of militant Islam which found its most vivid expression in the Iranian revolution. Both academic and journalistic writings on this event and resurgent Islam in general gave increasingly wider currency to the term, and gradually and imperceptibly, it came to be used as a label to describe broadly comparable phenomena associated with other religions, thus generalizing to the latter a usage once reserved for militant Islam. An important development in this generalization is the introduction of other variables, like ethnicity, territory and language, to the element of religion, making 'fundamentalism' almost synonymous with terms like 'cultural nationalism', 'ethno-nationalism' and 'religio-ethnic nationalism'.

Thus, religious fundamentalism in this new sense is a general and largely modern phenomenon easily fading into ethnic, linguistic, regional and other parochial expressions of group identity. It is important to keep in mind that in this new sense, the term carries the ideological position that what it believes in, and militantly strives for, is in fact no more than the restoration of the utopia allegedly embodied in the original message of the specific religion in question. It is in this new sense that contemporary Sri Lankan Buddhism can be said to exhibit traits of 'fundamentalism': it seeks to establish a Buddhist utopia of the majority Sinhala ethnic group, imagined to go back to the early era of Buddhism, but in fact only as old as the early twentieth century, with some antecedents going back a few decades, to the late nineteenth century. It is fair to say, however, that while in the 1970s legislative and executive measures were taken towards the establishment of that utopia in the form of a hegemonic social and political system of the Sinhala Buddhist majority, that attempt has had only limited success, and there are increasing national and international pressures for the politically dominant majority to return to policies that are more tolerant and accommodative of the minorities. This prospect makes the case of Sri Lanka less of a 'fundamentalism' in the sense in which the term is now popularly used.

Buddhism and fundamentalism

Among the great religions, Buddhism with its fundamentals of non-violence, compassion, avoidance of extremes, replacement of ritual with ethics, denial of any soteriologically meaningful external mystical agency, and the enthronement of human effort as the only path to liberation, is arguably the most tolerant and pacifist, and it would therefore be a very good thing if indeed there were truly a Buddhist fundamentalism (in the sense of a return to these Buddhist fundamentals). Unfortunately, we have no such thing.

If Buddhism is defined purely in terms of its analysis of the problem of existence and its recipe for liberation, there is little room in it for a fundamentalism in the popular sense in which the term is used today. But on the other hand, if we define Buddhism as what Buddhists do in the name of Buddhism, it is possible to say confidently that one striking development in early twentieth-century Sri Lanka was the articulation of a fundamentalism in the form of a call for return to a Buddhist utopia. In that movement, Buddhism is exclusively identified with the Sinhala ethnicity, and the resulting Sinhala Buddhist community is accorded hegemonic status in the Sri Lankan polity.

Buddhist fundamentalism in Sri Lanka in this sense can be further elucidated in comparison with developments in Burma (Myanmar) and Thailand, which along with Sri Lanka represent the *Theravada* or the orthodox of the two major schools of Buddhism (the other, later school being *Mahayana*). Among these three cultures, Burma and Sri Lanka belong in one category while Thailand in the other. This distinction is sociologically significant because the most obvious difference between Burma and Sri Lanka, on the one hand, and Thailand, on the other, is that Burma and Sri Lanka were colonized by European powers and Thailand was not. Thailand is the most stable of these three societies, and exhibits fundamentalist attributes the least, enabling us to connect Buddhist fundamentalism with the colonial experience and the associated social change.

The continuity of Thailand as a nation spared colonial rule enabled it to maintain intact its institutions while accepting Western influences voluntarily. Thus Thailand continues to have a stable and complex monastic organization that parallels the secular social order headed by the king. Through monastic networks, gifted and dynamic young monks can gain mobility, ultimately gaining an education at one of the monastic universities in the capital Bangkok.[2] Qualified monks have avenues for obtaining salaried employment in the monastic bureaucracy which is a major department of the government. Government-sponsored programmes of social work enable young monks to gain intellectually and morally satisfying experiences working as missionaries and development workers. The continuity of the monarchy and state patronage of the religion contribute to a degree of effective control over monastic discipline. Further, loyalty to the monarchy acts as a unifying factor so that the non-Buddhist minorities are not deprived of a sense of national belonging. The fact that Thailand is about 95 per cent Buddhist also helps. These factors add up to a picture of sharp contrast with Sri Lanka, where colonialism took away the monk's pride, and energetic and gifted monks were and are denied avenues of intellectually, emotionally and socially satisfying self-expression. It is partly due to this reason that such monks are lured to seek self-expression in the deviant area of 'fundamentalism'.

Buddhism in Burma is in many ways comparable to that of Sri Lanka.[3] While, broadly speaking, Burmese Buddhism goes back to about 200 BCE, the establishment of *Theravada* over other forms of Buddhism dates back only to the reign of King Anuruddha (Anawrahta) (1044–77). As in Sri Lanka, Burmese ethnicity was identified with Buddhism, but since Burma was ethnically more homogeneous than Sri Lanka, this led to no disastrous ethnic polarization. Targets of Buddhist activism in the colonial era were the British overlords, and their Indian accomplices who staffed the Burmese British administration, both non-Buddhist.

In early twentieth-century Burma a revivalist movement was launched, largely based on the Sri Lankan revival inspired by Anagarika Dharmapala and the American Buddhist Colonel Henry Steel Olcott, the founder of Sri Lankan Buddhist revivalism. As in Sri Lanka, Buddhist clergy, known as the *Sangha*, came to play an important political role, first as anti-colonialists, and later as a pressure group for a share of political and social power, a move opposed by the devout sections of the laity. There was in the post-independence period an attempt by some sections of both lay and monastic actors to blend Buddhism with Marxism, described as the higher and the lower truths respectively, and leading men to spiritual and material liberation respectively. The primary trend in the post-independence era was, however, to bring the monks increasingly under a systematic ecclesiastical organization, backed ultimately by the power of the state. This, however, failed, due to opposition from the monks. Thus in all the three major *Theravada* traditions, Sri Lanka, Burma and Thailand, there has been an attempt to systematize and regulate the *Sangha*, but this has been successful only in Thailand. Arguably, the most important reason for this is the continuity of the monarchy in Thailand as opposed to its abolition in Burma and Sri Lanka.

Given Burma's colonial experience and the militancy of the monks during British rule as well as during the early post-colonial era, its potential for a Buddhist hegemony was real and powerful. However, with the rise, about three decades ago, of a military dictatorship in Burma, this potential has been largely curbed, and monks are in no position to play any meaningful political role. Stated differently, as a dictatorship, Burma is able to bring its community of monks under state control in functionally the same way as Thailand as a monarchy does, although clearly for different reasons. Sri Lanka as a democracy is unable to do so. Indeed, it is widely held that in Sri Lanka the picture is reversed, and that it is the *Sangha* that controls the state. This is only appearance. The reality is more complex. There is certainly a relation between the *Sangha* and politics in Sri Lanka, and one of my concerns in this chapter is to suggest that the specific *Sangha*/politics relation as we find it today is a recent development. The relation, widely held to have existed historically between the *Sangha* and state, belongs to a quite different order of phenomena.

Within a few centuries of the founding of Buddhism, and especially in its migrations and establishment in lands outside India, Buddhism and the state entered into a complex of mutual relations, and the *Sangha* evolved into a class of influential social actors in their particular societies. In the case of Sri Lanka, times of foreign threat occasioned the espousal of a proto-nationalism by the *Sangha*, but this was ephemeral and superficial for a society which contained a deeper and more pervasive impulse for integrating incoming groups and accommodating ethnic and linguistic diversity. The role of the monk was religious and cultural, and any activist politico-nationalist role he played was not institutional but random and contingent. Thus, we must relate the much talked about activist political role of the Sri Lankan Buddhist clergy to recent developments. It is to this task and the consequences of that relation that I now turn.

A new role for the monk: a reformer's dream

It is now widely held by the Buddhist monks of Sri Lanka that their role is 'social service'. They further hold that this was their function always, going back to the beginnings of Buddhism in Sri Lanka. This view is also now tacitly accepted by the laity in Sri Lanka, especially the more literate classes, and indeed espoused by nationalist intellectuals as well, who have sometimes engaged in fierce debate over the issue. A correlate of this understanding of the role of the monk is the *power* of the monk, most commonly understood as the political power to make and unmake governments. On sober reflection we have no grounds to believe that the monk enjoyed that kind of power historically. And field experience tells us that they do not wield any such power today. We should then ask the question, how then did this belief in monastic power and invincibility come about?

I contend that the widely held conception of the central role of the monk in traditional Sinhala society is a myth that was invented by Anagarika Dharmapala, the most influential figure in the Buddhist revival of Sri Lanka. This myth was fostered by later advocates, both monk and lay. Monks did play a significant role in pre-colonial society, but as just observed, that role was nothing like the one that Dharmapala invented. The model for this newly invented role was the Christian priest with his access to positions of power in colonial Sri Lanka, and a specifically Christian conception of the pastoral role.

Dharmapala (1864–1933) was the son of a furniture maker who, through dedication and hard work, acquired considerable wealth. He was sent to Christian schools where he felt a great sense of humiliation at the hands of teachers who were Christian priests, presumably due to their denigration of Buddhism as a primitive and idolatrous religion. It would seem appropriate then, that he would grow up to show the world that Buddhism had all the nobility and modernity a religion could offer, and that it was in fact Christianity and other theistic religions that were deficient. The family habit of hard work was the other important factor that Dharmapala wove into his message. He changed his foreign name 'David' to 'Dharmapala', meaning 'Guardian of Dharma', which was his own definition of his destiny and mission. The first part of his name, Anagarika, meaning 'homeless', further defined his task, a semi-renunciation that was exteriorized in the garment he wore, which was a cross between the renouncer's robe and the layman's garb. He exhorted Buddhists to give up the ritualism characteristic of rural peasant Buddhism and instead cultivate morality, and to infuse themselves with methodical and relentless productive activity rather than be content with the mere subsistence characteristic of peasant life.

In numerous writings and speeches starting from about the last decade of the nineteenth century, especially as a columnist of the weekly newspaper he founded and edited, Dharmapala gradually unveils, mostly by means of his critique of the existing state, an ideal Sinhala Buddhist society that existed until the end of the Sinhala monarchy in 1815, and which now needed to be revived. It is in this ideal past society, constructed in Dharmapala's imagination and not in any Buddhist texts, that we must locate the origins of fundamentalism in the case of Sri Lankan Buddhism.

Dharmapala's image of the past society is based on the national chronicle *Mahavamsa*, although it is likely that the writings of British colonial authors, like Emerson Tennent whom he cites, gave him his first inklings into that society. The central political feature of that ideal past society was righteous and paternalistic kingship. The basis of the social order was Buddhist morality or righteousness. That morality was also magically powerful: so long as it existed, the nation prospered, and no foreign power could conquer it. At present, the absence of a king, which has resulted in the acceptance of foreign customs and mores, has caused a decline in Buddhist morality, keeping the society in subjugation to alien rule. Whatever the present depths are to which society has descended, morality can throw off the foreign yoke and restore it to its former ideal state. What is needed therefore is a return to righteousness. It does not take much: living in Buddhist morality for a mere five years would restore Sri Lanka to its former glory, but a glory that so accommodates and conforms to modernity that, except for its unique cultural stamp, it will appear no different from a prosperous, developed and modern nation. Here Dharmapala is envisaging a society that is technologically advanced, yet uncompromisingly moored within the moral and cultural frameworks of tradition.

The culprit that has caused the society's decline is the loss of purity, brought about by the incorporation of foreign political, physical and moral structures and substances, which corrupt and make unwholesome the individual body as well as the body politic. Foreign customs and mores corrupt the moral life and foreign foods, especially meat and alcohol, corrupt the physical life. The villages in particular are in a deplorable state of poverty, ignorance, lack of cleanliness and healthy habits. In addition, there is also decline caused by the superstitious ritualism of ignorant villagers. In the paradigm envisaged by Dharmapala, society is a non-political ethico-moral system where conformity derives from internal discipline and not from external coercion or threat of such coercion. In the absence of a king, no central authority emerges, and the polity seems to consist of conglomerations of innumerable village theocracies, where the monk is the most important and benevolent leader. It is the monk who has the duty and the ability to teach the villagers the true Buddhist way of life which has been now eclipsed due to foreign intrusions. The monk should instruct the villagers to abide by the precepts of Buddhism, to stay away from sinful activities, and where possible, try to cultivate meditation. With that as the non-negotiable moral base, the monk must instruct the people in good habits, such as health, manners, cleanliness, activity, diligence, prudence and punctuality. He must provide guidance in the proper scientific knowledge necessary for productive agriculture, craft and commercial activity, in short, in all ingredients of a prosperous, healthy, peaceful and happy civic life.

It is quite clear that this ideal society is a fusion of two broad components. The first is economic. The poverty and material want of the people, and their superstitions that inhibit the growth of a dynamic philosophy of life, must be alleviated. Dharmapala wants the people to abandon their laziness and develop productive habits. He is advocating what we would today call a 'work ethic'. He is envisaging a society with thriving agriculture and industries. He is talking about good health habits. In short, in our terms, he is dreaming of a developed society. This economic vision is to be realized through rational means, for example by educating young people in English and other international languages which carry modern knowledge, and training them in modern industry, crafts and modern ways of thought. Let us call this Dharmapala's 'economic agenda'.

The second component of Dharmapala's vision of an ideal society is political and cultural. It is a broad framework of ideology within which all else is encompassed. It is anti-imperialist and anti-foreign. It is to be based on an imagined indigenous culture which he considered 'Aryan'. The national ethos of the Sinhala people and of Buddhism will be supreme in the island, and Dharmapala is silent on the fate of the other cultures and ethnic groups. We can call this part of Dharmapala's vision his 'political agenda'.

Dharmapala conceived of his task of regenerating Sri Lanka as a war which needed an army of capable and dedicated leaders and foot soldiers. Many of his writings and speeches were in effect clarion calls for enlistment. These calls found enthusiastic response from some of the younger monks, particularly those enrolled at the two Buddhist monastic colleges, Vidyodaya and Vidyalankara. These two colleges were identical in their curricula and organization and were descendants of the same scholastic tradition. But in their political outlook they turned out to be drastically different from each other. Vidyodaya was conservative, and adopted the realistic and pragmatic attitude of accepting the British government as the properly constituted authority. Vidyalankara, on the other hand, was rebellious and took a radical and anti-imperialist stand. Though apparently contradictory, both perspectives, the conservatism of Vidyodaya and the radicalism of Vidyalankara, were derived from Dharmapala. To put it differently, the Vidyodaya monks took over the economic agenda of Dharmapala, and his more pragmatic and accommodating side. And the Vidyalankara monks took over his ideological, cultural and political agenda, and his hegemonic, exclusivist and dark side. So, Dharmapala's army consisted of two battalions of monks representing the duality of his agenda and the two sides of his personality. Let us call the sober, accommodating, Vidyodaya monks 'pragmatic monks' and the exclusivist, hegemonic monks of Vidyalankara 'ideological monks'.

Dharmapala's economic programme of rural regeneration meant a self-sufficient economy modelled on the imagined economy of traditional Sri Lanka whose backbone was agriculture. Industries and rural crafts constituted the rest of the economy. The main organizing mechanism of all activity is a rural association, to be founded in every village, called a Village Protection Society.

What Dharmapala envisages here is an idyllic moral community that is close to the idea of 'village communities' that fascinated Western writers like Henry Maine and B.H. Baden-Powell, and Indian reformers such as Gandhi and his disciple Jay Prakash Narayan. The only difference is the Buddhist moral basis of this society, symbolized by the pre-eminent position accorded to the monk who, along with the headman, holds power: it is a self-sufficient, self-governing, democratic community that is also responsible for educating its young in academic knowledge and the crafts.

Rural development: monks and social regeneration

In the 1930s and the 1940s, the monks of the Vidyodaya monastic college tried to put this idea of regeneration into action. This project was known as *Gramasamvardhana* or Rural Development. Two features are notable in the idea of rural development as put into action by these monks. First, it was non-ideological in that it did not blame colonial rule for the state of the peasant. Second, it was understood as an activity of the economic sphere that was independent of the political. Rural development in this sense was free of involvement in deliberately constructed issues of religion, language, culture and ethnicity, which constitute the second part of Dharmapala's agenda. Three monks from Vidyodaya stand out as the most illustrious activists of this movement: Kalukondayave Pannasekhara, Hinatiyana Dhammaloka and Hendiyagala Silaratana. It is as if these pioneers consciously separated the pragmatic and the ideological that were united in Dharmapala's thinking, and discarded the ideological and held on to the pragmatic.

The greatest achievement of these monks is their articulation in clear and effective form of a doctrine of religio-economic action that reminds us of Max Weber's 'inner-worldly asceticism'. This doctrine lay dormant in Dharmapala's theory of a Sinhala Buddhist utopia. In his theory of the regenerated Sinhala Buddhist society, Dharmapala had envisaged a hard-working peasantry, but it also envisioned a rigorous moral code which prohibited any form of mundane enjoyment. The people of Dharmapala's utopia were constrained to spend all their leisure in religious activity and meditation. According to Dharmapala, this exercise of honest and hard work together with an abnegating lifestyle would ensure happy rebirths and eventually *Nirvana*. The pragmatic monks of Vidyodaya elaborated this doctrine with great skill and made it the theme of the 'sermons' they delivered as they traversed the length and breadth of the country in the cause of rural development.

In taking upon themselves the economic part of the Dharmapalite agenda, these monks also articulated another idea dormant in the theory of Dharmapala, namely that the duty and role of the monk are to repay the laity's material support of the monks, not with religious instruction and ritual services alone, indeed not even primarily as traditionally understood, but with substantial positive activity towards the improvement of life in this world, especially of those in need. This refers to a broad spectrum of activity that helps the alleviation of poverty, the promotion of health, better housing, adequate nutrition, conflict resolution, crime eradication and temperance. While some of this was part of the monk's traditional moral instruction to the laity, the difference lay in the fact that these were advocated as functional for a better *this* world as opposed to being generative of merit for the *next* world. These monks interpreted Dharmapala as advocating that monks should primarily involve themselves in the *this-worldly* welfare of the laity. This even included the gift of material goods to the laity, constituting a radical departure from the unidirectionality of the flow of material goods from layman to monk that is the hallmark of the relation between monks and laity.

While these ideas are innovative, creative and socially meaningful, there is a central weakness in the rural development project, namely its romantic and idyllic nature. It was Dharmapala's imagined village community, inspired by European conceptualizations, that in the first place gave rise to the project. Dharmapala himself was well read in English, had travelled widely in India, Europe, America and Japan, and had gained first-hand experience of industrial and technological society and capitalist enterprise, an experience for which he also had preparation in his growing up in an enterprising family, in a dynamic colonial commercial city and in the Protestant missionary school. His followers, of whom the economic monks of Vidyodaya were the best exemplars, had none of this. While their early education was in Christian schools, this was elementary, and their broader education was confined to the doctrinal texts and Sinhala and Pali literature, which gave them no exposure to any kind of knowledge dealing with social and economic institutions. Their imagination could grasp only the idyllic and romantic village-based part of the Dharmapalite vision, which even under the best of conditions had no scope for accommodating a process of vibrant and self-generating economic development. Their vision bore a family resemblance to the village-based, anti-industrial, anti-capitalist system articulated by Gandhi and his disciples like Jay Prakash Narayan and Vinobha Bhave. Their rural communities were vulnerable to numerous forces that could and did nullify them within about two decades, ranging from state control to incentive-based alternatives, and from the appeal of ideology to the very cultural conditions that the project was supposed to combat in the first place. They simply had neither the vision nor the qualifications to launch the needed activist project.

But these monks had their hearts in the right place. Because they were convinced of the truth and feasibility of Dharmapala's message, they tried to do what he told them to do, to the best of their ability. They represented a pragmatic nationalism as opposed to a nationalist ideology with built-in propensities for degeneration into chauvinism and zealotry. Their education and socialization were traditional, as was their monkhood. They did not explicitly talk about their monkhood or have to define or defend it, because their lifestyle conformed to accepted rules of monkhood, and they had no personal or ideological reason to change that lifestyle. They were patriots without being narrow nationalists, and were able to conceptualize in principle a social order in which the economic was primary and triumphant over the ideological. They made accommodations to the colonial government which they knew fully well was alien and imperial, but which they chose to interpret as representing the familiar notion of kingship to which obedience was due. In this, too, they represented a pragmatism and a benevolent aspect of tradition.

These monks also accepted ethnic and cultural diversity as a fact of Sri Lankan life. They represented a conservative as opposed to a radical socialism, and a specific path of ethnic harmony and national development which, had it not been undermined by the ideology brewing at Vidyalankara, had a fair chance of guiding the different ethnic groups that comprise Sri Lanka towards harmonious nationhood. In this sense they represented continuity with the dominant current of history, which was inclusivist and accommodative, as opposed to the alternative current of exclusion and hegemony, which could and did exist only ideologically, given the non-centralized nature of the pre-modern polity. With the advent of British rule and *de facto* centralization, the path was cleared for the dormant exclusivist current to awaken with force and encompass the social order. The monks at Vidyalankara were in the forefront of this ideology-driven hegemonic project. Let us now take a brief look at their activities.

Monks and nationalist politics: invention of a heritage

Ideology and political activity have been brewing at Vidyalankara since at least the 1940s, but it was not until the 1950s that these monks launched themselves as a political power, contributing substantially to, if not enabling altogether, the election of a nationalist government in 1956, widely considered a watershed in the recent history of Sri Lanka.

The sequence of events that led to the rise of the ideological monks at Vidyalankara is as follows. In 1946, the year before the inauguration of a new constitution and the introduction of a full-fledged parliamentary system to the island, the Western-oriented and conservative ruling party was very anxious at the rising popularity of the Marxist parties. They were also aware that some Vidyalankara monks had connections with these parties and were speakers at their propaganda rallies. The ruling elite determined that it would be dangerous for them to let this alliance between the monks and the Marxists thrive, and launched a campaign to discredit the monks. In one of their campaign rallies, the conservative leader D.S. Senanayake stated that monks should not engage in political activity. This led to the scholar monk Walpola Rahula, a stalwart of Vidyalankara, refuting this theory first in public meetings, and later in a polemical treatise first published in Sinhala in 1946.[4] In this work Rahula attempted to show that monks had always participated in politics, and in fact were the kingmakers of ancient times. Contending that 'it is nothing but proper' that monks engage in politics, Rahula argues that the idea that the monk should be a cloistered ascetic and ritual specialist is an invention of the imperialists and Christian missionaries to keep the monks, who were the educated and most able section of society, apart from the people. The work argues for a politically activist role for the monk and defines the monk's role as 'social service'. The effect of this work, however, was paradoxical. It enthroned ideology and put an end to the real 'social service' that was being attempted by the pragmatic monks of Vidyodaya.

In the 1940s, the Vidyalankara monks actively organized themselves. Using their networks, they built a nationwide organization of monks for political purposes. As the general election of 1956 approached they intensified their propaganda and campaign activities. They were helped by a section of the Sinhala Buddhist elite, especially the nationalist All Ceylon Buddhist Congress, which appointed a commission to look into the state of Buddhism. This Commission, known as the Buddhist Commission, in its report, argued that Buddhism had been 'betrayed' by the British colonial government. It proposed rectification of this condition by, in effect, establishing Sinhala Buddhist hegemony over the island. The government elected in 1956 inaugurated such a programme. It made Sinhala the only official language of the country, and created a department of cultural affairs which gave official status to Buddhism. These policies were carried further when the new constitution of 1972 gave Buddhism a 'special place', and the Constitution of 1977 created a Ministry of Buddhism. English was dethroned not only as the official language, but also as the medium of instruction in schools. These developments clearly represent the fruition of Dharmapala's ideological agenda.

These monks continued to talk about socialism, but this has to be distinguished from what we generally understand by the term socialism. Theirs was rather a 'Buddhist Socialism'. Increasingly it became more 'Buddhist' than socialist, which by the mid-1950s turned into a hegemonic Sinhala Buddhist chauvinism. When these monks realized that the Marxist parties wanted no part of Sinhala Buddhist hegemony or the ideology of culture, they quickly abandoned the Marxists and joined hands with the extremist elements.

The writings of the Vidyalankara monks refer constantly to 'country, nation and religion'. This is a usage derived from Dharmapala. What they have in mind are Sri Lanka as a territorial unit, the Sinhala ethnic group, and Buddhism. The union of the three terms in this usage makes the territory of Sri Lanka the exclusive property of the Sinhala Buddhists. According to the worldview of these monks and their secular counterparts, Sri Lanka is a Sinhala Buddhist political entity. It is striking that no spokesman of this group has ever spoken clearly and specifically about the fate of the minorities in that political entity. Alternatively, it has been vaguely suggested by some in this group that the minorities would be part of this socio-political entity in so far as they merge their own cultural identity with that of the majority Sinhala Buddhists. Stated differently, the worldview expressed in the phrase 'country, nation and religion' envisages a hegemonic Sinhala Buddhist culture empowered to place its stamp on other cultures in order to bring about a homogeneous utopia.

The victory of the nationalist forces in 1956 is the most important single factor that empowered the monk, and gave credence to the mythical conception of monastic supremacy invented by Dharmapala, and disseminated by Rahula, in particular in his theory of the monk's ancient role as kingmaker. This empowerment was, however, an illusion, real power being concentrated in the hands of the governing lay elite. But the monks did get some rewards. In addition to exaggerated ceremonial recognition, which delighted them, they received booty in the form of grants for monastic schools and other cultural and religious projects. Most importantly they were rewarded with the granting of university status to the two monastic colleges: Vidyodaya and Vidyalankara.

These universities produced an important result: a substantial body of young monks educated in secular subjects who were employable on a salary basis or who could otherwise seek financially profitable activity. This has led to a further step in the evolution of the modern monk. This monk thinks of his salaried work or whatever other profitable work he does as 'social service', and his sense of 'self-respect' does not allow him to accept lay generosity. Correspondingly, he does not feel obliged to perform any religious or ritual service to the laity, although he might fulfil some such function on a selective basis. Because of his full-time occupation, he does not have the time to work for the laity anyway, even if he so desires. These changes have generated the new doctrine that the monk–lay relation is not a hierarchical exchange of economic goods for spiritual services, but an egalitarian exchange of goods, services and social favours. The effect of this is a secularization of the monkhood not seen since the decline in conformity to the Code of Monastic Discipline that led to the importation of ordination from Thailand in the eighteenth century. These monks hold the view that a monk can practise almost any art or craft, science or profession.

Today, there are monks who teach for a salary. Some are controlling directors of well-funded pre-schools. Some are investors. Some own car-repair shops. One is an importer of motor bicycles. Some are active in politics. Some practise astrology and occult sciences. One is the president of the Nurses Union. One is a songwriter with a good-sized fan club, and another writes stirring battle songs for the soldiers in the ethnic war. Some are novelists. One is a prolific painter and another a sculptor. Some have established meditation centres, but with the tourists in mind. One was recently elected President of the local Rotary Club.

It is not the task of the sociologist to say that any of these is wrong. But it certainly is the task of the sociologist to relate this development to social factors, and to point out that they arise from the definition of a new role for the monk envisaged in the writings and ideology of Anagarika Dharmapala and his followers. It is also the task of the sociologist to point out the striking displacement of goals that has taken place. The utopia and moral order envisaged in Dharmapala's empowerment of the monk has led to economic stagnation, assaults on the autonomy of the public service and the judiciary, denial of a free press, erosion of professionalism and professional ethics, dismantling of democratic institutions, and the violent call for a separate state.

Conclusion

From the point of view of Buddhist fundamentalism, the most important development arising from the Dharmapalite empowerment of the monk is the coming into being of the political or the ideological monk. This monk is the manifestation in flesh and blood of the ideological component of Dharmapala's project, which envisages a Sri Lanka which is Sinhala and Buddhist, in which the minorities are either entirely absent, or subservient to the hegemony of the Sinhala Buddhists.

This ideology was by no means embraced only by the monks. It was also immensely appealing to the indigenous elites who, either out of choice or for want of opportunities, remained alienated from the modernity and dynamism of the then British colony. It was the union of these two indigenous elites, monastic and lay, that led to the electoral victory of the nationalist forces in 1956. In the ensuing decades the Sinhala Buddhist hegemonist project was put into effect, but at great human and national cost, in particular at the cost of derailing altogether the arduous task of post-colonial nation-building. The main accomplishments of this hegemonic project are the effective establishment of Sinhala as the official language, the enthronement of Buddhism effectively as the state religion, and a politicization of the administrative machinery that has compromised the principle of equal opportunity for the minorities.

Among the developments in contemporary Buddhism that recent studies have identified are revivalism, the spread of Buddhism in the West and Buddhist modernism.[5] These inter-related processes have involved attempts to shore up Buddhism by means of new and rational methods, including the use of Western models, and confronting Christian missionaries with the help of the weapons of these missionaries themselves, such as the printing press and public debate; and cleansing Buddhism of what are considered to be external and superstitious accretions, and the corresponding attempt to restore Buddhism to its rational foundation. Such an elucidation of contemporary Buddhism is undoubtedly a perceptive one, but it ignores the most important of these developments in pragmatic and policy terms, namely the rise of fundamentalism in the sense defined at the beginning of this chapter. Stated differently, the commentary and analysis of these scholars are not broad enough to embrace the full range of the behavioural spectrum of the impact of modernity on Buddhism. It is inadequate from the point of view of considerations of peace, stability, minority rights and nation-building.

Notes

1   Some of the material I use in the second part of this chapter is derived from my book, H.L. Seneviratne, *The Work of Kings*, Chicago: Chicago University Press, 1999.

2   For a detailed account of the Thai Buddhist clergy (*Sangha*) see Stanley J. Tambiah, *World Conqueror and World Renouncer*, Cambridge: Cambridge University Press, 1976.

3   For a lucid account, see Heinz Bechert, '"To be a Burmese is to be a Buddhist": Buddhism in Burma', in Heinz Bechert and Richard Gombrich (eds) *The World of Buddhism*, London: Thames and Hudson, 1984, pp. 147–58.

4   An English translation appeared in 1974, nearly thirty years later, under the title *Heritage of the Bhikkhu*.

5   See for example, Heinz Bechert, 'Buddhist revival in East and West', in Bechert and Gombrich, *The World of Buddhism*, pp. 273–85; Tambiah, *World Conqueror and World Renouncer*, pp. 406–23; K. Malalgoda, *Buddhism in Sinhalese Society 1750–1900*, Berkeley, CA: University of California Press, 1976.

Select bibliography

Bond, George, *The Buddhist Revival in Sri Lanka*, Columbia: South Carolina University Press, 1988.

De Silva, K.M., *Managing Ethnic Tensions in Multi-Ethnic Societies: Sri Lanka 1880–1985*, Lanham, MD: University Press of America, 1986.

Gombrich, Richard and Obeyesekere, Gananath, *Buddhism Transformed*, Princeton, NJ: Princeton University Press, 1988.

Juergensmeyer, Mark, *The New Cold War? Religious Nationalism Confronts the Secular State*, Berkeley, CA: University of California Press, 1993.

Seneviratne, H.L., *The Work of Kings*, Chicago: Chicago University Press, 1999.

Spencer, Jonathan, *Sri Lanka: History and the Roots of Conflict*, London: Routledge, 1990.

Tambiah, Stanley J., *Buddhism Betrayed? Religion, Politics and Violence in Sri Lanka*, Chicago: University of Chicago Press, 1992.

Tambiah, Stanley J., *Leveling Crowds: Ethnonationalist Conflicts and Collective Violence in South Asia*, Berkeley, CA: University of California Press, 1996.

8

BEING HINDU AND/OR GOVERNING INDIA?

Religion, social change and the state

Chakravarthi Ram-Prasad

Over the past two decades, politics in India has seen an increase in the role of ideology based on appeal to features of the Hindu religious traditions. This has been read, especially in the West, as a growth in a Hindu version of religious fundamentalism, the parallel being drawn most obviously with Islam, but also to a lesser extent, with Buddhism; and ultimately, drawing on the very idea of 'fundamentalism', Protestant Christianity. The aim of this chapter is to clarify the nature of this phenomenon, by asking exactly how the role of Hindu thought in the Indian polity should be interpreted and by suggesting what the consequences of that role are.

The main conclusions that result from my analysis in this chapter are as follows:

1   Ideology based on Hindu religious thought should more accurately be understood as a form of cultural essentialism with nationalist goals. It is not helpful to see it in terms of religious fundamentalism.
2   The troubled nature of religion-derived social change in India can be traced to both the specific history of the land and the general features of a stressful modern political economy.
3   While ideological concerns about the nature of the Indian polity motivate political organizations associated with *Hindutva*, two connected factors have substantially changed and severely limited the role of religious ideology in actual governance.

  (i) Varied voting patterns and levels of support for parties constrain the scope for ideological action because of the demands of rule by coalition and alliances.

(ii) Demands of competence in a democracy (whether or not success-fully met) call for non-ideological governance in many substantive areas.

4   Strategies to secure individual and social rights primarily require the effective management of the globalizing forces of the political economy.

In terms of the general theme of this volume, what I have to say about the nature of this religious ideology is derived from a study of the social changes in India that have created the conditions for this phenomenon. At various points, issues of the individual, social, political and economic rights will also be considered, since the direct worries about the phenomenon are precisely about such rights.

Hindutva: an analysis of its claims and characteristics[1]

The central concept that we are interested in here is that of *Hindutva*. It means 'Hinduness', and has been used by proponents of a certain sort of ideology to characterize a position that, maximally, makes these three claims:

1   The Hindu religious traditions have some common essence.
2   This essential religion is the (constitutive) religion of India.
3   To be Indian is, in some sense, to be Hindu.

I say 'maximally' because not everyone associated politically with the *Hindutva* movement, and certainly not everyone who supports (let alone occasionally votes for) the democratic political parties who espouse *Hindutva*, actually holds all these tenets. Even more problematically, even those who hold these tenets give different interpretations of it. This variation is significant if we are to assess the actual societal impact and appeal of *Hindutva*, for treating it as a monolithic and doctrinal movement would severely mislead us.

In general, however, it would appear from this very general formulation of *Hindutva* that it combines religious fundamentalism with religious nationalism.

Fundamentalism, nationalism and Hindutva

Let us understand by 'fundamentalism' here the ideology that holds that every religion has a core of beliefs and values derived from some singular, authoritative text(s) and that life is truly or authentically religious only when it exemplifies those beliefs (and adheres to those values).[2] Originally, this idea of a textually given doctrinal core to a religion and a life lived only in accordance with that core, came from US Protestant Christianity.[3] While it has special features regarding the manner in which the doctrinal core is determined, other religions have had this term, interpreted in the general way above, applied to them as well. I propose to follow this widespread, general usage, always allowing for substantive variations in the fundamentalisms of different religions.

Religious nationalism here is the relatively straightforward ideology that nationhood is constituted by membership of a religion. Of course, the significance of this sort of nationalism is that it is usually to do with a nation–*state*, and therefore asks for territorial sovereignty and all the constitutional, legal, military and other institutional powers that that implies. Religious nationalism and fundamentalism are not necessarily connected. For one thing, many fundamentalists set themselves apart from the very conditions of material modernity that include the political concerns of nationality and statehood. Equally, the strictly doctrinal aspects of religion often play little part in nationalisms that invoke religion, for religion there is more vehicle for historical and cultural, and sometimes ethnic, collective identities.

My argument is that, regarding fundamentalism, *Hindutva* ideology cannot properly be understood as fundamentalist, given the nature of the Hindu religious traditions. As regards religious nationalism, *Hindutva* is indeed that, but I will argue that two considerations have to be kept in mind. First, many of the actual cases of mobilization through appeal to *Hindutva* ideology that result in violence are not really oriented to nationalism; they are about local concerns and they use fears and stereotypes that, while historical, do not turn on the idea of a Hindu nation as such. This makes *Hindutva* more than simple religious nationalism. Second, there is a contradiction between using *Hindutva* to exclude non-Hindus from membership of the nation–state (which is typical of nationalism), and using it to re-define Indians so as to include non-Hindus as already members of the nation–state (which flows from the logic of constructing a Hindu essence, as we will shortly see). Of course, in both cases, the aim is to create a Hindu hegemony over non-Hindus. Nevertheless, this inclusivistic reflex makes for at least a different sort of religious nationalism than we tend to encounter with other traditions.

The challenge of pluralism

The conceptual problem with searching for the fundamentals of Hinduism is obvious; and despite some persistent efforts to the contrary, widely accepted (even, as we will see, by *Hindutva* ideologues). There is no text commonly authoritative for all those who might be called Hindus. Even the *Vedas*, the corpus of ritual injunctions, myths, metaphysical metaphors and cosmogony, have only a notional authority among those who accept them, playing no role comparable in the daily worship of Hindus that the *Qur'an* and the Bible have in Muslim and Christian lives. Most of the ideas subsequently found in Hinduism do not occur in the *Vedas*. In any case, many who count themselves as Hindus do not have a place in their religion for the *Vedas*. The absence of any core text to serve as 'scripture' is matched by the absence of any single body of doctrines. No single idea is common to all and only Hindus. Some, like the ideas of consequential action and rebirth, are found in other Indian religions as well. But this, it must be admitted, actually helps the *Hindutva* case: Jainism and Buddhism, and even Sikhism, which do share certain concepts with the Hindu traditions, are routinely included in the *Hindutva* definition of Hinduism.

In the face of an irreducible diversity of authoritative texts, doctrines and sources of the religious life, one heroic *Hindutva* strategy has been to try and designate a text (and its teachings, suitably interpreted) as the core of Hinduism. Usually, this has been the 2,000-year-old *Bhagavadgita*, the 'Song of the Lord', being the teachings of Krishna, a manifestation of God, to the warrior prince Arjuna. But generally, it is exactly this lack of a core of texts and beliefs that has provided for a characteristically modern reading of Hinduism as a religion, a specific form of which constitutes the essence of *Hindutva* ideology. We will approach the matter of the *Hindutva* extraction of an essential Hinduism somewhat obliquely, through a short study of the very notion of Hinduism.

Hindutva *and the very category of 'Hinduism'*

There is a strangely double-faced critique of the very idea of 'Hinduism'. It has usually been represented, in Western scholarship, as an attempt to deconstruct the early modern project of creating out of diverse traditions of India a single tradition that can fall into the Western category of 'religion'. (This is, of course, a narcissistic tale, for it would seem that what the West builds, the West alone can tear down; Indians resident in the structure but watch.) This denial of a single religion called Hinduism, in this master narrative, is done for the sake of rescuing the authentic and authentically diverse Hindu traditions from an earlier, hegemonizing and constructing Western discourse.[4] But this liberal act tends to be construed by Hindus of various political persuasions as an attack on their religious identity. For modern Hindus exposed to issues of nationality, identity, modernity and globalization in its various forms, there is no fundamental question about their religion and religious identity – it is Hinduism and they are Hindus. Attempts to demonstrate that there is no single religion called Hinduism are seen, not as liberal attempts to give back autonomy to Hindus, but yet another act of Western colonization of Indian terrain, and a consequent denial of Hindu identity. Now, recent scholarship, Western and Indian, has pointed out that the construction of 'Hinduism' as a single religion and 'Hindus' as a single people was a nineteenth- and twentieth-century project to which Hindus themselves gave intellectual support and which they took over and sustained for their own ends. This makes matters more complex. On the one hand, the recognition of the agency of Hindus in the realization of a single religion would seem to indeed give back autonomy to Hindus in the development of their history.[5] On the other hand, the very emphasis on the constructive and modernist nature of this realization of a single religion calls into question the authenticity (especially the historical continuity) of Hindu unity.

In this contest of accounts, one fact is indubitable. Modern Hindus have certainly tried to define Hinduism through appeal to some unifying feature. It is this attempt at unification that makes it difficult to say exactly where the particular ideology of *Hindutva* differs from nineteenth- and twentieth-century Hindu attempts to define Hinduism. The significance of this difficulty, I will argue, lies in the fact that it helps explain the elusive and shifting nature of the appeal that political parties driven by *Hindutva* ideology have to the Hindu electorate. The conceptualizations of Hindu identity have themselves lacked any singular authority across Hindu society. Therefore, any acutely ideological formulation of these concepts, while having appeal because it simplifies those concepts, cannot gain any singular, and consequently unifying, hold over Hindu society.

In some ways, then, *Hindutva* is only an extreme and authoritarian rendering of modern Hindu conceptions of pan-Hindu identity.[6] This also helps to explain why public and intellectual resistance to *Hindutva* has so often come from those who reject the unifying themes of modern Hinduism. In other words, resistance to *Hindutva* ideology comes from those who usually reject dominant discourses on Hindu identity *per se*, either because they reject altogether the authority of religion in issues of identity or because they challenge the historical marginalization such discourses have perpetuated.[7]

In the course of 300 years of modern Western contact with and political dominion over India, the native traditions of artefacts, gods, rituals, codes of conduct, social stratification, abstract concepts of transcendence and morality, rational debates and a range of social customs, were collated and thematized by Westerners, usually with the cooperation and interpretive mediation of the priestly intellectual class of *brahmins*. By setting aside the self-proclaimed followers of other indigenous traditions, the Western students of this culture arrived at a body of vast and varied concerns that they called the Hindu religion, or Hinduism. The term, however, went back in a somewhat enigmatic fashion through Islamic travellers earlier in the millennium to the ancient Greeks themselves, who had talked of the people beyond the River Sindhu, which was hellenized into the 'Indus' and thus gave rise to the term 'Hindu'.

Through the nineteenth and the early twentieth centuries, Hindus themselves began to schematize their tradition into a religion. However, as has been mentioned, it always proved impossible to find a determinate body of doctrine in a commonly agreed set of texts, adherence to which could identify Hindus and Hindus alone. Gradually, the idea emerged of Hinduism as a 'way of life', a perennial order (*sanatana dharma*, to use the classical Sanskrit term that came to be applied as the native term for the modern religion). While not making the technical point of late twentieth-century academics that 'religion' itself is an inappropriate term for the Hindu tradition, modern Hindus have long recognized that Hinduism is not a religion in the sense in which Christianity, Islam and others are. The acceptance of this amorphous nature to their religion was not, however, of much use to Hindus who were attempting to develop a way of defining themselves; being told that they really could not define themselves did not help.

Modern and contemporary discussions of definition have tended to divide into the academic one of trying to provide a coherent justification for taking something to be Hindu, and the existential one of saying what makes one a Hindu. Hindu self-definition, for over a hundred years now, has concentrated on finding a value or attitude or belief under the commonly accepted religio-cultural diversity. The effort at self-definition was initially confined to a small number of influential intellectuals and leaders; over the past half a century or so, ideas of Hindu identity have become widely accepted among the educated urban middle classes. That is to say, the majority, indeed the vast majority of Hindus have not directly participated in this construction of the Hindu *imaginaire*. However, the political consequences of the *Hindutva* interpretation of Hindu identity have had major consequences.

Pluralism, Hinduism and the ideological essence of Hindutva

To put the matter briefly, Hindus, looking to find a common value or belief that would provide them with the determinant of Hindu identity, have by and large settled on the very fact of irreducible Hindu plurality and made a singular virtue of it. The abundance of often competing authoritative texts, the endless variety of rituals and customs, the many forms of God (and the proliferation of gods), are all matters of fact – the fact of plurality. But from this, many Hindus have extracted a doctrine of plurality. Simply put, they have argued that the continued existence of plurality actually points to what is common to all the elements of plurality – a deliberate doctrine of non-orthodoxy. What is supposed to define Hinduism, then, is not merely the fact of irreducible plurality but a doctrine propagating the value of plurality. To be Hindu is to be committed to the doctrinally enjoined acceptance of plural religious traditions. In the changing conditions of modern history, this has meant widening the circle of acceptance from the many groups and communities now called Hindu to include the religions of the world. To be Hindu is to acknowledge Christianity, Islam, and so on. Sometimes, this is characterized as the doctrine of Hindu tolerance. But, in fact, it is a larger claim, for Hinduism is not supposed to enjoin mere tolerance, which is just the acceptance of the right of others to hold different views. Hinduism is further held to enjoin the acceptance of the rightness of other religions. This doctrine is traced back not only to the fact of plurality mentioned above, but also to various teachings or sayings in various texts to the effect that there are many different ways to the same goal or that all people belong to the same family.

This doctrine of the acceptance of other religions, however, easily builds into a larger claim: Hinduism alone professes the rightness of other religions, whereas they are constrained by their inability to accept the legitimacy of others. This means not only that Hinduism is superior to other religions in its intrinsic liberality, it includes and is therefore conceptually larger than the exclusivist religions, which profess only their own rightness. Hinduism is the universal religion, because it doctrinally advocates the idea of religion as such, the eternal concerns for transcendence that all humans have; it offers more than one specific and jealously kept path.

This hegemonistic claim is then made more aggressive still: by asymmetrically allowing for other religions, in a manner they cannot or do not match, Hinduism is supposed to include these other religions within its doctrinal embrace. Its very nature is such as to allow for other religions, and they have not the means to reciprocate. They exclude, and therefore limit themselves; it includes and therefore rises above them.

Clearly, there is a continuum of ideologization here, from attempts to find the sources of religious identity to assertions of superiority. Such a continuum is hardly limited to Hinduism, although what is specific is the emergence of a doctrine of plurality from the plethora of religious and cultural sources. What cannot be determined easily is where perfectly understandable and reasonable attempts at definition (however unsympathetic Western academics are towards them) shade into ideological justifications for dominance (hence that fastidious lack of sympathy, one suspects). It is this curious and ambiguous relationship between the modern Hindu search for identity and the *Hindutva* articulation of it that makes for the latter's appeal to Hindus in search of identity. *Hindutva* ideology draws on many of the same ideas as more general Hindu conceptualizations of religious identity.

Many Hindu intellectuals would not subscribe to the doctrine of plurality; from the fact of historical plurality to the hypostatization of a universal doctrine is a major step. It is taken because of the search for a pan-Hindu identity, because the old, more specific categories of lineage, caste, class, group or community are deemed inadequate or partial. There can be many self-representations that are factually and historically Hindu without having a pan-Hindu signification, because they are tied to more local allegiances. It can also be added that that is a sense of self that the vast majority of people-called-Hindus have, derived from their immediate cultural resources. On the whole, however, attempts to find a unifying sense of being Hindu have involved finding an underlying principle of universality. Yet, many who would accept this intellectual case for Hindu identity, and who would even be prepared to think that in having this attitude Hinduism is unique and special, would not, and intellectuals need not, be committed to *Hindutva* ideology. All religions have their own claims to uniqueness and veracity, after all.

Hindutva ideology builds on this modern Hindu notion of a uniquely Hindu but universally applicable principle of plurality, but makes a specifically political extension of it. It identifies Hinduism with the people of the nation–state of India. Of course, *Hindutva* ideologues emphasize this principle of plurality as the doctrine that establishes the universality and superior morality of Hinduism, but that is only part of the rhetoric of their discourse. It is the identification of the religion with the nation–state that has substantive consequences. Once it has been argued that there is indeed some underlying principle to all the diversity of Hindu traditions, it is possible to claim that there is a single, unified religion. This stress on the unity of Hinduism, which results from the principle of plurality, is vital to *Hindutva*. For, if there is one single religion and that religion is the religion of the people of India, then, there is one Indian people, defined by their religion. Indians are unified and India is unified, and that unification is through a religion, which has been unified by extracting its essence, namely, the doctrine of plurality. Let us set out the steps in this thinking:

1   Hinduism is a single religion, because all its traditions commonly reveal the doctrine of plurality.
2   Hinduism is the religion of India.
3   There is a single religion and therefore a single people who belong to that religion.
4   The single religion is Hinduism and the single people are Indians.

The crucial and characteristic *Hindutva* claim is 2. What makes for Hindu-*ness* (Hindu*tva*) then, is not merely the unifying doctrine of universally applicable plurality, but the unifying identity of Indians as Hindus. The essence (the '-ness') of the religion is not just the principle of plurality but the nationality with which its practitioners are identified.

Religious authority in Hinduism and its consequences for Hindutva *ideology*

These conceptual details point to some conclusions about the type of authority possessed by figures within the movement. There is no scope for theocratic authority in Hindu society, in either a strong or a weak sense of the term. Strong theocratic authority comes from having both (i) a system of religious organization that provides justification for intervention in and mobilization for political activity; and (ii) a structuring of society in which it is normative for political power to have a foundation in religious sanction. The paradigm for this, of course, is the Iran of the ayatollahs. What I call weak theocratic authority has only (i); examples can be found in the Christianity in the Church of England and Buddhism in Thailand. There is no theoretical basis for such authority in Hinduism, for there is neither a recognizable and cohesive pan-traditional priesthood nor, indeed, any one pan-societal religion.

In some ways, *Hindutva* is like the political activity of Protestant fundamentalism in North America, in that there is an appeal to religion by ordained figures of authority in each case, but that appeal is restricted to followers of particular groups or denominations or sub-traditions. But the parallel breaks down because Protestantism at least has recourse to a putatively universal religious doctrine, which allows for appeal to a textual source and authority that could, in theory, be accepted by a majority of the polity that is outside a particular group. That attempt at universality, after all, is precisely what gives the American Religious Right its motivation. There is no such religious doctrine for Hindus, and so, even an otherwise respected leader of a religious group cannot be able to appeal to some source common to the majority that is supposedly part of the same religion. This has indeed been the case with the pronouncements of some of the *Sankaracharyas* who head monastic organizations in different parts of India dating back over a millennium. They are generally treated with respect by Hindus, but their religious authority is limited to those who worship God as Siva, and that too, usually in the particular region with which the organization is traditionally associated. This is not due to a contingent failure of authority, as with the ministers of the American Christian Right, but to an absence of any commonality to Hinduism.

This lack of universal appeal also affects politicians who hope to make use of religion. It is precisely because there is no religious authority that *Hindutva* politicians have to take recourse to the abstract historical meta-doctrine of Hindu plurality.

What all this amounts to is that Hindu society in India cannot be mobilized *en masse* through any unifying religious authority, even in theory. This should be kept in mind when predicting its future; and it perhaps explains the internal limits of its appeal.

The history of religious and social change: the context of *Hindutva*

There is no neutral way of stating the historical circumstances from which *Hindutva* ideology emerged, for part of the issue precisely is the contestation of history.[8] My summary of the history of Islam in India will, doubtless, be open to the charge of prejudice (at the very least, in the strict hermeneutical sense of inescapable pre-judgement).

Prologue: pre-Islamic India

The reading of pre-Islamic Indian history is contested, in a way suggested by our previous discussion of the nature of Hinduism. What is at issue is whether the history of the sub-continent before the coming of Islam should be read as an irreducibly plural and varied series of political formations, social changes and religio-philosophical texts, or as a unified account of a single if complex religious culture. It should be noted that modern accounts of Hinduism, even given by Western academics, tacitly simplify ancient Indian history in order to given some coherence to the very idea of

Hinduism. The diverse strands of the classical past are separated, at least into Hindu, Buddhist and Jain traditions; and while this limiting of Hinduism might be rejected by some Hindus, nonetheless, the modern categories of the different religions and their histories are perpetuated. It is admittedly an extremely difficult task to give a sustained account purely through the plurality of indigenous texts, movements, languages, regions and the like, without using modern categories. Besides, modern Buddhist and Jain historiographies, too, equally resist a non-denominational reading of the classical past. The reading of the past, then, is a contemporary concern, and we have seen how both Hindus and others have read the past in various ways.

Nonetheless, the contemporary relevance of *Hindutva* thought is given by the presence of Islam (and secondarily, Christianity) in India. So the history is from the coming of Islam to India.

Islam and India

Islam came primarily to the Indian sub-continent, to what is now the Pakistani province of Sindh, in the eighth century, in the form of early Islamic Arab armies. But there had also been a variety of trading relations between the Arab world and the southern Indian region of Kerala for centuries. For the next four hundred years, several Islamic military formations penetrated farther into the sub-continent, mainly raiding the rich but weak kingdoms of Western India but not attempting to settle or convert. This slowly changed until, by the thirteenth century, Delhi was in the hands of Muslim rulers who had originated in West Asia, although there were also Turks among them. From this time onwards, there were constant wars in North India, as successive rulers of the Sultanate in Delhi sought to expand their power and secure their borders against indigenous kingdoms. This military situation was usually complex, as alliances and counter-alliances formed between the Muslim rulers, their sometimes recalcitrant governors and the native rulers, most notably the Rajput kingdoms. Gradually, either directly through generals of the Delhi Sultanate or indirectly through autonomous provincial governors, kingdoms ruled by Muslims extended into South India, as older, native imperial formations crumbled there as well. By the sixteenth century, the sub-continent was a *mélange* of political formations, with a dominant but weakening imperial centre in Delhi and a complex mix of kingdoms and autonomous provinces, forming and re-forming, ruled by Hindu dynasties or by the Muslim elite mostly descended from the nobles who first came to Delhi. It was into this situation that armies from southern Central Asia, with an ancestry that went back to the

Mongols, arrived and, through a series of military victories, established themselves in Delhi. But the history of the Mughals was remarkably like that of the earlier Sultanate, for they extended control over the sub-continent as much through alliances as through conquest, and now over Muslim-ruled areas as well as Hindu ones. (The Mughals were the Muslim imperial ruling dynasty in India between the sixteenth and eighteenth centuries, descended from Mongol chieftains in Central Asia. The empire, its court and the age itself are named after them.)

During those six or seven centuries, by the sword, through the pressure of taxes that favoured Muslims, or from constant contact with rulers, armies, civil servants and religious figures, part of the native population became Muslim. At the same time, the comparatively small number of soldiers and even fewer nobles from outside the sub-continent intermingled with the native population, both of Hindus and Muslims. In brief, the majority of Muslims were native to the sub-continent, and had become Muslims for a variety of reasons; the non-native Muslims were a small minority and they quickly became assimilated into the composite culture that they had helped to create.

The West and the question of Hindu/Indian identity[9]

As the Mughal empire collapsed rapidly from its apogee as the supreme imperial power across the sub-continent, the European traders who had first come at the end of the fifteenth century moved into the post-imperial vacuum. European wars were fought by proxy on the sub-continent, while Indian successor states interacted with the Europeans in the pursuit of their own military and economic ends. By the late eighteenth century, the native states had mostly lost out in their strategic alliances with the Europeans, the other European empires had lost out to the English (or, by then, the British), and the British had become the dominant political presence through the English East India Company. In the middle of the nineteenth century, the Company was disbanded and the sub-continent came under the British Crown.

The Mughal successor states had been both Muslim and Hindu, widely ranging in size, wealth and cultural mix. As the British exerted direct or indirect control, they took up the study of the land and culture that earlier European powers, especially the Catholic Church under Portuguese patronage, had initiated; but the British made that study also a means of control. Cultural practices were recorded, ancient codes of conduct legalized, rituals recorded and tolerated or abolished. Islamic laws and customs were comparatively easy to organize, as they had some common sources of authority (although that could not be extended to many practices, beliefs and customs that had grown up in the composite culture of India). But the task was more complicated with the amorphous native traditions. To organize and systematize was already to define. And so Hinduism was defined, even as the material that was held to constitute it was gathered. The same construction of a systematized religion also happened to the other traditions – Sikhism, Buddhism, Jainism, Zoroastrianism (and Christianity in India).

This objectifying was in part an Enlightenment project, in part political control. In any case, by the end of the nineteenth century, processes of control in British India, like civil law, were organized according to the objectified resources of the different religions. When pressure for political representation at the turn of the century started growing, that too was granted on the basis of religious 'communities'.[10] The fundamental development of giving identity through systematically organizing (through objectifying) cultural beliefs and practices was not challenged; for the imagination of identity had become of paramount importance to Indian intellectuals and leaders of all backgrounds. By the end of the nineteenth century, Indians were beginning to think of the nature of the political dispensation under which they wished to live, and demands for autonomy from London grew in stages from local representation to Home Rule to Independence (and thereafter from Dominion to Republic).

The issue of Indian identity, however, was vexed from its very birth.[11] What exactly were these subjects of the British Empire to look back on, to draw from, when searching for their sources of national selfhood? Here was a history, but which of it was Indian? Without doubt, there was a disjuncture in it, dating to the coming of Islam to the sub-continent. So, what to make of the presence of Islam in the making of India? Two broad types of responses to this question developed.[12]

1   One sought to anchor national identity in the whole of the history of the sub-continent, taking its trans-religious history as the source of a modern national identity. This again had two broad variants.

  (i) One emphasized the role of particular religions in the immediate inspiration for seeing oneself as an Indian, but allowed that different religions would eventually lead to a common sense of being Indian, since all these religions were part of the history of India. Gandhi was the exemplary proponent of this view, but it had a distinguished history of advocacy, including Bal Gangadhar Tilak, Aurobindo, Rabindranath Tagore, S. Radhakrishnan and others.

(ii) The other, later variant, saw religions as being problematic sources of nationhood, since they were many while the nation–state was to be one; this variant sought commonality in a cultural history that de-emphasized the religious dimension. Commitment to this view is the now contested secular legacy of Jawaharlal Nehru.

2   The other type of response boldly acknowledged the consequences of the religious history of India, and argued for a political identity that was derived from the specificity of religious identity. In this at least, the *Hindutva* thinkers agreed on the basic premise with Mohammed Ali Jinnah, the Muslim League and all those who argued for the Islamic state of Pakistan. The sources of the national self were to be found in religion and religious history; India could be found only in the essence of Hinduism, according to V.D. Savarkar, K.B. Hedgewar, M.S. Golwalkar and others.[13]

Hindutva, *modern India and Pakistan*

At the birth of modern India, in the early and mid-nineteenth century, there were individual kingdoms, nominally independent of British rule but under British influence, that were ruled by Hindu or Muslim kings. The rest of the sub-continent was directly under British rule. Across this imperial domain, religious demography was mixed. Despite British classification of the religions of people, from the first census in 1851 onwards (which was notable in creating a unified category of 'Hindus'), the actual mix of the population was complex. Many parts of India, especially in the North, had composite cultures, where literature, music, dress, food and even festivals drew on Hindu and Muslim elements. Despite the vestigial presence of Muslim nobility that traced its origin back to non-Indian lands, local cultures were immemorial mixtures and interactions of religious cultures. Systematic organization of Indian history gave Hindus and Muslims, or at least the small proportion that was literate, access to a history of warring states and rulers from different religions. This relentless 'history from above' presented a story of clashing civilizations, and forced from intellectuals a decision on how they were to read their past and their present. This reading of history was not usually challenged. The question, rather, was whether to see differences as internal to a nation or as between religious nationalities. We have seen the broad division of responses. Ideological implications have now penetrated the reading of history to its depths. To even point out that (i) political and military relationships cut across

Hindu–Muslim divisions; and (ii) the lives of the masses of people, given the native origins of most Indian Muslims, might have been very different from apparently polarized leaderships, is already to be seen as denying the specificity of religions; it is already to be some sort of a non-religious nationalist or a 'secularist', and to stand against both Islamic and *Hindutva* constructions of nationhood.

It was always going to be the case that once political movements were mobilized on the basis of these convictions, the historical relationship between religious communities was going to be affected. That indeed happened. Broadly, there was an asymmetry in the dominant politicization of religion through nationalism. The Indian National Congress attempted to present a case for a nation that was at once constituted by all religions but transcended them. This attempt cut obliquely across the communal identities created by British rule, through the census and in newly created legislative assemblies (and even in cricket tournaments involving teams from different religions!). Already, there was a sense of being a 'Hindu', a sense created by classifying all those not specifically members of other religions as belonging to this one, single (albeit indefinable) religion called Hinduism. To this emergent identity, the Indian National Congress responded by evolving a discourse of Indian identity that accepted the idea of Hinduism but attempted to place it, its demographic majority notwithstanding, as one among the many religions of India. The Muslim League, in contrast, was self-evidently a political movement for the rights (and later, the independence) of Muslims; the very demographic dominance of 'Hindus', it felt, made the Congress discourse of religious equality or neutrality an illusion. A nation with a Hindu majority would always be a Hindu nation. While some in the Congress made precisely this claim, it was in no way part of Congress policy. It was left to individuals largely outside the main nationalist movement to articulate this view from the Hindu perspective. By the 1920s, an ideology developed that matched for Hindus the Muslim League argument for a religion-based nationalism. Drawing on late nineteenth-century expressions of the special place of Hindus in the history and identity of India, *Hindutva* was an ideology that called for a Hindu nation.

As is well known, for complex reasons, largely resulting from political mobilization, the Islamic nation of Pakistan was born at the same time as the non-religiously specific state of India. Both before and after Independence, Hindu nationalist ideology was uncertain about its attitude to Pakistan. On the one hand, as I have suggested, the argument for Pakistan usefully matched the argument for a Hindu India: one nation is for Muslims and the other is for Hindus. The very argument for a separate

Muslim state was premised on the intrinsically Hindu nature of the original, undivided, pre-Independence India. Therefore, the creation of Muslim Pakistan seemed to open the way for a Hindu India; only the neutralist myth of the Congress had led to the creation of a 'secular' India in which the state treated all religions equally. On the other hand, the older and bolder argument was that India – the undivided, pre-Independence India – was the original, Hindu India; to grant Pakistan was already to grant too much. All Muslims in the original Indian had to be part of the greater Hindu India.

The latter response was dominant among the politically weak Hindu nationalists at the time of Independence; they therefore opposed Partition (the division of British India into Muslim Pakistan and secular India), seeing it as capitulation by Hindus to Muslims. Rejection of the principle of Partition was a doctrinal commitment of Hindu nationalists for much of the fifty years following Independence; they dreamt of an Undivided India (*Akhand Bharat*). The rhetoric of Undivided India was used into the 1990s even by politicians like Lal Krishna Advani, who led the re-constituted *Bharatiya Janata* Party into political relevance and the parliamentary mainstream. But this commitment had steadily become more and more symbolic, both among those concerned with the realities of political power-sharing in the late 1990s and among ideological strategists who, recognizing that re-uniting Pakistan into a greater India was an idle fantasy, focused on changing the nature of the Indian polity within existing borders.

The contemporary concern of *Hindutva*, therefore, is with the identity of Indians in India as it is now, an identity that they wish to derive directly from a Hindu past. Setting aside the theoretical issue of Pakistan's right to exist, they concentrate on Hindu history as the foundation of the present Indian State. They read that history in broadly two parts: an ancient period, in which the land was a Hindu land; and Islamic (and colonial) times, in which Hinduism was enslaved by alien religions and cultures. The common domination of both Hinduism and Islam by the British is not central to this narrative; instead, colonialism becomes merely the time in which another alien religion was introduced into the Hindu land, namely, Christianity. In this way, the divide is between the classical Hindu past and a subsequent subordination of Hinduism by Islam and Christianity.

The Hindutva *reading of history*

The central features of the *Hindutva* reading of history, simplified, are as follows:

1   There was a single, albeit pluralistic and tolerant religion indigenous to the land of India. It was Hinduism, and the other native traditions are in fact derivative parts of it.
2   The coming of Islam was the coming of an alien culture, a culture that clashed with the indigenous tradition and eventually dominated it. This was followed by the coming of a Christian culture, which equally subjugated the native religion.
3   With political independence, the golden opportunity was lost of regaining a Hindu land, for the alien traditions were accepted as part of the new nation–state.
4   The eventual aim, therefore, should be to make this nation–state the modern successor to the ancient land of a single culture.

Hindutva *in the twentieth century: the socio-political picture*

A brief study and analysis of the political history of *Hindutva* is required if we are to understand the current significance of Hindu nationalism.[14] The core *Hindutva* organization has always been the non-political *Rashtriya Swayamsevak Sangh* (RSS), which traditionally concentrates on cultural activism and social service, according to the ideological convictions of Golwalkar and Hedgewar, two of the founding exponents of *Hindutva*. They believed that securing a Hindu state was a matter of changing the attitudes of Hindus, of making them feel strong and united in their private and public practices as Hindus. This apparently idealistic ideology has been the dominant theme of RSS discourse. The other stream of *Hindutva* activity follows the conviction of Savarkar, the other seminal *Hindutva* ideologue, that mass political mobilization was the key to the transformation of the Indian polity. In pre-Independence India, it took the form of the Hindu *Mahasabha*, which was initially an interest group under the umbrella of the Indian National Congress, arguing for greater attention to be paid to specifically Hindu-defined interests in the freedom struggle. After Independence, this stream of Hindu nationalism took the form of the parliamentary party, the *Jana Sangh*. The RSS was implicated in both the assassination of Mahatma Gandhi and in violence during the Partition, and was banned for a while. It was always viewed with extreme distrust by the leader of the Congress.

After the formation of the *Jana Sangh*, the RSS occasionally became more directly engaged in its political affairs, but generally maintained its role as the ideological training ground of the parliamentary party. In the 1960s, another organization, the *Vishwa Hindu Parishad* or World Hindu Council (VHP) was formed to pursue a more activist role in the importation of religio-cultural issues into political debate. Other organizations have been formed over the years that are part of the *Sangh Parivar* or family of organizations. The most notable is the vehemently *Hindutva Shiv Sena* or Army of Shiva, which is a political party in the western Indian state of Maharashtra, whose capital is the financial first city of India, Mumbai (Bombay).

The *Jana Sangh* was marginalized by the Congress, never getting more than a handful of seats in Parliament, until it became part of the curious coalition of nationalist, socialist and other parties that came briefly to power in protest against Congress Prime Minister Indira Gandhi's lapse into undemocratic rule in the mid-1970s. After the squabbling coalition lost power to Mrs Gandhi, the *Jana Sangh* was reconstituted as the *Bharatiya Janata* Party (BJP) in the early 1980s, and remained a mostly isolated party during the 1980s, although it gradually gained more seats at successive general elections. It finally came to power, but only in a coalition with regional and even left-wing parties, in the late 1990s, retaining power through a slightly different range of alliance partners in the last election of the 1990s.

Throughout this time, the relationship between the RSS, the *Jana Sangh*/BJP and other members of the *Sangh Parivar* was close but problematic. It was problematic primarily because of issues of political strategies, but also because of ideological differences. Since strategy and ideology are inter-related, we can look at them together. The problematic is best expressed through two intersecting dichotomies: the 'cultural–political' and 'hard–soft'.

The cultural–political tension is over the question of whether *Hindutva* ideals should primarily be concerned with the transformation of national culture and society, or whether they should be about the management of the functions of state. Of course, the official view has always been that cultural training is to be applied to governance or the management of matters of state; hence the RSS background of virtually all the main leaders of the *Jana Sangh*/BJP. But the different imperatives have often worked against each other. To put it briefly, cultural concerns have tended to produce elitist, abstract, inflexible strategies premised on the virtues of consistency and ideological purity; while political aims have called for populism, pragmatism and the flexible morality of co-option and compromise. When

Hindu nationalist parliamentary parties were in opposition and with low levels of support, their political orientation called for agitation and mass mobilization that involved attempts to locate and exploit the resentment of whichever groups could provide electoral support to increase the number of seats in Parliament. The ideologues of the RSS were focused on matters of personal conduct, rigorous discipline and the internalization of designated Hindu values; they often found the demotic discourse and the opportunistic search for mass support, even (or especially?) by politicians trained by them, distasteful and valueless. On the other hand, when the parliamentary party moved into government, its courting of potential partners with very different ideological inclinations and its acceptance of technocratic individuals without *Hindutva* credentials were virtually unacceptable to the pure ideologues.

The hard–soft divide does not exactly parallel the cultural–political one. It is mainly over matters of strategy, although sometimes 'soft' strategies also seem to have weak ideological commitments behind them. 'Hard' strategies are based on enunciating uncompromising ideological principles, both of assertions and rejection. They are premised on retaining the support of people who hold similar views, and gaining that of people who do not share that commitment but are nevertheless drawn by appreciation of the strength with which those principles are held. 'Soft' strategies take flexibility to be vital to the holding of ideological principles, and are premised on the conviction that only flexibility will simultaneously retain those of strong commitment and attract others without such commitment.

The RSS has always followed a 'hard' strategy. In principle, this meant that its leaders and cadres uncompromisingly worked on personal cultivation of 'Hindu' culture and the social uplift of all, as demonstrations of the vitality and potential of Hindu-derived values. But, in fact, this has often meant the – usually autonomous but ruthless – involvement of grassroots workers in violent attacks on Muslims, Christians and, sometimes, *Dalits* ('the oppressed', the traditional Untouchables). Of course, the inflammatory consequences of the speeches and writings of RSS leaders should always be taken into account when considering the role of the ideologues in riots and other acts of violence.

The majority of leaders in the *Hindutva* political parties have followed the simple prescription of hard strategies in opposition and soft ones in power. This is most obvious with the *Shiv Sena*, the dominant *Hindutva* party in the state of Maharashtra, led by the hardline Bal Thackeray. While clearly involved in fomenting communal violence in Bombay/ Mumbai – to the extent of Thackeray facing prosecution that even the *Sangh* publications admitted was legitimate – the *Shiva Sena* has been conspicuously cautious in handling communal relations since it was able to form a government. The same goes for its switch from traditional RSS-derived autarkic ideology to investor-friendly economic liberalism after coming to power.

It is the BJP, of course, that most concerns us, and here the tensions and changes in strategy are telling and important. The conventional distinction since the 1980s has been between the soft strategies exemplified by the veteran *Jana Sangh* politician and BJP Prime Minister, A.B. Vajpayee, and the hard ones adopted by L.K. Advani, Home Minister in the BJP-led government. While both were trained in RSS culture, Vajpayee has for long attempted to reach an eclectic variety of voters, asserting the cultural significance of *Hindutva*, but generally eschewing the political goal of somehow forcibly transforming the Indian polity into a purely Hindu one. In the elections in which the BJP was able to come to and retain power, Vajpayee's strategy clearly worked. In the 1999 election, it was his presidential image that contributed to the success of even regional parties that were part of the National Democratic Alliance of which the BJP was the senior partner. The success of Advani's strategy by contrast, is contested. He was the national politician who most clearly gave an aggressive political reading of *Hindutva* ideology, promising to remove constitutional provisions that were supposed to discriminate against the Hindu 'majority' by protecting the rights of 'minorities'. He was closely involved with the tactic, in successive elections, of projecting fiery extremist anti-Muslim orators at mass rallies. He was, of course, instrumental in the escalation of the *Hindutva* demand in the late 1980s and early 1990s for the 'restoration' of putatively Hindu holy sites on which medieval Islamic rulers had built mosques. The destruction of the mosque at Ayodhya, supposedly built on a temple marking the birthplace of the divine *avatar*, Rama, was the culmination of a process that Advani and others like him had initiated but over which they apparently lost control. The cycle of rioting and murder that resulted from it morally implicated the whole Indian political establishment, including the Congress government that had prevaricated in its response, not only Advani and the *Hindutva* movement. In charge of a powerful ministry after the BJP came to power in a coalition, Advani was expected to start implementing the strong demands of the *Hindutva* ideologues. He did no such thing. Indeed, in certain crucial situations in which *Hindutva* ideology might have seemed especially at stake, as with a uniform civil code that would remove the special rights of Muslims to follow their own laws of marriage, divorce, etc., Advani has assiduously stuck to the coalition programme that has none of the standard *Hindutva* demands. It would seem that Advani has 'gone soft'. Indeed, the standard view in the Indian media is that he mediates between the BJP-in-government and the RSS, precisely because of this equivocation between dyed-in-the-wool ideology and pragmatic interpretations of governance.

It is clear that as far as being in government is concerned, the Hindu nationalist parties have more or less no room for manoeuvre. They came to power only by seriously compromising on their programme of trans-forming the Indian polity. For one thing, they got the votes they could, which have in any case levelled off, only by reaching a wider constituency that was uncomfortable with hardline *Hindutva*. For another, and rela-tedly, they could form a government only through a coalition that vigor-ously rejected all of the *Hindutva* demands and demanded that the BJP function as a party without an ideology.

The consequence of this pragmatization of the BJP has been the chan-nelling of virtually all ideological energies into extra-parliamentary and often plain unlawful activity. We will look at the BJP's transformation through the demands of governance and the ways in which *Hindutva* has been forced to express itself when we look at the nature of the political economy and society in India at the start of the twenty-first century. But, first, we must try to understand what social and political changes lay behind the growth of Hindu nationalism in independent India, for only then can we see how those changes have been handled by Hindu nation-alists.

The state, national resources and social change: a theory to explain the rise of Hindu nationalism

After independence, the Congress under Jawaharlal Nehru evolved a system of governance that attempted to meet the complex demands of a country of such diversity, illiteracy, poverty, history and competing social structures. To put it briefly, the Nehruvian strategy attempted to institu-tionalize competing demands through a flexible system of allocation of resources, management of competition, negotiation of demands and an apportionment of power to local elites and potential lobby groups. This institutionalization was largely possible because Nehru himself and his associates in power had a historic and charismatic appeal to the electorate that removed threats to their power. It must be added that it was very likely that many of them genuinely preserved an idealistic sense of national mission in which the preservation of personal power was not a significant factor. Although *dirigiste* policies depressed economic growth, available resources were perceived to be spread across the country through the insti-tutionalized dispersion of power which originated at the centre. This made

179

political opposition difficult, as there was no uniform constituency for the opposition to address. This, more than anything else, allowed little scope for the *Jana Sangh* to extend its power.

The *Jana Sangh*'s participation in government in the late 1970s was directly a result of the changes in, and failures of, Indira Gandhi's governmental strategies. Politically weak at the time of her accession to power, she saw a threat in the status of political leaders who had had regional and local bases under her father. She tried to by-pass them through a range of populist tactics aimed at focusing attention on her, making her seem the sole source of power. In any case, the eighteen years of Nehruvian rule had ossified the systems of negotiation, and the passing of the first generation of leaders gradually reduced the acceptability of that elite allocation of resources which had depended on their aura of disinterest. Governance began to be de-institutionalized under her, and made more a matter of directly dealing with enough regions, groups, lobbies and special interests to enable her to sustain personalized governance. This populism, inevitably, meant allocating resources selectively. The structures of resource management that had kept the Nehruvian state intact, by allowing sufficient numbers of local elites to mediate between the state and the people (while benefiting from it in often corrupt ways), crumbled. The components of the *Janata* government of the late 1970s gained what power they had by meeting the demands of specific constituencies that felt excluded from Indira Gandhi's dispensation. The *Jana Sangh* was one of them.

During Mrs Gandhi's last term of office, and in Rajiv Gandhi's time after his mother's assassination, populist strategies continued. Muslims, for example, were also treated as a specific competing group, often ostensibly allocated resources to keep their support, sometimes vilified and marginalized in order to reallocate resources to local Hindu groups when the latter's affiliation to the Congress was in question. Through the 1980s, then, Indian democratic governance increasingly became a matter of targeting groups for resource allocation, and the older and more subtle way of knitting different groups into institutions of mutual entitlement was all but forgotten. But this strategy, while having the merit of directly and swiftly garnering support among those who benefited, increased the probability of disempowered groups venting their frustrations through counter-populism; but that could be articulated, and its fruits harvested, only through antinomian discourse and practice. The groups targeted for increase in their benefits had to have attention drawn to their good fortune; and that meant, conversely, a rhetorical rejection of the claims of competing groups. The radicalization of Muslim communities and the growth of support for Islamic fundamentalism were partly a result of the deliberate and open transferral of economic, educational and political resources from them to competing, largely Hindu, groups accompanied by negative characterizations of the rights of Muslims within the Indian polity. But ironically, when there was a perception that Muslims were allowed special benefits under this strategy of targeted populism, anti-Muslim sentiments were sharpened too, as various groups felt neglected or hard done by, and formulated their protest in terms of religious discrimination. The BJP was perfectly positioned to tap into this resentment.

My argument here is that the growth of the BJP, through exploitation of resentment formulated in the religious terms of Hinduism, was in this period one example of political counter-strategies brought about by the frenetic and targeted populism of the Congress. This can clearly be seen in the other problematic cases, of caste and region. The unravelling of the old Nehruvian elite-based management of demands allowed Backward Castes, and especially the Scheduled Castes (the *Dalits*, listed in the schedule of the Indian Constitution) to emerge as protesting political movements, competing for resources seen to often be arbitrarily allocated away from them. They formed constituencies for anti-Congress leaders who came from either within these castes or had left the Congress. The central or federal hold on competing regional demands had also weakened almost from the beginning of Indira Gandhi's prime ministership (in the mid-1960s), as her opponents came from regional strongholds. By the end of the 1980s, regions – usually the constituent states of the Indian republic, sometimes sub-regions of the states – had routinely begun to build local political movements premised on their being discriminated against. There are, of course, other sources of regionalism, but they arise from assertions of older, usually linguistic and even ethnic identities, and have a different aetiology. Therefore, caste-based political movements and regionalism resulted from the very same de-institutionalization of power management in the Indian polity as did Hindu nationalism.

This analysis is meant to show that the growth of the *Hindutva* movement was not some primal resurgence of religious sentiment, but largely a result of astute exploitation of failures of governance. Of course, it was not accidental that counter-populism, that is, the mobilization of people against a government, through appeal to unmet, real or constructed demands, could take the form of *Hindutva*. Two inter-related factors made possible the formulation of *Hindutva* populism in the late 1980s and early 1990s. One was the long-term, indeed historical emergence of something like a pan-Hindu identity, carrying with it an acute distinction between Hinduism and other religions, especially Islam. This we have already seen.

The second was the way in which various resentments over loss (and more rarely, lack) of privileged access to national resources could be expressed as justifiable responses to a threat to Hindu identity.

It has been mentioned that two prime constituencies for targeted populism were the Muslim communities and various socially disadvantaged caste groups (the Scheduled Castes, that is, castes designated in the schedule of the Indian constitution, and various Backward Castes, also constitutionally specified). In the Nehruvian dispensation, special provisions for them were both (i) indicated as provisional; and (ii) managed through intermediate elites, who benefited from devolved control. In direct populism, these intermediate groups were dispensed with. The net amount of resources (material and political) that filtered through to Muslims and Backward Castes was much less than necessary to combat disadvantage. However, the very rhetoric of populism through which these groups were courted and their corresponding demands articulated, created an impression among those who could not place themselves in these categories that they were being discounted in the allocation of resources. These groups, to put it briefly, were neither Muslims (or other 'minorities') nor from the Backward Castes. The religious 'minorities' were, of course, not Hindus. And the Backward Castes, precisely because of their social standing traditionally associated with religious sanction, were at best ambivalent about the religion within which they were held to have this inferior status. Even more so, the Scheduled Castes, usually *Dalits*, who were literally outcastes, found that their attempts at identity formation precluded appeals to the very religious tradition that had made them liminal to its hierarchical *imaginaire*, however much Hindu social reform sought to treat discrimination within traditional conceptions of group (that is, caste) identity. The two categories of non-Hindus and *Dalits* have often overlapped. The great constitutional lawyer, B.R. Ambedkar, who was an 'untouchable', led in the 1940s and 1950s a movement for conversion to Buddhism among those who shared this outcaste status.

The newly resentful groups were those who had most internalized historical constructions of pan-Hindu identity and most unproblematically saw themselves as Hindus. They came from the Forward Castes, from the urban educated and the rural powerful. The nineteenth- and twentieth-century articulations of a pan-Hindu identity drew upon precisely the texts, rituals, forms of worship, religious exemplars and social forms that conditioned their cultural lives. They had few or no problems in identifying with the central features of the emergent Hindu identity. Consequently, they were least resistant to the sharply ideological rendering of that identity that *Hindutva* offered.

It was the mobilization of significant segments of these strata of society that led to the rise of Hindu nationalism.[15] The violence that drew the attention of the world to *Hindutva* was the result of the overlay of *Hindutva* appeal to the historical tensions between communities. In other words, the *Hindutva* leaders took the existing ideas of religious difference – born of the colonial construction of communal identity and deformed by the traumas of the Partition of India and Pakistan – and focused them on the contemporary contestation of resources brought about by the growth in targeted populism. We have looked at both these processes, but it is their combination that enabled the *Hindutva* movement to gain wider appeal than it ever had. Inevitably, this combined the type of violence that had its historical roots in the creation and crystallization of communal and then national identities with the type of violence expressive of deinstitutionalized contestation of resources. Muslims could be seen both as unnatural elements of a Hindu-based national society (for had they not insisted upon the creation of a nation–state for their own religion?) and as unfair beneficiaries of state allocation of resources. Secondarily, lower castes could be seen as gaining an unfair share of national resources (for had they not continued to enjoy the benefits of reservations for education and jobs, and other policies of apparent reverse discrimination?). In either case, groups were 'being pampered' at the cost of the 'mainstream'. (Any number of resonances can be found in the history of anti-immigration and minority discourse in the West to this day.) Mobilization based on these potent possibilities could be achieved only by organizations that had the relevant ideological base in the notion of a Hindu India. In the disgruntlement of certain sections of Hindu society, the *Sangh* found precisely what it wanted for the realization of its aims.

The surge in support for the BJP in the late 1980s and early 1990s was purely a matter of counter-populism. Agitation, propaganda and mass mobilization were aimed at fomenting and expressing resentment among those Hindus who felt they had been cut out of the national apportionment of resources. They were people who had held secure places in the state apparatus and took their share through participation in disbursement, or people who were beginning to think that they should be entitled to what they wanted by virtue of their place in the polity. The aim of the *Hindutva* organizations was to channel this resentment into a rejection of the Congress and the Left parties which were in power in the 1980s and early 1990s.

Violence erupted in two ways. One was when large-scale symbolic activities aimed at unifying people behind political parties, like rallies and marches, got out of emotional control and demanded catharsis in the destruction of the excluded.[16] The most potent example of this, of course, was the agitation over the mosque at Ayodhya. The other was when communal feelings were manipulated by appeal to religious nationalist sentiments for local, and often illegal, purposes, like eviction of slum-dwellers for real estate speculation, or intimidation of labourers to squeeze out higher profits. This pattern led to, and continues to perpetuate, an unresolved battle of accusation and self-justification. Critics of the *Hindutva* organizations, in particular the BJP, implicate them in the violence. *Hindutva* leaders deny that their political agitation was morally responsible for any violence that happened afterwards, and argue that the local communal violence was in no way organizationally connected to them. They have had legal success in distancing themselves from many of the violent incidents that occurred in their inflammatory rise to influence, despite several court cases accusing them of involvement. This has become a moral issue, in which interpretation is everything, and hence avoids formal resolution.

Assessing the present and future of *Hindutva* politics

At the time of writing, the BJP has been in power, although in coalition, for nearly three years, and has won two elections. The alliance of which it is a part could well see out the term of office; and it looks likely that the BJP will be part of the Indian political system for the foreseeable future, although the party-political landscape is quick-changing in twenty-first century India. It is therefore worthwhile looking at the recent past and near future of India and come to some conclusions about *why* (we have just seen *how*) the BJP – and the *Hindutva* movement – have come to occupy this position in the Indian polity. This will also, I think, allow us to cautiously predict how the very demands of the polity will constrain the functioning of *Hindutva* in the democratic sphere. But first, we must keep in mind the political power situation in which the BJP has operated since it has been in government.

The political situation of Hindutva *at the start of the twenty-first century*

Despite its tacit support of an anti-Congress Left government in the late 1980s, the BJP was clearly seen as the political arm of the RSS and largely isolated in parliamentary affairs. The BJP's isolation was both the cause and the effect of its highly emotive appeal based on Hindu religious identity. Often, violence was endemic to its strategy, since the religious nature

184

of its appeal tended to inculcate in those who responded to it a highly communalized view of social and political relations.

By the mid-1990s, however, the collapse of the Congress as the natural party of government had led to the inexorable rise of coalitions. When the non-Congress United Front government was formed, the BJP could not find any partners, since its strategy was still seen as unacceptably communalist, that is, based on radicalizing relations between the religious communities. A doomed thirteen-day stint in government allowed the BJP little scope for governance, but convinced its leaders that the hard strategy was not going to allow them to break through to the critical levels required for single-party government. There simply were not enough Hindus willing to vote directly for the BJP. In the next election, the BJP played a delicate game, still catering to the radicalized section of Hindus in certain states with histories of communal tension by giving a platform to fiery *Hindutva* figures, while projecting a nation-wide front of moderation and political compromise. There were enough regional and sub-national parties that thought power-sharing with the BJP on this basis acceptable; a minimum common programme was entirely without any of the BJP's standard *Hindutva* commitments. The narrow margin of the coalition's victory showed both the limits and possibilities of the BJP, and the limits were entirely about *Hindutva*, for the possibilities opened up only through promises of governmental competence and balance between regions.

The domestic woes of the coalition could not be resolved, and the nationalism briefly created through the conducting of nuclear tests quickly subsided into realistic debates over the virtues of nuclearization. The coalition fell because of the unpredictability of a regional partner. New alliances were formed for the next general election, and the distinctive ideological claims of the BJP were, if anything, even less in evidence. In previous elections, the BJP leadership had sought to combine hard and soft strategies; this time, almost all the ideologues were either removed or kept on tight leashes. The tensions within the *Hindutva* movement were usually higher than between the BJP leadership and its alliance partners. The BJP could not significantly increase either its share of the popular vote or seats in Parliament. Only the astute mix of parties in alliance ensured the numbers required for government. The BJP did not lose its standard appeal to urban middle-class Hindus, but it made a stronger show in rural areas and significantly increased its share of the Muslim vote from a low base. It could not increase its share of votes from the Backward Castes.

The government which came to power in 1999 included a broad range of partners, from across various states and including the largest Sikh party and the main pro-Indian party in Muslim-dominated Kashmir. Practically all the main cabinet posts, External Affairs, Finance, Information and Broadcasting, Defence, Commerce, were held by either reformist BJP members held in deep suspicion by RSS ideologues or by coalition partners with often strongly anti-*Hindutva* views.

On a series of issues, *Hindutva* strategies have been curtailed by the realities of coalition. A significant example was in early 2000, when the BJP government in the state of Gujarat attempted to remove the legal ban on state employees being members of the RSS. The BJP at the centre came under such strong pressure from its own partners that the Gujarat government saw it wise to retreat. This issue was significant because it seemed a minor *Hindutva* demand, compared to such major and traditional demands as the 'return' of a series of sites held to be holy to Hindus, on which mosques had been built in the past; or a uniform civil code removing the right of Muslims to their own personal law; or the removal of the special rights of Muslim-majority Kashmir where the freedom to move and own property for all Indians does not hold. Yet the BJP could not secure even this aim. When the BJP is asked as to why it has jettisoned its traditional demands, its ingenious answer is to say something important about Hindu nationalism. It maintains that it is bound by the common manifesto of the alliance and aims to maintain its integrity and its commitments to its partners. Even setting aside the cynical thought that it would otherwise not survive in power, it is significant that the BJP chooses to emphasize its moral qualities rather than its ideological ones. There are well-publicized spats between the RSS and the BJP (and within the BJP between its ideologues and various reformist ministers). We are not in any position to authoritatively predict the future of this struggle for dominance, but the very fact of the divergence between what hard *Hindutva* strategists want and what the politicians in power are willing and able to do points to a conclusion. The realities of democratic power in India are the greatest constraints on ideological aims.

Anxiety *and* Hindutva

The appeal that the BJP has and the extent to which the electorate is willing to support it can be understood by looking at what motivates the BJP's constituency: anxiety and its corollary, ambition. There are two different types of anxiety over social change, carrying with them ambitions that are thought to be in danger of not being realized. The *urban middle-class* anxiety is over global competitiveness, India's role as a major player and the consequent economic benefits of enhanced status. There are two intimately connected issues here. One is about international political influence, the other is about economic power and the ability to deliver prosperity at home. The demand of the educated classes in India is that the government of the day deliver on these matters through having a strong presence in international negotiations, political or economic. There is often an ideological hankering after the abstraction of national status; Indians of very different political persuasions have long thought that India should have a seat on the UN Security Council, that it should be a leader in world affairs, that it should be consulted on major international affairs, and so on. Indeed, one can risk a crass generalization and say that the dominant modern Indian intellectual mentality has been to take approbation from the international community as the goal of diplomacy and international discourse.[17] A rough comparison may be with China, whose leadership concentrates, rather, on getting maximal freedom to pursue its own instrumentalist ends and only seeks to manage international reactions in this regard. Successive Indian governments have sought to gain some sort of 'respect', through having a voice in international affairs, with little thought of direct economic benefits to the state. Until well into the 1990s, the economic dimension of international influence, so well grasped by East Asian countries, was utterly ignored by the Indian foreign policy establishment; it is still viewed with extreme suspicion by rigorous anti-capitalist intellectuals who are more active in India than in practically any other country. This is not a party political issue. The idea of 'swadeshi' or 'self-nationhood', originally an idea due to Gandhi concerning economic and political independence but later coming to imply a protected domestic economy, has appeal to socialists as much as to the protectionist wing of the Hindutva movement. Every government since 1991 has pursued a policy of opening India up to the international economy and deregulating the domestic economy, while facing stiff opposition from unions, anti-capitalists and anti-internationalists, the latter two from both within party cadres (but outside government) and the political opposition.[18] By the turn of the century, however, economic policy had become central to international strategy; the Marxist-led government of West Bengal has been an enthusiastic seeker of foreign direct investment.

However, there is also a great deal of worry, across the political spectrum, about liberalization. One type of worry is cultural and concerns the perception of threat from the West regarding everything from sexual mores, food and clothing to patterns of worship. The other is economic: job losses through competitiveness, environmental degradation and population displacement through development. A good deal of the resistance to governmental strategies comes from sources that are intrinsically suspicious of all statal activity and regard nation-based ambitions as irrelevant or even dangerous. But our analysis of the source of the appeal to Hindu nationalism concerns those who respond to these issues through electoral choice.

The debate, then, is complex, for it combines (i) the issue of how India's status in the world can be secured with (ii) concerns over whether economic liberalization is the way to secure either international power or domestic prosperity. The common factor in all this is the question of whether any political party in power can secure any of these ends. Can it make India strong in the world? Can it do so by managing the globalization of the economy? Can it resist the destabilizing consequences of such globalization?

Hindutva ideology is thought by those who support the BJP to possess a vision of a strong state appropriate for these ends. Originally, untested in governance, the BJP could invariably call for a hawkish stance on a variety of international issues. In power, the BJP briefly fulfilled expectations (and fears) by conducting nuclear tests in May 1998, although previous governments (especially the non-Congress United Front in 1996–7) had come close to doing so. But subsequent events have shown the BJP to be no different from any other Indian government in its general strategic attitudes and failures. The BJP-led government came closer to gaining security in Indo-Pakistan relations than any previous government, through direct and high-level diplomacy. This resulted in a relaxation of intelligence gathering that allowed for the incursion of Pakistani-supported militants into Kashmir in 1999. In the subsequent war, despite *Hindutva* demands for extreme action, the government allowed the Indian Army to fight with one arm tied, by refusing to allow counter-incursions to Pakistan to secure the heights commanded by the intruders. This incurred higher casualties and caused domestic uproar, but decisively changed Western governments' attitudes to the Indo-Pakistani conflict over Kashmir in favour of India. The irony lay in a Hindu-nationalist party garnering support for India through militarily risky restraint; geo-strategic calculations had won over ideological urges.

Support for the BJP from the middle classes is calibrated through perceived efficiency (allowing cynically for political rhetoric and the compromises of power). There is much on this in the Indian English-language media, and commands support in the intelligentsia. The economic strategy of the National Democratic Alliance, of which the BJP is the dominant partner, is scrutinized, supported or opposed by this economically powerful section of society with these concerns in mind, rather than any possible religious implication; after all, there seldom is any. As the international benefits – especially through United States, British and French commitment to greater economic and political cooperation – of the unideological restraint during the Kargil War became evident, this section of Indian society began to see the BJP as a reasonably responsible leader of a coalition government. This attitude to the BJP, and *Hindutva* indirectly, dominates the popular Western media picture of India as supportive of religious ideology (even though, as we have just seen, some of the problems of the BJP domestically have been precisely because it is thought to have jettisoned its ideology). But it does not directly alter the ground realities of communal conflict, and indeed constrains it through demands of efficiency.

The wider, *semi-urban and rural* anxiety is caused by immediate pressures over scarce resources. *Hindutva* has been used to mobilize Hindus by blaming continued scarcity on the supposedly disproportionate share of resources enjoyed by the 'minorities'. In the survey of the BJP's rise to power, we saw how important, indeed central, this was to *Hindutva* political strategy. This type of support for *Hindutva* is at local and state level, often extra-parliamentary and the locus of violence. Indian-language newspapers, especially in the North, articulate and motivate these forces. The violent result is reported (rightly with horror) in Indian-English and international media.

The economic standing of this section of the population is uncertain. Unlike the urban middle classes who aspire to international standards of living and are quick to evaluate any government's achievements, this section of society feels threatened by caste- and religion-based groups in its socio-economic vicinity. The growth of targeted populism that we described earlier has allowed many disadvantaged groups to articulate protest through the political process, using the ready-made constituency of the caste to propel local leaders into positions of state and central power. The so-called 'cow-belt' of North India, where the BJP first started building its strength, has been characterized precisely by this process. The Congress struggled to keep the support of groups which realized that they did not need its traditional intermediation. New parties directly based on the electoral strength of these groups arose, and the BJP attempted to address those who felt left out in this bidding war. However, after being in power in the most populous state in India, Uttar Pradesh, the BJP has had to answer to the electorate and has been punished nearly as much as the Congress, which in the decades after Independence was unassailable there. Parties catering to and arising out of Backward Caste considerations dominated politics in this and neighbouring states by 2000. So, it is quite reasonable to conclude that the BJP has been able to come to power by claiming to be able to assuage the anxieties of middle- and upper-caste Hindus, but it cannot sustain its base on ideology alone. It is just as vulnerable to the calculated decisions of the electorate as any other party.

The biography of the BJP is now no longer the story of *Hindutva*. In power at the centre, it is now the target of discontent when it is unable to deliver on economic promises implicit in its rhetoric of an India in which Hindus have their fair share. (For what other share than of economic goods ultimately matters for most people in a developing society?) It is left to other, non-political elements (some organized, others chaotic) to express and channel the anger of discontented Hindus. At most, this is left to back-bench members of the BJP, who have specific constituencies where such inflammatory rhetoric is worthwhile in political terms; but they have a delicate and problematic relationship with members of the government, whose interests they indirectly threaten by encouraging communal disorder.

The BJP can preserve its base here only by actually delivering on its economic promises. But in this, it cannot do anything radically different; all Indian governments now have to balance the demands of the globalizing economy of India with the imperatives of social justice. The appeal of the BJP, then, is shaky in this constituency. Here are the numbers required for it to be a national party; but that is insufficient for power, which can be had only through a delicate and complex coalition of parties, each with its own constituency. There could be cause to think that if more people in India felt unequivocally like the core semi-urban and rural supporters of the BJP, the party would be tempted to cash in on its ideological reserves of communalism. But as three successive elections have shown, not only is there a limit to the core appeal of the BJP, its chances of doing well are increased precisely when it is constrained by alliances with different types of appeal. The BJP can, then, do little but negotiate with its partners for a sufficient share of resources to preserve its base; and they will compromise with it because their own hopes of national power rest on alliance with it. But this painful transactional process is far removed from the urgent violence which first drew the attention of the world to the BJP.

Pure ideology and the demands of governance

Violence against religious minorities since the BJP came to power potentially threatens to be a more elusive problem to diagnose and respond. As I have mentioned, the exact relationship between the BJP and the violence caused by its oppositional rhetoric in the 1980s and 1990s is still debated in India, especially in legal terms. The moral responsibility of many in the BJP is clear. The connection with other elements in the *Sangh Parivar* is unquestionable. The complexity at the start of the twenty-first century lies in the continuation of ideologically expressive violence under a BJP-led government.

This state of affairs is evident when we look at the comparatively new victimization of Christians. As the BJP government leadership sees little value and, indeed, much harm in explicitly anti-Muslim rhetoric, a vacuum has been created in discourse on the Other. The local economic and social anger that was in the past manipulated against Muslims is now often directed against Christians. For example, when missionary activity is accompanied by infusions of money into converted communities, the simple fact of differential wealth is expressed as a threat to Hindu society, where the account has it that Hindus become Christians because of money. All Christians are then targeted, as they are alleged to be complicit in this erosion of culture. This sort of violence, however, is a matter of law and order, and the BJP-led government has no choice but to pursue the perpetrators; indeed, the BJP's partners specially pressure it to respond quickly, so as to demonstrate that they are not communally tainted by association with the BJP.

While it is certainly true that some of the violence against religious minorities is driven by local manipulation of religious identities for crude economic ends, many other instances are not so easily explicable. It must also be kept in mind that, in all this time, while violence may have been encouraged and motivated by economic ends, its actual occurrence has often been without obvious reductive explanation; the violence just happens, through sociopathic patterns whose study is beyond the remit of this chapter. But what is difficult to deal with here is that many cases of incitement to and perpetration of violence seem to be 'genuinely' driven by ideology. The analysis of the situation, when the BJP has been in power for some time, shows that the motivational roots of violence have thickened ideologically and withered instrumentally.

This raises the question of treatment. If violence is a tactic adopted by a party to gain political power, then, opposing the party and stopping it getting power would seem the obvious thing to do. Diagnosis of communal violence and opposition to *Hindutva* attempts to gain power have gone together for some time. But now, communal violence is a problem precisely for the BJP, for it is in charge of law and order and it has to account for itself to an electorate impatient for it to govern competently. Purely ideological violence is highly problematic because it is not clear in what practical way opposition to its perpetrators can be expressed. Of course, immediate and highly local counter-marches, vigilance, grassroots protective mobilization of vulnerable groups, and so on can take place, but by their very nature, they are specific in locale and participation, where outside involvement only complicates matters by throwing up questions about motives. What to make of people prepared to commit violence purely through convictions about religion and identity?

191

This is the challenge as much to the BJP-led government as to anyone else. The very fact that this is so alters our understanding of communal violence in India today. It is possible that in the future, a Hindu national- ism party may remobilize and propagate violence as an instrument for the attainment of power; but that does not seem the mostly likely scenario to project from the present situation. For now, our study suggests that continuing violence is because there is still scope for articulating resent- ment in religious terms. What can a BJP-led government do?

It would seem that, while purely ideological violence exists, the poten- tial for it to spread still remains a matter of economic anxiety. To treat communal tension requires efficiency on the part of the state in delivering resources to those in conflict and in deformative social competition. The great struggle in the political economy is between the compulsions of tar- geted populism, which we have looked at, and the demands of global com- petitiveness. That is why illegal redirection of electricity and water to favoured people is tolerated through bribery and the complicity of politi- cians, even while India becomes the most competitive provider of high-skill software. (But complexity is a matter of political scale: consider how strange it is that 'Europe' can have appalling war and absurd luxury cars within it; but that is the range 'India' encompasses.) Any government in India has to work with the deinstitutionalized corruption of governmental systems while attempting to create the infrastructure for both wealth- creation and social redistribution. In brutally reductivist terms, it is the betterment of the economic prospects of the populace that removes the immediate catalysts for violence: anxiety over scarce resources, the percep- tion of threat over access to those resources, the calculation that the cer- tainty of violence now can remove the uncertainty of negotiation later. In brief, in a richer country, there would be less urgency to violence. It is only then that the institutions of good governance could have the wherewithal: police forces with sufficient training, the national Human Rights Commis- sion with sufficient resources, a basic social security net. Practically all the procedural failures to respond to social breakdown effectively could be corrected with 'mere' money. The social argument for liberalization is driven by the conviction that working with the global economic order, albeit with national interests in mind (incidentally, the anodyne re- definition of 'swadeshi' by the BJP foreign and finance ministers), will bring such growth in national resources as can treat social pathologies. As problems of economic justice and environmental sustainability (which the rich countries have effectively and unfairly bypassed) are intrinsic to the economic process, the implications of the effort to ameliorate communal tensions through liberalization are ramifying.

This falls far short of any grand plan for removing communal violence from India but it goes further than the facile condemnation of Indian political processes, especially among Western academics and the popular media. The advances of the material conditions of life will lessen the pressure on interpreting scarcity in terms of religio-cultural ideology. Whatever the outcome of the revaluation of the nature of the Indian polity, *Hindutva* could become a matter of 'mere' prejudice (such as most Western democracies seem prepared to sustain) rather than violation of the rights of Indians from different socio-religious groups.

Afterword: Gujarat and after, or *Hindutva* at the cross-roads

At the time of writing the chapter, a different tension – which became bleakly evident in the violent events in Gujarat in early 2002 – had not become clear, although it had developed over the period of the BJP-led government at the Centre. This tension is the *Hindutva* version of the long-standing Indian dialectic between the Centre and the federal states, with similar resulting ambiguities of political interaction and ideological variation. In brief, when violent Hindu groups began targeting Muslim localities ostensibly in revenge for the burning by a Muslim group of nearly sixty Hindus on a train, the government of Gujarat, run by a Chief Minister who had been formerly general secretary of the BJP and an apparently technocratic moderate, appeared to let the violence run its course for two days. Worse, he said that the brutal anti-Muslim program had been a 'natural response' to the original massacre. The Central government, in the surprising form of the so-called 'hardliner', the Home Minister, L.K. Advani, initially took an unsympathetic stance against the Gujarat government, and the Prime Minister talked of a 'national shame'. This attitude appeared to exemplify the Central government's recognition of larger interests – the pressure from its coalition partners as well as India's international image – and the post-ideological demands of successful governance. But gradually, as it began to emerge that the core of the *Hindutva* constituency in Gujarat (and, less so, elsewhere) thought well of Chief Minister Narendra Modi, the BJP high command, which had not yet given into demands for his dismissal, refused to move against him. At the time of writing, it was striking that the violence, while still simmering in Gujarat (where the *Hindutva* movement appeared to have progressed further in its ideological aims than elsewhere), had not spread to even other communally mixed areas of India. The *Hindutva* movement, as a whole, would appear to be at a cross-roads. During its term of office, the

BJP has lost most of the states that it held before coming to shared power at the Centre. Some of the erosion could be precisely because it has not been as ideologically focused on *Hindutva* as its extreme supporters had hoped; but in the main, this is because it has not been evaluated highly by the electorate on the tests of governance. Gujarat, therefore, presents a problem. Does the support that has firmed up for the Gujarat state BJP as a result of the violence against Muslims indicate the need for a return to inflammatory mobilization at the national level? Or does the apparent exceptionalism of Gujurat during and after the riots of February 2002 indicate exactly the limits of *Hindutva*'s appeal? After all, the effort on the part of the non-parliamentary sections of the *Hindutva* movement to re-ignite the issue of a temple at Ayodhya on the site of the destroyed Babri *masjid* in 2001–2 garnered hardly any new support. There may be no clear decision within the BJP on whether to relapse into violently ideo- logical attempts at mobilization or whether to gain a more sustainable range of support through political moderation in an irreducibly pluralistic parliament. This uncertainty may well be manifested in the next general election and thereafter. Every instance of a Gujarat-style eruption puts back the time when *Hindutva* might be 'just' ideology; that time might well be only asymptomatically reached. The spiralling of anti-immigrant prejudice in 'rich' Europe indicates that few exclusionisms ever disappear through economic prosperity. But the progressive integration of many sec- tions of the BJP into the tumultuous but democratic parameters of Indian governmentality appears, still, to indicate that the imperatives of gover- nance might yet come to subsume those of communal ideology. But the story is far from complete.

Notes

1 For a full analysis, see Chakravarthi Ram-Prasad, '*Hindutva* ideology: extract- ing the fundamentals', *Contemporary South Asia*, vol. 2, 1993, pp. 285–309.
2 This formulation suggests exclusivity because only that life is regarded as truly religious which is guided by the fundamentals of that religion, and con- ceivably, this need not be the case. There can be a fundamentalism which holds that while being guided by the fundamentals of a particular religion makes a life truly dedicated to that religion, other lives can be truly religious in other religions when they are guided by the fundamentals of those other religions. Such an inclusivist fundamentalism is rare, but also problematic. After all, the primary justification for adherence to the fundamentals of a particular religion is that they, rather than those of another religion, are *right*.
3 See Chapter 5 in this volume, Nancy T. Ammerman, 'Re-awakening a sleeping giant: Christian fundamentalists in late twentieth-century US society'.

4 H. von Stientencron, 'Hinduism: on the proper use of a deceptive term', in G.D. Sontheimer and H. Kulke (eds) *Hinduism Reconsidered*, Delhi: Manohar, 1989, pp. 11–27.

5 R. Inden, *Imagining India*, Oxford: Blackwell, 1990.

6 P. Chatterjee, 'History and the nationalization of Hinduism', in V. Dalmia and H. von Stietencron (eds) *Representing Hinduism: The Construction of Religious Traditions and National Identity*, New Delhi: Sage Publications, 1995, pp. 103–28.

7 S. Sarkar, 'Indian nationalism and the politics of *Hindutva*', in D. Ludden (ed.) *Making India Hindu: Religion, Community, and the Politics of Democracy in India*, Delhi: Oxford University Press, 1996, pp. 270–94, especially on lower-caste aspirations.

8 R. Thapar, 'Imagined religious communities? Ancient history and the modern search for a Hindu identity', *Modern Asian Studies*, vol. 23, 1989, pp. 209–32.

9 For a modern Islamicist perspective on this period, see *A History of the Freedom Movement (Being the Story of Muslim Struggle for the Freedom of Hindu-Pakistan, 1707–1947)*, Karachi: Pakistan Historical Society, 4 volumes, n.d.

10 See G. Pandey, *The Construction of Communalism in Colonial North India*, Delhi: Oxford University Press, 1990, on this process for the entire period leading up to Independence.

11 For a fluent and accessible treatment of this question, see S. Khilnani, *The Idea of India*, London: Penguin, 1998.

12 Although this is my own analysis, for a range of views on modern India and religious pluralism (especially the presence of Islam), see H.G. Coward (ed.) *Modern Indian Responses to Religious Pluralism*, Albany, NY: State University of New York Press, 1987.

13 For the seminal study of the rise of Hindu nationalism, see W.K. Anderson and S.D. Damle, *The Brotherhood in Saffron: The Rashtriya Swayamsevak sangh and Hindu Revivalism*, Boulder, CO: Westview, 1987.

14 C. Jaffrelot, *Hindu Nationalist Movement in India*, New York: Columbia University Press, 1996.

15 T.B. Hansen, *The Saffron Wave: Democracy and Hindu Nationalism in Modern India*, Princeton, NJ: Princeton University Press, 1999.

16 For a sophisticated study of violence, see Stanley J. Tambiah, *Leveling Crowds: Ethnonationalist Conflicts and Collective Violence in South Asia*, Berkeley, CA: University of California Press, 1996.

17 On a succinct academic statement of the political case, see J. Manor and G. Segal, 'Taking India seriously', *Survival*, vol. 40, 1998, pp. 53–70.

18 J.D. Sachs, A. Varshney and N. Bajpai (eds) *India in the Era of Economic Reforms*, Delhi: Oxford University Press, 1999.

Select bibliography

Bagchi, A., 'Predatory commercialization and communalism in India', in S. Gopal (ed.) *Anatomy of a Confrontation: Ayodhya and the Rise of Communal Politics in India*, London: Zed Books, 1993, pp. 193–218.

Crossman, B. and Kapur, R., *Secularism's Last Sigh? Hindutva and the (Mis)rule of Law*, Delhi: Oxford University Press, 1999.

Gold, D., 'Organised Hinduism: from Vedic truth to Hindu nation', in Martin E. Marty and R. Scott Appleby (eds) *Fundamentalisms Observed*, Chicago: Chicago University Press, 1991.

Hansen, T.B., *The Saffron Wave: Democracy and Hindu Nationalism in Modern India*, Princeton, NJ: Princeton University Press, 1999.

Jaffrelot, C., *Hindu Nationalist Movement in India*, New York: Columbia University Press, 1996.

Ludden, D. (ed.), *Making India Hindu: Religion, Community, and the Politics of Democracy in India*, Delhi: Oxford University Press, 1996.

Madan, T.N., *Modern Myths, Locked Minds: Secularism and Fundamentalism in India*, Delhi: Oxford University Press, 1997.

Ram-Prasad, Chakravarthi, '*Hindutva* ideology: extracting the fundamentals', *Contemporary South Asia*, vol. 2, 1993, pp. 285–309.

Ram-Prasad, Chakravarthi, 'Hindu nationalism and the international relations of India', in K. Dark (ed.) *Religion and International Relations*, Basingstoke: Macmillan, 2000.

9

RELIGIONS, HUMAN RIGHTS AND SOCIAL CHANGE

R. Scott Appleby

As the Cold War ended, religious communities were presented with challenging new opportunities to serve the cause of peace. The context for this development was a renewal of 'rights talk' around the world that had its beginnings in the 1960s. The states of Latin America and Eastern Europe, whose political discourse was impoverished of human rights discourse and characterized by 'excessively strong and simple duty talk', embraced democracy and moved to strengthen legal protections of the rights of individuals and minorities. The discussion of democracy and human rights became *de rigueur* in the Middle East, Africa and Asia as well – even for governments that preferred to avoid it. In the United States, social critics reassessed an 'American rights dialect' that had been impoverished by absolute formulations and excessive concentration on the autonomous and self-sufficient individual at the expense of the community.[1]

In the 1980s and 1990s religious leaders and scholars initiated internal debates and external dialogues on the religious sources and meanings of universal human rights. Policy-makers as well as scholars came to see religious communities as cornerstones of cultures of non-violence and civic tolerance. These communities often obliged, by claiming a long-standing witness to 'human rights' in ancient scriptures and ethical traditions. Some appropriated elements of the new rights talk or hastened to formulate their own parallel discourses in which rights talk was challenged or complemented by the delineation of responsibilities to religion and society. Protestant, Catholic and Jewish leaders responded to the excesses of radical individualism in North America, for example, by promoting a countervailing discourse of civic responsibility in service to the common good, and by reminding their fellow citizens of the long-standing contributions of religious communities to the cultivation of civic virtues and social accountability.[2] Muslims initiated a far-reaching debate over 'Islamic

197

democracy' and 'Islamic human rights' in the Middle East, Africa and South Asia.[3]

In regions experiencing rapid social and political transitions which opened spaces for religious innovation, differentiation and growth, the role of religions in defining and protecting human rights was hotly contested. 'Soul wars' erupted between Roman Catholics and Evangelical Protestants in Latin America, between Christians and Muslims in Africa, and in the countries of the former Soviet bloc, where the explosion of religious diversity tested the region's capacity to tolerate religious diversity and accommodate genuine pluralism under the law.[4]

Religious institutions and actors who serve as agents of human rights face considerable opposition, not least from their own co-religionists. Religiously motivated actors on both sides of the Arab–Israeli conflict are prominent among the uncompromising 'rejectionists' who oppose peace accords, negotiated settlements and power-sharing agreements. States ruled in whole or part by a religious coalition are major violators of human rights. Extremist versions of Islam, usually seen as an opponent of women's rights in particular and human rights in general, have held power in Iran, Sudan and Afghanistan; other manifestations pose a serious threat to secular regimes in Egypt, Algeria and Pakistan. Human rights groups have long campaigned against the Arab-led Islamic government of Sudan, for example, accusing it of genocide because of its brutal repression of black African Sudanese southerners, who are Christians or followers of traditional religions. And even in places like Indonesia, South Africa and Nigeria, where they are a small minority, religious extremists are grouped in cadres or militias dedicated to destabilizing religiously tolerant governments and harassing religious and ethnic minorities. Similarly, Hindu nationalism, a form of ethno-religious chauvinism, exerts considerable influence on the Indian state and its current policies.

The fundamentals of fundamentalism

Nevertheless, the sweeping judgement that all 'fundamentalists' are alike, and dangerous to Western interests, trades in hyperbole. First of all, tarring every religiously orthodox, literate, and committed believer with the pejorative label 'fundamentalist' erases the enormous distance, for example, between ordinary, pious Muslims and bomb-throwing 'Islamic terrorists'. It also flies in the face of the fact that many pious Muslims, Hindus, Christians, and Jews strenuously object to the implication that their extremist co-religionists, who are a minority in every religious tradition, are the only believers actually upholding or defending the basic tenets of the faith. And it also conveniently overlooks the fact that radical or extremist religious movements, even those rooted in transnational 'world' religions such as Christianity or Islam, are inherently local in character, and incoherent as regional or global entities.

For all these reasons, religious extremism must be analysed not as a civilizational or transnational force, but on a case-by-case basis. And the framework for such analysis must rest on an understanding of the distinction between the two major forms of religious extremism: 'fundamentalism' and 'ethno-religious nationalism'.

Used properly, the term 'fundamentalism' refers to an identifiable pattern of religious militance in which self-styled true believers attempt to arrest the erosion of religious identity by outsiders, fortify the borders of the religious community, and create viable alternatives to secular structures and processes. Their definition of 'outsiders' tends to be elastic, frequently extending beyond missionaries of other faiths and foreign troops stationed on the country's sacred ground to Western businessmen, educational and social service volunteers, relief workers and professional international peacekeepers. In addition, the extremists count among their enemies their own co-religionists – fellow Muslims or Jews or Christians or Hindus – who advocate pluralism and tolerance, as well as government officials and those with no religious faith at all. In each of these categories, the religious extremists are the sworn enemies of pluralism, the legally protected co-existence of a variety of religious and secular practices and ways of life.

Fundamentalists perceive their opponents as either intentional or inadvertent agents of secularization, which they see as a process through which traditional religions and religious concerns are gradually relegated to the remote margins of society. There they can die a harmless death, eliminated by what the Iranian intellectual Jalal Al-e Ahmad called the 'sweet, lethal poison' of 'Westoxication'.

To counter these 'attacks', fundamentalists instinctively turn to a selective retrieval of the sacred past – lines or passages from the group's holy book, the traditional teachings of a guru or prophet, or heroic deeds or episodes from a mythologized golden age (or moment of tragedy). These stories and lessons help justify a programme of action designed to protect and bolster the besieged 'fundamentals' of the religion and to fend off or conquer the outsiders. The agenda expands to include the attainment of greater political power, the transformation of the surrounding political culture, the moral purification of society and, in some cases, secession from the secular state or the creation of a 'pure' religious homeland.

Ideologically, fundamentalists see sacred truths as the foundation of genuine knowledge, and religious values as the base and summit of morality – a trait they generally share with traditional believers. But because the fundamentalists themselves have been formed by secular modernity, or in reaction against it, they are in self-conscious competition with their peers in the secular sciences. Yet they also set the terms of the competition by presenting their sacred texts and traditions – their intellectual resources, so to speak – as inherently free from error and invulnerable to the searching critical methods of secular science, history, cultural studies and literary theory. Having subordinated secular to sacred epistemology, fundamentalists feel free to utilize and even develop new forms of computer and communications technology, scientific research, political organizations, and the like.

No matter how expertly or awkwardly they imitate secular moderns, however, fundamentalists remain dualists at heart; they imagine the world divided into unambiguous realms of light and darkness peopled by the elect and reprobate, the pure and impure, the orthodox and the infidel. Many if not all fundamentalists further dramatize this Manichean worldview by setting it within an apocalyptic framework: the world is in spiritual crisis, perhaps near its end, when God will bring terrible judgement upon the children of darkness. When the children of light are depicted in such millenarian imaginings as the agents of this divine wrath, violent intolerance towards outsiders appears justified on theological grounds.

Whatever specific theological resources the host religious tradition may (or may not) have for legitimating a departure from normal operating procedures, fundamentalists believe themselves to be living in a special dispensation – an unusual, extraordinary time of crisis, danger, apocalyptic doom, the advent of the Messiah, the Second Coming of Christ, the return of the Hidden Imam, etc. This 'special time' is exceptional not only in the sense of being unusual; its urgency requires true believers to make exceptions, to depart from the general rule of the tradition.[5]

This provides an answer to the puzzling question: How does a religious tradition that normally preaches nothing but peace, compassion, forgiveness and tolerance, adopt the discourse of intolerance and violence? It does so in the belief that 'These are not normal times.' Thus certain Zionist rabbis in Israel invoked the *halakhic* norm of *pikuach nefesh* in ruling that the Oslo Accords threatened the very existence of Israel and Judaism itself. This interpretation impelled several '*yeshiva* boys' to carry out the 1995 assassination of the 'traitorous' Prime Minister Itzhak Rabin. Similarly, Ayatollah Khomeini made the extraordinary ruling that the survival of the Islamic Republic of Iran demanded that parts of the Islamic law putatively governing it were to be suspended in deference to the Supreme Jurist's (that is, Khomeini's) own *ad hoc* rulings.

Organizationally, fundamentalist movements form around male charismatic or authoritarian leaders. The movements begin as local religious enclaves but become increasingly capable of rapid functional and structural differentiation and of international networking with like-minded groups from the same religious tradition. They usually recruit rank-and-file members from the general population, but they are often particularly successful in appealing to young, educated males who are unemployed or underemployed (and, in some cases, from the universities and the military). The movement imposes strict codes of personal discipline, dress, diet and other markers that serve subtly or otherwise to set group members apart from others in the society.

Fundamentalism: strong religion, weak nationalism

The salient characteristic of fundamentalism is its concern with religious erosion. Fundamentalist militancy borrows *animus* and attitudes from age-old religious orthodoxies; it is born and thrives within the context of the more widespread and diffuse social phenomenon known as a religious revival. And, like a cult or new religion, a fundamentalist movement may depend heavily on charismatic leadership and innovative religious practices. Drawing on all these religious streams, fundamentalism is identical to none of them. Rather, it is a distinctive religious phenomenon, shaped profoundly by the conservative religious encounter with secular modernity – and by the fateful decision, taken by the 'angry religious conservatives' who became fundamentalists, to battle secular modernity on its own turf.

Practically, that decision meant that fundamentalists draw on radio, television, audiocassettes, faxes, the Internet, Stinger missiles, black markets, think tanks, paleontological 'evidence' for the young earth theory, identity politics, and modern marketing techniques, to terrorist tactics – all turned to militant or extremist religious ends. Yet fundamentalists' organizational and ideological power remains rooted in the host religious tradition.

If fundamentalists are committed to the consolidation of the host religion's political hegemony within the state, they are weak in the art of 'nation-building', in bringing together into a viable political coalition the various groups and peoples living within the boundaries of a 'nation'. As political actors fundamentalists are exceptionally vulnerable to fissure, fragmentation and political instability. They are faced with a serious dilemma: abandon the absolutism and exclusivism that inspired and fuelled the movement in its formative phase and made it 'fundamentalist', or relax religious and moral standards to allow for a broader coalition that enables effective governance.

Their core activists are literate in, and practitioners of, the host religious tradition. This inner core, peopled by religious 'zealots', causes problems for fundamentalist governance of ethnically and/or religiously hetero-geneous populations – that is, for the governance of most populations existing around the world in the twenty-first century.

Ethno-religious extremism: weak religion, strong nationalism

The other major expression of religious extremism, ethno-religious nationalism, also fails to produce effective political leaders from the religious community, but for different reasons. Here the religious component is often weak, under-developed and dependent on secular nationalist politicians and parties. Rather than produce national religio-political leaders, these movements lend religious prestige to ethnic and nationalist leaders.

As the pattern of religious violence in Northern Ireland, India or the former Yugoslavia makes clear, religious actors may identify their tradition so closely with the fate of a people or a nation that they perceive a threat to either as a threat to the sacred. While the primary focus of funda-mentalist energies is the host religion, which they seek to defend, bolster, re-interpret and revive, religious nationalists feel that the most direct route to purifying or strengthening the host religion is the establishment of a political collective within which the religion is privileged and its enemies disadvantaged. The nation-building project of the post-colonial era pro-vided opportunities for some communal groups in South Asia, for example, to monopolize the state apparatus and to dominate, incorporate or diminish other groups. Communalism attracts both majorities and minorities, elites and masses, who complain that the post-independence secular order has left them 'victimized' and grasping for their share of edu-cational opportunities, capital assets, occupational training and jobs. The proliferation of communal politics, in turn, has arisen out of the political arithmetic of majority rule: the competition for resources and benefits requires the formation of coalitions of 'ethnic concerns and interests acting as a monolithic principle, vertically integrating a people differentiated by class'. Majoritarian dominance, experienced as exploitation and oppres-sion by an ethno-religious minority, lies at the root of the conflicts in Northern Ireland and Sri Lanka as well.

In such settings religion can become a powerful means of binding together racial, linguistic, class and territorial markers of identity. In the process of 'hardening', religion provides not only the dedicated cadres of young extremists but also the public rituals and processions that bind religious and ethno-nationalist sentiments together and become occasions for intolerance and arenas of collective violence.

The *Hindutva* movement in India has configured itself as one such collective. Allied with secular politicians in the governing *Bharatiya Janata Party* (BJP), its goal is the creation of a representative structure resembling the secular nation–state but pursuing a policy of civic intolerance towards 'outsiders' (that is, non-Hindus). Yet as the host religion for the nationalist movement flying the saffron flag of Hindustan, the imaginary Hindu nation, Hinduism is a weak vessel for religious fundamentalism. It lacks a strong historical sense of itself as an organized religion, with a body of revealed religious law and a concept of God acting dramatically within history to bring it to a definitive conclusion. Perhaps for the same reasons, however, Hinduism does lend itself powerfully to the cause of nationalist movements constructed around the fluid categories of 'religion' and 'ethnicity' and drawing on a mix of secular and religious symbols and concepts, religious and non-religious actors.

In fact, like 'Hinduism' itself, Hindu nationalism is clearly a construct designed to challenge the secular, pluralist order in India. It has borrowed from the Abrahamic traditions both an eschatology of ultimate destiny (with the Hindu nation depicted as the realization of the mythical Kingdom of the Lord Ram) and the notion of a righteous elect representing the Aryan race: the celibate and highly disciplined staff of the National Union of Volunteers (RSS) and the World Hindu Party (VHP), many of whom are *brahmins* or members of other 'twice-born' castes.

The central concept of *Hindutva* – 'Hindu-ness' – defines the geographic, racial and religious boundaries of Hinduism and India alike. Sadly, the resulting inflammatory and diffuse appeals to 'Hindu national pride' in the face of perceived Muslim encroachments have produced a great deal of uncontrolled mob violence. Hindu nationalists calculate the potential advantages of such violence, including the opportunity a crisis situation presents for recruiting and mobilizing young men. They seek platforms for disseminating their ideology and create 'events' that publicize their cause. They redefine sacred land and sacred space in a controversial way, using the mass media coverage of their activism as a means of grabbing attention and mobilizing followers. The destruction by Hindu nationalists of the Babri mosque in Ayodhya followed a series of fiery speeches given by RSS leaders.

A similar dynamic shaped Serbian Orthodox extremists' alliance with Slobodan Milosevic in the run-up to the Bosnian War of 1991–5. 'The genocide in Bosnia was religiously motivated and religiously justified', Michael Sells writes:

> Religious symbols ... myths of origin (pure Serb race), symbols of passion, and eschatological longings (the resurrection of Lazar) were used by religious nationalists to create a reduplicating Milos Obilic [the assassin of Sultan Murat], avenging himself on the Christ killer, the race traitor, the alien, and, ironically, the falsely accused 'fundamentalist' next door.[6]

Although war in the former Yugoslavia featured a prominent religious element, this was a case not of fundamentalism, but of the manipulation of 'folk religion' to construct ethno-national legitimations for violence. The seeds of Serbian, Croatian and Bosnian religiosity were not stamped out under communist rule, even among the so-called secularized masses, but neither were they nurtured. Scattered and left untended, they were eventually planted in the crude soil of ethno-nationalism, ultimately coming to terrible fruition in the Bosnian genocide.

Religious actors as agents of human rights

In each of the settings described above, religious actors qualified as expert witnesses, so to speak, of human rights violations, as well as advocates of the extent and kind of religious human rights deserving protection. In some cases, they were prepared to relieve (or help prevent) the state from assuming the full burden of responsibility for defining and developing civil and political rights, 'second generation' social, cultural, and economic rights (for example, rights to education, employment, health care, child care, etc.) and 'third generation' environmental and developmental rights. Uniquely poised to mediate the encounter between the universal and culture-specific elements that must co-exist in any viable regime of human rights, religions are increasingly compelled to re-examine their practices in light of this new role and place in civil society. What does it mean, Christians are asking, for example, to disciple all nations when one accepts a universal regime of human rights and affirms its values of tolerance and respect for cultural integrity and belief?

The establishment of constitutional democracies around the world and the proliferation of international laws, treaties, covenants and other instruments devoted to the articulation and protection of human rights, promoted this kind of religious soul-searching. Jews, Muslims, Hindus and Christians have taken special note of Article 18 of the Universal Declaration of Human Rights, Article 18 of the International Covenant on Civil and Political Rights (ICCPR), and Articles 1 and 6 of the 1981 Declaration on the Elimination of All Forms of Intolerance and Discrimination Based on Religion or Belief.[7] Yet international covenants and laws, they also realize, are largely irrelevant to societies lacking a culture in which individual and minority rights are valued. Religions, contends John Witte, Jr, 'must be seen as a vital dimension of any legal regime of human rights. . . . Religions will not be easy allies to engage, but the struggle for human rights cannot be won without them.'[8]

The salient question is whether and how the scale of values governing local understandings of rights and responsibilities is generalizable across cultures and religions. The language of 'universal' human rights has inspired resistance from various quarters, including religious communities that see the attempt to build an international regime of human rights law as a new form of Western colonialism. The Universal Declaration of Human Rights and subsequent conventions impose post-Enlightenment ways of knowing and Western cultural assumptions and ideologies, opponents charge, which are no more universally binding than any other culturally determined set of principles. Asian leaders meeting in Bangkok in 1993, for example, voiced strenuous opposition to 'the universal human rights regime' because they perceived that such rights talk, formulated primarily by Westerners, reflects what they considered to be an excessive penchant for personal autonomy – a value given little priority in Asian cultures. By way of contrast, the Bangkok Governmental Declaration of 1993, issued during the same meeting by a group of Asian nations in advance of the Vienna World Conference on Human Rights, emphasized the principles of national sovereignty, territorial integrity and non-interference.[9]

Religious support for universalism

Certain principles are true apart from their level of inculturation in any given society. Accordingly, a regime of universal human rights necessarily transcends and thus stands in judgement of every particular social embodiment and normative order of rights and responsibilities. This, in fact, is what it means to honour a universal standard: all other normative orders of justice and rights must concede to its priorities. The forty-eight nations that voted to ratify the Universal Declaration of Human Rights in 1948 (none opposed, eight abstained) understood and accepted these fundamental notions. Furthermore, the objections of the fundamentalist critics notwithstanding, the post-war process of formulating universally binding principles and norms drew not only upon 'Western' conceptualizations of rights but was genuinely inclusive of a variety of cultural and religious perspectives around the world. In 1998, on the occasion of the fiftieth anniversary of the Universal Declaration, a prominent group of human rights activists, scholars and international lawyers reminded cultural relativists of this fact, and reinforced it with historical studies of the drafting of the document.[10]

Yet even among the nation–states, transnational agencies and moral communities that reached consensus on universal human rights and responsibilities, the specification of practices that violate or uphold them remains an arena of controversy. Basic questions are unresolved. Which practices fall within universal norms, which are left to cultural arbitration? Must a local regime of human rights be predicated on the priority of individual rights, or do the rights of a community take precedence? And what of nations and religious or sub-national ethnic communities not formally bound by the Universal Declaration of Human Rights and its principles – how and by whom are their interpretations and observances of 'human rights' to be evaluated and sanctioned? Cultural relativists argue, furthermore, that a uniform interpretation of basic human rights provisions is neither possible nor desirable. They point, for example, to Article 5 of the Universal Declaration of Human Rights, which stipulates that 'No one shall be subjected to torture, or to cruel, inhuman or degrading treatment or punishment.' Because understandings of human dignity tend to be indeterminate and culturally contingent, they contend, the precise meaning of this provision is not self-evident; practices defined as 'torture' in one culture may be absolved or approved by another.

There is, however, a middle course between the imposition of a universalist discourse and regime of law, and deference to a sort of indigenous cultural imperialism. Cultures can participate in the formulation and interpretation of universal human rights norms binding upon them. The human rights scholar Theo van Boven has recommended that the implementation of human rights instruments such as the Declaration on the Elimination of All Forms of Intolerance and Discrimination Based on Religion or Belief, should be accompanied by consultation and dialogue among interested groups, organizations, and movements from across a broad sociopolitical and religious spectrum.[11]

Can the world's religious communities be expected to take a leading – and constructive – role in such efforts? Organized religion has a mixed record. After World War II Jewish and Christian denominations were vigorous advocates of human rights, issuing bold confessional statements and assigning significant institutional resources to the cause. Jewish NGOs such as the World Jewish Congress made important contributions to the early development of human rights law, while individual religious leaders devoted their careers to advocacy, diplomacy and the reporting of human rights violations. Religious actors shaped the civil rights movement in the United States and revolted against oppressive colonial rule in Africa and Latin America.[12] Christian democratic movements contributed to the evolving discourse on human rights in Europe.[13]

In the 1980s and 1990s, as globalization both displayed and deepened the multicultural and religiously plural character of most developed and developing societies, a greater number and variety of religious actors and religious communities participated at each level of the cultural discourse on human rights. Religious NGOs developed expertise in human rights advocacy and monitoring,[14] human rights education consciousness-raising or 'conscientization',[15] humanitarian assistance to victims and legal representation for victims of human rights abuses,[16] and inter-religious and ecumenical relations.[17] Progressive leaders and activists from different religious traditions and communities found similar ways to sacralize human rights. They celebrate the memory of virtuous and holy 'progressives' from the religion's past, their lives interpreted and projected as embodiments of the tradition's core human rights values. Hindu human rights advocates, for example, hold up for emulation not only Gandhi, but also Rammohun Roy (1772–1833), the first able spokesperson of modern reformist Hinduism and a crusader against the practice of burning widows alive (*sati*). Roy, the founder of the *Brahmo Samaj*, a theistic, unitarian religious society open to all, devoted his life to clarifying and promoting the humane ethical values of ancient Indian spirituality.[18]

Progressives, in addition, gave much-needed attention to the elaboration of women's rights, freedoms and responsibilities. A generation of Jewish, Christian, Muslim, Buddhist and Hindu scholars and advocates – and their colleagues outside the tradition(s) – reinterpreted what they judged to be outdated teachings and practices, and pressed religious leaders to battle male chauvinism in religious communities.[19] Progressives produced an apologetical literature that attempted to account for and de-legitimate the expressions of extremism within their respective religious communities.[20]

Finally, progressives plumbed the tradition's teachings on war and peace, with the intent of strengthening aspects that amplify the religion's voice as an advocate of human rights and non-violent conflict transformation. In the wake of the 1990–1 Gulf War, Christians (and their non-Christian colleagues) reconsidered the viability of the just war theory and gave renewed attention to theologies of non-violence and pacifism, while Muslims (and their non-Muslim colleagues) revisited the concept of *jihad* with an eye to lifting up and thereby strengthening the scriptural and traditional warrants for non-violent resistance to oppression and injustice.[21] Jews drew together elements of a theory of conflict resolution from biblical *mitzvot* and rabbinic rationales.[22] Buddhists formed social movements which challenged the anti-democratic, corrupt and oppressive regimes of Burma, Thailand, Vietnam and Cambodia. Hindus challenged India's traditional caste-based economic and social discrimination, supporting the Mandal Commission's recommendation, in 1990, to reserve a larger number of federal and state jobs and admissions to educational institutions for the so-called backward castes at the expense of the upper castes.[23]

Whereas religious actors were among the notable champions of justice during the first half-century of the human rights era, the formal or official religious leadership too often failed to support the religious witness by giving it permanent institutional expression. Religious officials and institutional leaders, because they are charged with preserving and defending the faith in its concrete social, institutional (and bureaucratic) forms, tend in general to be more conservative – and more adverse to taking risks – than activists, scholars and community leaders. Yet the official leadership, more than other actors in the religious sector, command the material resources and enjoy the public prominence necessary to legitimate and deepen the faith tradition's commitment to social justice and the common good.

In the 1970s, however, religious officialdom squandered the momentum that had gathered in the 1960s. Most religious groups made only modest contributions to rights activism and to the theory and law of human rights. Religious leaders, with some notable exceptions, did not develop specific precepts or programmes to implement the general principles set out in the religious manifestoes of the 1960s, nor did they follow up their general endorsement of human rights instruments with effective lobbying and litigation. The relatively greater awareness and participation of religious communities in human rights campaigns in the 1980s and 1990s mainly served to underscore the fact that the world's major religious bodies possess the necessary conceptual and organizational resources to accomplish much more by way of imbedding the discourse and observance of universal rights more deeply in local cultures.

The religious leaders in the 1970s, to be fair, suffered a withering of support and encouragement from secular human rights activists, who were directing their inadequate resources to the most egregious violations of human rights – the physical abuses associated with war crimes, torture, imprisonment, rape, and so on. Religious groups and their rights were assigned a low priority, behind freedom of speech and press, race and gender issues, and provision of work and welfare. Left to their own devices, John Witte explains, many religious communities failed to muster the will or resources to oppose the oppression of belief and religious practice, or even to document the spiritual and moral abuses accompanying such oppression.

The exclusivist tendencies within most religious communities also impeded progress towards human rights advocacy. Perhaps the most difficult prospect for a religious community to contemplate is its own diminishment or displacement. Religious opponents of dialogue and conciliation with outsiders predicted that 'diminishment and displacement' would be the likely results of 'liberalizing' and tolerance-building measures. Enclave-builders portrayed the religion's truths, 'rights' and responsibilities as being inherently superior to those of their rivals. In their judgement the strength of the religious community's claim to the loyalty of its adherents rested on the community's ability to present itself as the exclusive bearer of specific moral and/or material benefits. Comparisons with other normative communities were invidious, and therefore useful in sustaining a climate of mistrust and mutual antagonism that reinforced the necessity of membership in the elect community.

Despite the propensity of embattled religious actors to exploit hostility towards the 'other', there are influential religious leaders in all major religious traditions who believe that commitment to one's own normative system can be compatible with openness to the 'other'. One can be fully committed to a religion and identify with co-believers for that purpose, they maintain, while also being fully committed to another normative system for its purposes. 'People can and do have multiple or overlapping identities,' writes a leading Muslim intellectual, 'and can and do cooperate with the "us" of each of their identities without being hostile to the "them" of one level of identity.'[24]

The challenge for religious supporters of universal human rights in the new century is to translate into popular religious idioms their vision of religion as a non-violent, tolerant and rights-bearing sacred trust. The challenge for their supporters is to bring that vision to life in local, national and regional institutions in settings where people are threatened by religious violence.

Islam's internal human rights debate

Who is correct – the proponents of Islam's compatibility with democracy or Muslims who claim that Islamic core values are antithetical to

Western-style democracy and the Universal Declaration of Human Rights and other human rights instruments? There are elements of truth in both descriptions of contemporary Islam.[25] Moreover, many of the questions posed of Islam could also be posed of other religious traditions at various times in their history, including the contemporary period – indeed, they can be posed of religion itself.

Islam's, or any other religion's, capacity for bestowing legitimacy on political leaders who advance policies conducive to civic and non-violent tolerance depends upon the situation of its progressive religious leaders and intellectuals – their status within the religious community and the nation, the binding authority of their interpretations of Islamic law, and the popular appeal of those interpretations. It also depends upon the flexibility of the religious tradition on the matter in question, the range of possibilities contained within the scriptural and traditional sources. The contemporary debate over Islamic polity and the future of Islamic politics demonstrates that shared commitment to the observance of Islamic law does not lead to uniformity or even commensurability of method among Islamists or among Muslims in general. Like any complex legal code, the Shari'a admits of many interpretations and diverse applications, each of which is unavoidably selective.[26]

The life and thought of Abdullahi Ahmed An-Na'im illustrate the dynamics of Islam's internal pluralism. As a young man in his thirties An-Na'im, then a Professor of Comparative Law at the University of Khartoum in his native Sudan, became a leader of an Islamic reform movement called the Republican Brothers. He argued eloquently for a retrieval and construction of Islamic law that would both demonstrate and advance its compatibility with 'universal' human rights. He also denounced Sudanese President Numeiri's brand of Islamic fundamentalism, shared in its broad purposes by *Sunni* extremists from Tunisia to Pakistan and by *Shi'ites* in thrall to Iran's Ayatollah Khomeini, as a mistaken and ill-fated attempt to impose the *Shari'a* as an antidote to Western neo-colonialism. For his patriotism An-Na'im was imprisoned without charge in 1984. Nevertheless he continued, while in prison and after his release, to insist that the elements of *Shari'a* invoked by Numeiri and Khomeini – namely, the guidelines on penal law, civil liberties, and the treatment of minorities and women set forth by the Prophet at Medina – promoted a 'historically dated Islamic self-identity that needs to be reformed'. Islamic social justice and the exercise of legitimate political power depend, according to An-Na'im, upon the retrieval of the teachings of the Prophet in Mecca, which constitute 'the moral and ethical foundation' of the tradition. 'The Medina message is not the fundamental, universal, eternal message of Islam. That founding message is from Mecca', he wrote. 'This counter-abrogation [of the Medina code] will result in the total conciliation between Islamic law and the modern development of human rights and civil liberties.'

Rare is the interpreter of religion who does not claim to be upholding its 'fundamentals'. Rather, the battle is often over what they are, where they are to be found, how and by whom they are to be interpreted. In demanding the retrieval of the Mecca prophecy, An-Na'im concluded, 'we [Republican Brothers] are the super-fundamentalists'.[27]

Professor An-Na'im went on to serve as Executive Director of Human Rights Watch/Africa and to teach human rights and comparative law in universities in Europe, Africa and North America; at the time of writing, he is Professor of Law and Fellow in Law and Religion at Emory University. Like several other gifted Muslim activists and intellectuals, An-Na'im is committed to the elaboration of an Islamic discourse of human rights by which Muslims might engage other rights traditions in mutually useful dialogue.[28]

An-Na'im defends the orthodoxy of this project even as he acknowledges the considerable opposition to it among powerful circles. 'I see the possibility and utility of overlapping identities and cooperations as integral to my faith as a Muslim, in accordance with verse 13 of Chapter 49 of the *Qur'an*', he writes, translating the verse as follows:

We [God] have created you [human beings] into [different] peoples and tribes so that you may [all] get to know [understand and cooperate with] each other; the most honourable among you in the sight of God are the pious [righteous] ones.

To An-Na'im this verse means that 'human diversity or pluralism (be it ethnic, religious or otherwise) is not only inherent in the divine scheme of things, but also deliberately designed to promote understanding and co-operation among various peoples'. The last part of the verse, he believes, indicates that one's morality is to be judged by the person's conduct, rather than by his or her membership of a particular ethnic or religious group.

Does this reading of the *Qur'an* reflect the sensibilities of Muslims caught in the crossfire in Bosnia, Kashmir, or Gaza, much less those who have taken up arms against the ethnic or religious other? Does it, in fact, reflect the sensibilities of most Muslims in general? In Islamic states, where there is no formally recognized separation between religion and law, mosque and state, *Shari'a* is enshrined and presented (if not always consistently implemented) as the final and ultimate formulation of the law of

God, not to be revised or reformulated by mere mortal and fallible human beings. The preamble to the Universal Islamic Declaration of Human Rights (1981) asserts that 'Islam gave to mankind an ideal code of human rights fourteen centuries ago.'[29] 'When Muslims speak about human rights in Islam', a Pakistani commentator noted, 'they mean rights bestowed by Allah the exalted in the Holy Koran; rights that are divine, eternal, universal, and absolute; rights that are guaranteed and protected through the *Shariah*.'[30] Whenever there is a conflict between Islamic law and international human rights law, according to this view, Muslims are bound to follow the former.[31]

An-Na'im readily admits that his choices and interpretations of *Qur'anic* passages 'are premised upon a certain orientation which may not be shared by all Muslims today'. Muslims 'of a different orientation', he notes, 'may choose to emphasize other verses of the *Qur'an* which do not support the principle of overlapping identities and cooperation with the "non-Muslim other", but are, instead, clearly exclusive in discriminating between "believers" and "non-believers"'. Indeed, one need not be an extremist to interpret the verses cited by An-Na'im as referring to diversity and pluralism *within* the *umma* rather than among humanity at large.[32]

How and by whom are the interpretive principles to be specified and defined for a transnational religious community without a centralized hierarchy such as Islam? How and by what criteria are those principles revised? Who, ultimately, has the authority to arbitrate and mediate between competing claims about the frame of interpretation and its application? The various schools of Islamic theology and jurisprudence, and the numerous opinions within each school, testify to the fact that Muslims have always differed, and will always differ, in their choice and interpretation of verses and laws to cite in support of their views. History indicates that a minority view can gain greater acceptance as Muslim politics and social orientations change, and as exposure to other worldviews – including alternate interpretations of Islam – alters Muslim perceptions of the behaviours and attitudes properly constituting the straight path.[33] If the force of a new idea grows strongest where social and political circumstances have rendered it plausible, it is also true that Muslims' orientations to the world are influenced not only by concrete gains but also by their hopes and struggles for improvement in existing social and political conditions.

Indeed, An-Na'im believes that a new Islamic hermeneutics for human rights can become a powerful tool for Muslims striving for a more just and equitable society. The new method of determining what constitutes authentic human rights under Islamic law, if not exactly more 'democratic' than traditional methods, would be more inclusive of 'the comprehension, imagination, and experience of Muslim peoples'. An-Na'im comments:

> In my view, the community of believers as a whole should be the living frame of interpretation and ultimate arbiter and mediator of interpretative rules, techniques and underlying assumptions. This seems to have been the case during the founding stages of major religions. Over time, however, a few tended to appropriate and monopolize the process of interpretation and turn it into an exclusive and technical science or art. Thus, the process of religious revival and reformation is often about breaking the monopoly of the clergy or technocrats of hermeneutics and reclaiming the right of the community to be the living frame of interpretation for their own religion and its normative regime.[34]

Today, in contrast to previous eras, the agency of the Muslim peoples themselves is 'simply unavoidable' in understanding the sacred sources, and in deriving from them ethical norms and legal principles to regulate individual behaviour and social relations. At the dawn of the twenty-first century, that is, the Muslim peoples live within the specific historical context of cultural modernity – the new global reality of political, economic and security interdependence that shapes the patterns by which they interact with other cultures and strive to improve their concrete circumstances.

The contemporary human rights discourse within Islam is a response to the demands and opportunities of this 'globalized' context. Muslim advocates of human rights, insisting that Islam comes to know itself more profoundly through interaction with other traditions, have collaborated with non-Muslim scholars of Islam and entered into dialogue with Christian and Jewish scholars on topics such as 'Western and Islamic perspectives on religious liberty'.[35] *Sunni* Arab Muslims have echoed the late King Hussein's call for an inter-religious dialogue on the religious and humanitarian values underlying the positions of the parties to the Arab–Israeli conflict, and they participated enthusiastically in cross-cultural conferences and symposia on secularity, Islam and human rights in the 1990s.[36] Human rights violations by Islamic authorities are often opposed and criticized by Muslims themselves.[37]

The Islamic Republic of Iran provides perhaps the most striking example of the emergence of Islamic 'rights talk' under the conditions of cultural modernity. With his brilliantly argued advocacy of human rights and democracy, formulated from the depths of the *Shi'ite* as well as the larger

Islamic jurisprudential tradition, Abdolkarim Soroush, the Iranian philosopher and public intellectual, has sparked a fascinating political debate in the home of the first 'fundamentalist' revolution. Popular among Iran's youth and technocratic elite but opposed by the ruling clerical elite, Soroush challenges the latter's political legitimacy and takes issue with the doctrine of *vilayat-i faqih* (guardianship of the Supreme Jurist), which stood at the heart of the Ayatollah Khomeini's religious ideology. For Soroush, religiously imposed ideology is a distortion of religious values. He holds up human rights as the criterion for governance of the Islamic state – the criterion that guarantees the state's religious as well as its democratic nature.

How does Soroush justify this seemingly radical reversal? While Islam as a religion is unchanging and eternal, he acknowledges, 'religious knowledge' (*ma'rifat-i dini*) – a branch of human knowledge produced by scholars engaged in the study of the sacred *Shi'ite* texts – is always in flux, conditioned by history and adaptive to the scientific understanding of the time. Shaped in the contemporary era by intense cultural interaction and popular awareness of political options, religious knowledge has found Islam and democracy to be compatible, Soroush believes.[38] In a democratic state, furthermore, human rights cannot be restricted to religiously derived rights alone. Muslims as well as non-Muslims derive their human rights not from their faith but from 'their membership within the larger group of humanity,' as Valla Vakili, a disciple of Soroush, puts it. Many Muslim opponents of democracy refer to it as *dimukrasi-yi gharbi* (Western democracy), thereby identifying it with the threatening 'other'.[39] Soroush, by contrast, considers democracy a form of government that is compatible with multiple political cultures, including Islamic ones. In Muslim societies, governments which derive their legitimacy from the people necessarily will be religious governments, duty bound to protect both the sanctity of religion and the rights of man. In defending the sanctity of religion, Soroush warns, the government must not privilege a particular conception of religion, lest it sacrifice human rights for ideological purity. The guiding criteria for governance must be human rights themselves rather than any particular religious ideology; indeed, Soroush argues, a society embraces religion in large part because it upholds the society's sense of justice. 'We do not draw [our conception of] justice from religion,' Soroush writes, 'but rather we accept religion because it is just.'[40] Today that includes a respect for human rights.

This appeal to external (that is, extra-religious) criteria to evaluate religion's fulfilment of its proper purposes, is perhaps the most striking and controversial aspect of Soroush's thought. It constitutes an invitation – an imperative – to cross-cultural and cross-disciplinary dialogue. Politically charged matters such as the relationship between religion and justice, though addressed by the *Qur'an* and other religious texts, can be defined for the present age, Soroush teaches, only by Muslims entering into a theological debate that includes philosophical, metaphysical, political, secular and religious discourses.

Soroush has been a powerfully influential thinker because of the quality of his ideas – and because they come from a man who was an insider in the Iranian revolutionary government. After attending the Alavi secondary school in Tehran, one of the first schools to combine the teaching of the modern sciences and religious studies, he studied pharmacology at the university and then attended the University of London for post-graduate work in the history and philosophy of science. A confidant of Ali Shariati, the intellectual whose writings on Islamic governance were appropriated by Khomeini, Soroush returned to Iran in the midst of the Islamic revolution and took a high-ranking position on the Committee of the Cultural Revolution, which was charged with Islamicizing Iran's higher educational system. In 1992, five years after he resigned from the Committee in protest, Soroush established the Research Faculty for the History and Philosophy of Science at the Research Centre for the Humanities in Tehran and began to lecture extensively to both lay and theological audiences at universities and mosques in Tehran and at seminaries in Qum. His academic training, revolutionary credentials and connections with key figures in the government empowered Soroush to speak with an authority shared by few among the Iranian religious intelligentsia. In 1997 Soroush, despite being threatened by hardliners and hounded by young extremists from *Ansar-e-Hezbollah*, publicly applauded the election of Mohamed Khatami. But he also criticized the new president for indecision in the face of his 'fundamentalist' opponents, and urged him to stand up for human rights and academic freedom.[41]

Soroush and An-Na'im are part of a new set of modern Muslim intellectuals formed not by the traditional system of religious education but trained in both Islamic intellectual traditions and Western schools of thought. As religious authority experiences fragmentation throughout the Muslim world, these 'post-fundamentalist' thinkers are making a substantial impact on religious thought in their respective societies. There is no longer one voice of the traditional *ulama* speaking for Islam, but many competing voices, the existence of which contributes to the evolution of thought and political culture in Muslim societies. Indeed, Soroush and An-Na'im personify the worldwide multiplicity of Islamic voices arguing that pluralism and popular political participation are inherent to Islam.[42]

If thinkers like An-Na'im and Soroush continue to win hearts and minds in the Islamic world, significant progress towards building a trans-cultural regime of human rights seems likely. The idea that human rights belong to humanity itself rather than to a specific religion provides a foundation not only for the necessary intra-religious dialogue on values, rights and responsibilities in an interdependent world; it also establishes the framework for fruitful inter-religious dialogue on human rights. The re-location of human rights in humanity itself, rather than in religious identity, was Roman Catholicism's breakthrough in human rights in 1965. Other religious communities have also moved towards consensus around the affirmation that humanity itself is the source of the universality of human rights.[43] That understanding appears to be the *sine qua non* for a rights discourse sufficiently nuanced culturally but also capable of winning assent from a broad spectrum of religious, ethnic and cultural communities.

Religious human rights: mission, persecution and tolerance

Religious human rights must be at the core of any viable cross-cultural rights regime. The right to religious freedom, the oldest of the internationally recognized human rights, was a cornerstone of the Peace of Westphalia (1648). Over the next 150 years a number of pathbreaking statutes in North America and Europe enshrined religious liberty, and after World War II the right found its way into most of the world's constitutions. Nonetheless, religious human rights became the 'neglected grandparent' of the human rights movement, vulnerable to several variables on the ground: the history of relations between a particular religion and a state, the stability of the political regime, the degree of religious pluralism at the local level, and the attitudes and political influence of the dominant religion or religions.[44]

Religious actors and institutions, as we would expect, were both defenders and violators of religious human rights. In the twentieth century Christians, Muslims and Jews, for example, have all been accused of violating the religious human rights of others; and Christians, Muslims and Jews have also been part of a persecuted minority group somewhere in the world. Muslim minorities in Western Europe, Yugoslavia, the new states of Central Asia, India, China and Russia; Christians in Egypt, Sudan, Nigeria, Pakistan, India and China; Jews in the Arab Middle East, Europe and the Soviet Union; *Baha'is* in Iran; *Shi'ites* in Iraq and Lebanon; Tibetan, Cambodian and Thai Buddhists – this is only a partial list of religious groups and individuals persecuted or denied civil rights on account of their beliefs.

During 'the human rights era' the atheistic communist states of China and the Soviet Union repressed Buddhists, Christians, Muslims, Jews and other religious minorities. After the collapse of the Soviet Union, former communists continued their repressive campaigns against religious actors in the new states of Central Asia, while communist leaders in Vietnam, China, North Korea and Cuba continued their Cold War-era policies of religious persecution.[45]

Elsewhere, nationalistic religions themselves stood behind the most egregious oppression of religious minorities. In the 1980s and 1990s Sudanese *Sunni* Muslims engineered the persecution of Christians, indigenous religions and Muslim groups, while *Shi'ite* extremists of Iran targeted *Baha'is* and dissident *Shi'ites*. Pakistan's notorious Blasphemy Law, which outlaws Christian proselytism and makes speech against the Prophet a capital offence, reflected and aggravated social tensions between Muslims and Christians in that Muslim society, where numbers of Christians have been driven from their villages by Muslim mobs and have seen their homes and churches destroyed.[46] Hindu nationalists of India, as mentioned, formed youth vanguards (the RSS, or National Union of Volunteers), cultural movements (the VHP or World Hindu Party), and political parties (the BJP) dedicated to asserting Hindu hegemony over Muslims and other religious minorities of India; the communal riots and pogroms against Muslims in 1990 and 1991 following the destruction of the Babri mosque in Ayodhya was one of the bitter fruits of this burgeoning religious nationalism.

Christianity also contributed to a climate of religious discrimination in the former Soviet Union and in parts of Europe – often by supporting or advocating the repression of other Christians. In the 1990s the Russian Orthodox Church pressed the post-communist Russian state to discriminate against religious minorities and to prevent foreign churches and other religious organizations from attempting to attract converts. Russia's 1997 law protecting the religious freedom of the Russian Orthodox Church, at the expense of all other forms of belief, was a case in point of domestic policy compromising universal human rights norms.[47]

Similarly, the established religious bodies of Europe, Latin America, and the Middle East focused their ire on the explosion of the so-called 'sects' vying for converts in their native lands – a variety of religious groups including the Church of Jesus Christ of Latter-Day Saints (Mormons), the Church of Scientology, Jehovah's Witnesses and independent evangelical Christian movements. Belgium, France, Germany and Austria, in response to reports of supposed 'cult-like' activity, established commissions of inquiry on sects; in Germany, the Enquete Commission subjected members of the Church of Scientology and a Christian charismatic community to intense scrutiny, leading in some cases to harassment, discrimination and threats of violence against these 'sects'.[48] The Austrian Parliament passed a law restricting religious minorities according to the government's judgement regarding their level of patriotism and commitment to democracy.[49] In short, the liberties which established religions demanded for themselves, they frequently attempted to deny to other 'sects'.

The religious human rights record of states, religions, and religious NGOs was by no means uniformly negative, however, and there were signs that the issue had attracted the attention and energies of progressive activists in each of these spheres. Mexico repealed anti-clerical provisions in the Mexican Constitution that date back to 1917. The US Congress debated the provisions of the 'Freedom from Religious Persecution Act' and other proposed legislation to impose sanctions on countries that deny their citizens religious rights, restrict worship and otherwise persecute believers.[50] The Orthodox Christian churches of Eastern Europe held several national and international ecumenical conferences dedicated to the themes of non-violent conflict transformation, religious human rights and religious peace-building.[51] Roman Catholic and Protestant mission boards and relief-and-development NGOs devoted resources to community development and cross-cultural understanding.

Perhaps the most important positive development, however, has been the increasing importance of the international human rights documents – the evolving human rights canon – in providing a framework for local and national measures to strengthen protection of religious human rights. These documents define freedom of religion as including the right to 'change of religion' – a tendency being recognized increasingly by national law and international usage.[52] Although missionary faiths have argued that the act of preaching to non-believers is constitutive of their religious identity, the more compelling rationale for proselytism – compelling to secular states, at least – places it under the canopy of free speech. Thus Article 19 of the International Covenant on Civil and Political Rights (ICCPR) protects proselytism as the freedom to 'impart information and ideas of all kinds, regardless of frontiers'.

In 1993 the United Nations Human Rights Committee, which supervises the application of the ICCPR, issued an important 'General Comment' on the question of conversion and proselytism. The Committee observed that the freedom to 'have or to adopt' a religion or belief 'necessarily entails the freedom to choose a religion or belief, including, *inter alia*, the right to replace one's current religion or belief with another or to adopt atheistic views, as well as the right to retain one's religion or belief'. Article 18(2) of the ICCPR bars coercion that would impair the right to have, to adopt – or to reject – a religion or belief. Impermissible impairment, the Committee noted, includes the use (or threat) of physical force or penal sanctions to compel believers or non-believers to adhere to their current religious beliefs and congregations, to recant their religion or belief, or to convert. The Committee also identified and condemned some particular policies and practices, such as those that restrict access to education, medical care, employment, or the rights to vote or participate in the conduct of public affairs guaranteed in the ICCPR.[53]

Such practices are usually state-sponsored, as they are in the Sudan and Iran; but relief agencies with a missionizing purpose may also employ a subtler form of religious discrimination by withholding services or showing favour to members of and converts to the faith of the relief agency in question. The clarity of the ICCPR definitions notwithstanding, certain states and the dominant religious communities within them continued to press the issue of proselytism. What kinds of acts, they asked, are legitimate in the attempt to convince or induce other persons to change their religion or beliefs? How can a 'right to proselytize' be balanced with the right to privacy and with other religious rights equally deserving of protection, such as the right to educate, worship and practise one's beliefs and precepts? In some cases, opponents of proselytism argued, the right to practise one's religion entails the obligation to avoid or openly reject other belief systems. Such rights are impaired, they maintain, by coercion or by preaching or propaganda designed to erode traditional religious beliefs. Is it not therefore appropriate for states in which one religion prevails to grant the members of that religion certain privileges and advantages – including limitations on the proselytizing rights of other religions?[54]

The articulation and defence of religious human rights are only beginning. Despite signs of both formal agreement and practical action to define and protect religious rights, substantial variation exists in the way that 'church–state' relationships are institutionalized and religious freedom is observed around the world. Religions and states alike contribute to limitations on religious human rights. Some religions do not accept the right to abandon one and adopt another religion or the right to remain without a religion; states where such religions hold sway consider apostasy or heresy to be crimes and punish offenders severely. Other states demand that individuals follow formal steps in order to change their membership in a recognized religious community or congregation and even criminalize attempts to induce other persons to change their religion or join a different religious group. 'At the threshold of a new millennium,' Natan Lerner writes, 'tolerance and pluralism are far from a reality in many parts of the world. Defining the exact meaning and limitations of the right to change one's religion and to proselytize is critical to the achievement of greater toleration and pluralism.'[55]

Conclusion

The internal pluralism of Christianity, Islam and other major religious traditions enables religious actors to select and develop theologies and moral precepts that accommodate universal human rights norms and enhance the building of local cultures of peace. To the extent that religious leaders, educators and ordinary believers come to be influenced by the progressive thinkers and scholars within their own traditions, the latter have the capacity to transform popular attitudes towards 'the other'. The implications of such evolution of popular religious attitudes for conflict resolution are significant, to say the least.

Theologies of redemption have dramatic social consequences. Does the Christian minister pour energies and resources into facilitating reconciliation between peoples, or does he 'save souls' by preaching acceptance of the atoning death of Christ on the cross? Both options are plausible within a Christian worldview, but they bespeak different interpretations of the divine will and different orientations to the world. While they are not mutually exclusive, these two basic Christian orientations to the world promote different pastoral goals and methods of dealing with conflict. They yield at least three basic approaches to conflict transformation, each the expression of a lived religious witness, each likely to produce its own distinct political or social consequences.

The spiritualist approach sees the commitment to conflict transformation as a self-authenticating gospel mandate, an end-in-itself. It is rooted in the progressive or 'ecumenical' trends that emerged in mainline Protestantism beginning in the 1920s and in Roman Catholicism beginning in the 1960s. Fostering dialogue among peoples is the Christian way of life in conflict settings for groups of this mentality. One example is *Silsilah*, a small network of primarily Roman Catholic sisters and lay women living in the southern Philippines island of Mindanao who dedicated themselves to reconciliation with Muslims during the late 1980s and 1990s, a time when religious extremism gained a foothold in the region. Such groups view reconciliation as a spirituality, not a strategy, still less a technical or professional process. While conversant in the literature and some of the techniques of conflict resolution, these groups tend to be loosely organized and low-maintenance, their members often living an apostolic lifestyle of poverty or modest means. Although spiritualists leave concrete outcomes to the Holy Spirit, the relationships they promote can contribute to the stabilization of societies plagued by economic inequalities and communal tension.[56]

In recent years some Christian peacebuilding communities have moved away from an exclusive reliance on this outlook, although it remains powerfully appealing in its purity of intent and spiritual expression. The historic Christian peace churches, for example – the Society of Friends (Quakers), the Mennonites, and the Church of the Brethren – attempt to retain the ethos and piety of this outlook even as they have moved decisively in the direction of ends-oriented, world-transforming modes.

By contrast to the spiritualists, the conversionist model seeks to bring the world more closely into conformity with the reign of God in Jesus Christ, primarily by spreading the good news of salvation and, where possible, converting people to Christianity. The fundamentalist, Pentecostal and conservative evangelical missions of the Cold War era (and after) exemplified this worldview, as do indigenous evangelical movements such as *El Shaadai*, the so-called 'Catholic fundamentalists' of the Philippines. Church organizations, NGOs and para-church groups in this mode tend to be highly organized, well funded, and politically sophisticated. Their theology of conflict differs from that of the spiritualists, who tend to be pacifists or disciplined practitioners of non-violent resistance. For the conversionists, conflict may be inevitable in a world divided between children of darkness and children of light; 'spiritual warfare' is a common theme.

Such Christians argue that the act of proclaiming one's faith in the public forum is a fundamental human right, and they appeal to Western human rights traditions and enforcement instruments to make the mission field safe for their divinely ordained labours. Advocates of Christian religious rights, who claim that Christians are the primary victims of religious persecution in the twentieth century (a claim that Jews and Buddhists, among others, contest), invoke the UN Declaration on the Elimination of All Forms of Intolerance and Discrimination Based on Religion or Belief, which guarantees the right of everyone (including Christians) to worship freely, as well as the right to teach religion, write and disseminate religious publications, designate religious leaders, communicate with co-religious at home and abroad, solicit and receive charitable contributions, and educate children in religion and morality according to parents' wishes.[57] In their view 'conflict transformation' is not irrelevant, but it assumes a distinctive purpose, that is, removing impediments to the 'free market of ideas' and freedom of assembly, speech and religion. Those Roman Catholics, evangelical Protestants, Mormons, Seventh-Day Adventists and others who continue to seek to make converts, continue to risk their lives in doing so.[58]

Although adherents to the liberationist model also endeavour to change the world, they seek to usher in a non-sectarian, inclusive order of social and economic justice, which they believe to be the *sine qua non* of lasting peace. Progressive and 'liberationist' Roman Catholics, socially liberal evangelicals and mainline Protestants work towards this end. Advocates of structural change on behalf of the poor and marginalized, they often serve local communities, non-Christian as well as Christian, as educators and, increasingly, as trainers in conflict prevention and mediation. The cutting edge for liberationists is 'holistic community development', an approach which entails paying close attention to social relations among community members of different religious, ethnic or tribal backgrounds, to their spiritual and psychological needs and cultural trends, as well as to their material needs. It is in this context that conflict resolution is emerging as an invaluable service and skill offered by religious NGOs and liberationist-minded missioners.

These Christian actors are considered to be the most promising agents of peace-making. They promote religion's civic, tolerant, non-violent presences; they articulate and defend religious and other human rights. Political and military powers perceive conflict mediators of this sort as partisan. Indeed, the liberationists are inclined to take the side of the disenfranchized and disempowered, and they seek to restructure the conflictual relationship in such a way as to redress the imbalance.[59] Ecumenical and inter-religious as a matter of principle, the liberationists include some evangelical Protestant churches, most mainline Protestant churches, the United States Catholic Conference, NGOs such as the World Council of Churches, Pax Christi, Catholic Relief Services, and the International Conciliation Services of the Mennonite Central Committee.

The variety of attitudes towards human rights, proselytism and conflict found in contemporary Catholicism and Protestantism has its counterparts in Orthodox Christianity, Judaism, Hinduism and Buddhism. Indeed, Robert Traer writes, the support for human rights among religious leaders is 'global, cutting across cultures as well as systems of belief and practice ... Clearly, something new is occurring when women and men of different faith traditions join with those of no religious tradition to champion human rights.'[60]

No religious tradition speaks unequivocally about human rights; none earned an exemplary human rights record over the centuries. Their sacred texts and canons devote much more attention to commandments and obligations than to rights and freedoms. Paradoxically, their prelates, supreme guides, theologians and jurists have cultivated human rights norms while resisting their consistent application.[61] All this being said, human rights discourse has become the moral language of cultural modernity, in part as a result of its justification and advocacy by members of different religious traditions.

Each religion (and its specific schools or sub-traditions) has justified and advocated human rights in its own distinctive way and on its own terms, however. Each, as noted, has its own theological and philosophical framework for interpreting human rights, its own constellation of doctrines and precepts modifying the canon of rights, and its own exemplars or champions of human rights. The respective frameworks, or doctrines, or models of emulation are not readily reconcilable in every respect; even where different religions proclaim essentially the same luminous core truths, this basic unity is not always transparent to themselves or to others. The challenge of the next phase of the human rights era will be for religious leaders from these different traditions and sub-traditions to identify and enlarge the common ground they share.

Religious communities, in short, must be engaged, consistently and substantively, in the international discourse of universal rights and responsibilities. This engagement should include active and vigorous participation in efforts to build local cultures of religious and other human rights. Second, religious traditions with strong missionary outreach must promote missiologies, or theologies of mission, that foster respect for universal human rights norms, including the right to religious freedom. All religious traditions, in turn, must encourage the practice of civic tolerance of religious outsiders, including the revivalists and proselytizers among them. Finally, religious leaders must give priority to establishing and supporting ecumenical and inter-religious dialogues and cooperative ventures at local and regional sites of religious and ethnic conflict. Each of these monumental tasks depends, in turn, on the willingness and ability of religious officials, educators and community leaders to retrieve, articulate and apply religious concepts, norms and practices that promote human rights and non-violent conflict transformation.

Notes

1 Mary Ann Glendon, *Rights Talk: The Impoverishment of Political Discourse*, New York: The Free Press, 1991, p. 17. Parts of this chapter are adapted from Chapter 7 of my book: R. Scott Appleby, *The Ambivalence of the Sacred: Religion, Violence and Reconciliation*, Lanham, MD: Rowman & Littlefield, 2000.

2 For a sampling of the opinions of leading American conservatives on the need for a revitalization of religion in the public sphere, see 'The national prospect', *Commentary*, vol. 100, no. 5, November 1995, pp. 23–116. For a communitarian perspective which includes but does not privilege religious participation, and emphasizes the importance of core religious values that are compatible with secular humanitarian values, see Amitai Etzioni, *The New Golden Rule: Community and Morality in a Democratic Society*, New York: Basic Books, 1996, pp. 252–7.

3 For an overview of the debate, see John L. Esposito and John O. Voll, *Islam and Democracy*, New York: Oxford University Press, 1996.

4 See W. Cole Durham, Jr and Lauren B. Homer, 'Russia's 1997 Law on Freedom of Conscience and Religious Associations: an analytical appraisal', *Emory International Law Review*, vol. 12, 1998, pp. 101–246; and Harold J. Berman, 'Freedom of religion in Russia: an *amicus* brief for the defendant', in ibid., pp. 313–40.

5 Gabriel Almond, Emmanuel Sivan and R. Scott Appleby, 'Fundamentalisms comprehended', in Martin E. Marty and R. Scott Appleby, *Fundamentalisms Comprehended*, Chicago: University of Chicago Press, 1995.

6 Michael A. Sells, *The Bridge Betrayed: Religions and Genocide in Bosnia*, Berkeley, CA: University of California Press, 1996, p. 26.

7 Article 18 of the 1948 Universal Declaration of Human Rights provides that: 'Everyone has the right to freedom of thought, conscience and religion; this right includes freedom to change his religion or belief, and freedom, either alone or in community with others and in public or private, to manifest his religion or belief in teaching, practice, worship and observance.' Article 26 contains a provision calling for education to promote 'understanding, tolerance and friendship among all religious groups'. Freedom of religion is also upheld in Article 2 of the Convention on the Prevention and Punishment of the Crime of Genocide, Article 9 of the 1950 European Convention for the Protection of Human Rights and Fundamental Freedoms, Article 1 of the 1950 UNESCO Convention Against Discrimination in Education, Article 4 of the 1965 International Convention on the Elimination of All Forms of Racial Discrimination, Article 18 of the 1966 International Covenant on Civil and Political Rights, Article 12 of the 1969 American Convention on Human Rights, Principle VII of the 1975 Final Act of the Helsinki Conference on Security and Cooperation in Europe, Article 8 of the 1981 African Charter on Human and Peoples' Rights, and Article 7 of the International Convention on the Elimination of All Forms of Discrimination Against Women. Irwin Cotler, 'Jewish NGOs and religious human rights: a case-study', in John Witte, Jr and Johan D. van der Vyver, *Religious Human Rights in Global Perspective: Religious Perspectives*, The Hague: Martinus Nijhoff Publishers, 1996, p. 236.

8 John Witte, Jr, 'Law, religion, and human rights', *Columbia Human Rights Law Review*, vol. 28, 1996, p. 3.

9 See 'Final Declaration of the Regional Meeting for Asia of the World Conference on Human Rights', in *Human Rights Law Journal*, vol. 14, 1993, p. 370. Also see Joseph Chan, 'The task for Asians: to discover their own political morality for human rights', *Human Rights Dialogue*, vol. 4, March 1996, p. 5; Joseph Chan, 'The Asian challenge to universal human rights: a philosophical appraisal', in James T.H. Tang (ed.) *Human Rights and International Relations in the Asia-Pacific Region*, New York: St Martin's Press, 1995.

10 A preview and sampling of these arguments is found in *First Things*, April 1998, p. 82. See the following articles therein: 'The Universal Declaration of Human Rights fifty years later: a statement of the Ramsey Colloquium', pp. 18–22; and 'Reflections on the Universal Declaration of Human Rights', by Mary Ann Glendon and Elliot Abrams, pp. 23–7.

11 Theo van Boven, 'Advances and obstacles in building understanding and respect between people of diverse religions and beliefs', *Human Rights Quarterly*, vol. 13, 1991, pp. 437–52.

12 On the religious leadership of the US civil rights movement, see Charles Marsh, *God's Long Summer: Stories of Faith and Civil Rights*, Princeton, NJ: Princeton University Press, 1997; David Halberstam, *The Children*, New York: Random House, 1998; and John Lewis with Michael D'Orso, *Walking with the Wind: A Memoir of the Movement*, New York: Simon and Schuster, 1998. On Latin America, see Scott Mainwaring and Alexander Wilde (eds) *The Progressive Church in Latin America*, Notre Dame: Notre Dame Press, 1989.

13 See the following essays in Johan D. van der Vyver and John Witte, Jr (eds) *Religious Human Rights in Global Perspective: Legal Perspectives*, The Hague: Kluwer Law International, 1996: Peter Cumper, 'Religious liberty in the United Kingdom', pp. 205–42; T. Jeremy Gunn, 'Adjudicating the rights of conscience under the European Convention of Human Rights', pp. 305–30; Martin Heckel, 'The impact of religious rules on public life in Germany', pp. 191–204.

14 Examples include the World Council of Churches, the Vatican's Commission on Justice and Peace, and the National Conference on Soviet Jewry. See Cotler, 'Jewish NGOs'. On the contributions of secular NGOs such as Amnesty International and Asia Watch, see Michael Roan, 'The role of secular non-governmental organizations in the cultivation and understanding of religious human rights', in Van der Vyver and Witte, *Legal Perspectives*, pp. 135–59.

15 Examples include the Mennonite Central Committee, Catholic Relief Services and the Jacob Blaustein Institute for the Advancement of Human Rights, an organization of the American Jewish Committee.

16 In this area, religious NGOs worked closely with secular NGOs; see Roan, 'The role of secular non-governmental organizations', pp. 154–5.

17 Examples include the World Conference on Religion and Peace and the International Jewish Committee for Inter-religious Consultations.

18 Victor A. van Bijlert, 'Raja Rammohun Roy's thought and its relevance for human rights', in Abdullahi A. An-Na'im, Jerald D. Gort, Henry Jansen and Hendrik M. Vroom (eds) *Human Rights and Religious Values: An Uneasy Relationship?*, Grand Rapids, MI: Eerdmans Publishing, 1995, pp. 93–108.

19 For a review and sample of this work, see the following essays in Witte and van der Vyver, *Religious Perspectives*: Michael S. Berger and Deborah E. Lipstadt, 'Women in Judaism from the perspective of human rights', pp. 295–321; Riffat Hassan, 'Rights of women within Islamic communities', pp. 361–86; Jean Bethke Elshtain, 'Thinking about women, Christianity, and rights', pp. 143–56.

20 With regard to Islam, see, for example, Fatima Mernissi, *Beyond the Veil: Male–Female Dynamics in Modern Muslim Society*, 2nd edn, Bloomington: Indiana University Press, 1987; Shahla Haeri, *Law of Desire: Temporary Marriage in Shi'i Iran*, Syracuse: Syracuse University Press, 1989; Fazlur Rahman, *Islam and Modernity: Transformation of an Intellectual Tradition*, Chicago: University of Chicago Press, 1982, pp. 130–62. For Christianity, Lloyd J. Averill, *Religious Right, Religious Wrong*, New York: Pilgrim Press, 1989. For a response to Jewish extremism, see David Landau, *Piety and Power: The World of Jewish Fundamentalism*, New York: Hill and Wang, 1993; and, from a different perspective, Yossi Klein Halevi, *Memoirs of a Jewish Extremist*, Boston: Little, Brown, 1995.

21 For an overview of the Christian debate, see Lisa Sowle Cahill, *Love Your Enemies: Discipleship, Pacifism and Just War*, Minneapolis: Fortress Press, 1994. For Islam, see Sohail H. Hashmi, 'Interpreting the Islamic ethics of war and peace', in Terry Nardin (ed.) *The Ethics of War and Peace*, Princeton, NJ: Princeton University Press, 1996, pp. 141–74.

22 Reuven Kimelman, 'Nonviolence in the Talmud', *Judaism*, vol. 17, 1968, pp. 318–23.

23 For a discussion of the Hindu nationalist backlash against this measure, see Sudhir Kakar, *The Colors of Violence: Cultural Identities, Religion and Conflict*, Chicago: University of Chicago Press, 1996, pp. 158–69.

24 Abdullahi A. An-Na'im, 'Toward an Islamic hermeneutics for human rights', in An-Na'im, Gort, Jansen and Vroom, *Human Rights and Religious Values*, p. 231.

25 The debate about Islam raged with particular intensity in the decade following the end of the Cold War. For a summary of the various positions, see John L. Esposito, *The Islamic Threat: Myth or Reality?*, New York: Oxford University Press, 1992.

26 See, for example, John Kelsay's discussion of the disagreement involving the statements of representatives of Saudi Arabia and Pakistan at the United Nations with respect to the Universal Declaration of Human Rights. John Kelsay, 'Saudi Arabia, Pakistan, and the Universal Declaration of Human Rights', in David Little, John Kelsay and Abdulaziz Sachedina, *Human Rights and the Conflicts of Culture: Western and Islamic Perspectives on Religious Liberty*, Columbia: University of South Carolina Press, 1988, pp. 33–52.

27 Ahmed An Na'im, 'The reformation of Islam', *New Perspectives Quarterly*, Fall 1987, p. 51.

28 See Abdullahi Ahmed An-Na'im and Francis M. Deng (eds) *Human Rights in Africa: Cross-cultural Perspectives*, Washington, DC: Brookings Institution, 1990; Francis M. Deng and William Zartman, *Conflict Resolution in Africa*, Washington, DC: Brookings Institution, 1991; Leonard Grob, Riffat Hassan and Haim Gordon (eds) *Women's and Men's Liberation: Testimonies of Spirit*, New York: Greenwood Press, 1991.

29 *Universal Islamic Declaration of Human Rights*, London, 1981.
30 Khan Bahadur Khan, 'The word of Islam', in *Proceedings of the Third World Congress on Religious Liberty*, quoted in Johan D. van der Vyver, 'Legal dimensions of religious human rights: constitutional texts', in van der Vyver and Witte, *Legal Perspectives*, p. xxx.
31 Ann Elizabeth Mayer, 'Current Muslim thinking on human rights', in An-Na'im and Deng, *Human Rights in Africa*, p. 133; Abdullahi A. An-Na'im and Francis Deng, 'Law and religion in the Muslim Middle East', *American Journal of Comparative Law*, vol. 35, 1987, pp. 127, 130; Abdullahi A. An-Na'im, 'Religious minorities under Islamic law and the limits of cultural relativism', *Human Rights Quarterly*, vol. 9, 1987, pp. 1, 10.
32 See also the *Qur'anic* verses 3:28, 4:139, 8:72–73. Abdullahi A. An-Na'im, 'Toward an Islamic hermeneutics for human rights', p. 233.
33 For examples, see Ira Lapidus, *A History of Islamic Societies*, Cambridge: Cambridge University Press, 1988, pp. 500–8, 911–15.
34 An-Na'im, 'Toward an Islamic hermeneutics for human rights', pp. 236–7.
35 Little, Kelsay and Sachedina, *Human Rights and the Conflicts of Culture*.
36 Egyptian Muslim lawyers and intellectuals were among the enthusiastic hosts of an international conference on democracy and the rule of law held in 1995 in Cairo; they participated vigorously in a discussion of topics such as 'secularity, Islam and human rights'. David Little, 'Secularity, Islam and human rights', *Proceedings of the Conference on Democracy and the Rule of Law*, December 1997, pp. 22–4.
37 In his treatise *Faith in Human Rights*, Robert Traer collected an impressive list of Muslim protagonists of the human rights ideal. Robert Traer, *Faith in Human Rights*, Washington, DC: Georgetown University Press, 1991.
38 Ibid., p. 22. On Soroush, see Robin Wright, 'Islam and liberal democracy: two visions of reformation', *Journal of Democracy*, vol. 7, April 1996, pp. 64–75.
39 Wright, 'Two visions'. Also, see Bernard Lewis, 'Islam and liberal democracy: a historical overview', *Journal of Democracy*, vol. 7, April 1996, pp. 52–63.
40 Abdolkarim Soroush, quoted in Wright, 'Two visions', p. 27.
41 Robert Fisk, 'Iran's leader urged to stand up for human rights', *The Independent* (London), 8 December 1997, p. 6.
42 James Piscatori and Riva Richmond, 'Foreword', in Valla Vakili, *Debating Religion and Politics in Iran: The Political Thought of Abdolkarim Soroush*, Council on Foreign Relations Study Department Occasional Paper Series, no. 2, New York: Council on Foreign Relations, 1996, pp. 3–5.
43 See, for example, Michael J. Broyde, 'Forming religious communities and respecting dissenter's rights: a Jewish tradition for a modern society', in Witte and van der Vyver, *Religious Perspectives*, pp. 203–34.
44 W. Cole Durham, Jr, 'Perspectives on religious liberty: a comparative framework', in Witte and van der Vyver, *Legal Perspectives*.
45 Paul Marshall, *Their Blood Cries Out: The Untold Story of Persecution against Christians in the Modern World*, Dallas, TX: Word Publishing, 1997, pp. 71–96, chronicles 'Communism's continuing grip'.
46 On the Pakistan Blasphemy Law, see 'Bishop's suicide: A "protest death"', *Origins*, vol. 28, no. 1, 21 May 1998, pp. 1, 3.

47 The Russian Federation law on 'Freedom of Conscience and Religious Associations' took effect 1 October 1997. It places Islam, Protestant and Roman Catholic Christianity, Buddhism and Judaism in a 'second tier' classification, below the specially privileged (Russian) Orthodox Christianity. Donna E. Arzt, 'Historical heritage or ethno-national threat? Proselytizing and the Muslim *Umma* of Russia', *Emory International Law Review*, vol. 12, 1998, p. 469.

48 *Advisory Committee on Religious Freedom Abroad: Interim Report to the Secretary of State and to the President of the United States*, 23 January 1998, p. 11.

49 David Little, 'Religion and global affairs: religion and foreign policy', *SAIS Review*, vol. 18, no. 2, Summer-Fall 1998, p. 27.

50 *Advisory Committee on Religious Freedom Abroad: Interim Report*, p. 15.

51 For an example, see Károly Tóth (ed.) *Steps toward Reconciliation*, trans. Ecumenical Study Centre, Budapest: The Ecumenical Council of Churches in Hungary, 1996.

52 Thomas M. Franck, 'Clan and superclan: loyalty, identity and community in law and practice', *American Journal of International Law*, vol. 90, 1996, p. 482.

53 Human Rights Committee, 'General Comments Adopted Under Article 40, Paragraph 4, of the International Covenant on Civil and Political Rights: General Comment No. 22 (48) (art. 18)', UN GAOR, Human Rights Committee 48th Sess., Supp. No. 40, at 208, UN Doc. A/48/40 (1993). In April 1996, a seminar organized by the Office for Democratic Institutions and Human Rights (ODIHR) of the Organization for Security and Co-operation in Europe (OSCE) on 'Constitutional, legal and administrative aspects of the freedom of religion', devoted considerable attention to the issue of change of religion or belief. See Consolidated Summary of the Seminar, Warsaw: OSCE, 1996.

54 Franck, 'Clan and superclan', p. 486. Also, see Asher Maoz, 'Human rights in the State of Israel', in van der Vyver and Witte, *Legal Perspectives*, pp. 349, 360. Also see Silvo Ferrari, 'The new wine and the old cask: tolerance, religion and the law in contemporary Europe', *Ratio Juris*, vol. 10, 1997, pp. 75–83.

55 Natan Lerner, 'Proselytism, change of religion, and international human rights', *Emory International Law Review*, vol. 12, 1998, p. 478.

56 'Chain', the *Silsilah* Newsletter, provides bi-annual accounts of the work of this mission group.

57 Nina Shea, *In the Lion's Den: A Shocking Account of Persecution and Martyrdom of Christians Today and How We Should Respond*, Nashville, TN: Broadman & Holman Publishers, 1997, p. 7.

58 For other examples and details on the cases mentioned, see Marshall, *Their Blood Cries Out*, pp. 45–6; Shea, *In the Lion's Den*, pp. 27–51.

59 Cynthia Sampson, 'Religion and peacebuilding', in I. William Zartman and J. Lewis Rasmussen (eds) *Peacemaking in International Conflict: Methods and Techniques*, Washington, DC: US Institute of Peace Press, 1997, pp. 278–9.

60 Traer, *Faith in Human Rights*, p. 1.

61 Witte, 'Law, religion, and human rights', p. 4.

Select bibliography

An-Na'im, Abdullahi A., Gort, Jerald D., Jansen, Henry and Vroom, Hendrik M. (eds), *Human Rights and Religious Values*, Grand Rapids, MI: William B. Eerdmans, 1995.

Almond, Gabriel A., Sivan, Emmanuel and Appleby, R. Scott, 'Explaining Fundamentalisms', in Marty, Martin E. and Appleby, R. Scott (eds) *Fundamentalisms Comprehended*, Chicago: University of Chicago Press, 1995, 425–44.

Marshall, Paul, *Their Blood Cries Out: The Untold Stories of Persecution against Christians in the Modern World*, Dallas, TX: Word Publishing, 1997.

Mayer, Ann Elizabeth, *Islam and Human Rights: Tradition and Politics*, Boulder, CO: Westview Press, 1995.

Traer, Robert, *Faith in Human Rights*, Washington, DC: Georgetown University Press, 1991.

Van der Vyver, Johann and Witte, John, Jr (eds), *Religious Human Rights in Global Perspective: Legal Perspectives*, The Hague: Martinus Nijhoff Publishers, 1996.

Witte, John, Jr and van der Vyver, Johan D. (eds), *Religious Human Rights in Global Perspective: Religious Perspectives*, The Hague: Martinus Nijhoff Publishers, 1996.

10

POLICY RESPONSES TO
RELIGIOUS FUNDAMENTALISM[1]

James J. Busuttil

The authors in this volume have examined the phenomenon of religious fundamentalism. They have done so usually within the frame of reference of a particular religion and a particular country. Nonetheless, the analyses they have applied and the conclusions which they have drawn can be reflected upon to determine if the existence and growth of fundamentalist movements lead to certain policy implications for those concerned with their impact on social change and particularly on human rights.

Deconstructing fundamentalism

In this analysis, as in the others in this book, we must acknowledge the question, raised in Scott Appleby's chapter and examined in depth in Gerrie ter Haar's chapter, 'What is religious fundamentalism?' The answer is neither simple nor straightforward, and deserves detailed examination in each individual case. Fundamentalist tendencies and manifestations are in themselves of little practical interest to non-members of the fundamentalist group, assuming membership is voluntary and not coerced, until fundamentalists move into the political arena and begin to engage in policy proposals or policy-making that affect persons outside their group. It is, at the latest, at this stage that other actors must assess their attitude towards both the fundamentalists and their proposals and consider whether they should take any action in response. Those other actors include the government, other groups in the society including adherents of other religions, politicians, non-governmental organizations, human rights activists, the media, other states and, if relevant, development workers and organizations present in or concerned with the state where fundamentalists are asserting a role.

One of the most important features which underlies the present analysis is that religious fundamentalism and certainly fundamentalist tendencies can be found in any religion and in any part of the world. Fundamentalism is not the domain of any particular faith, people, state, region or level of economic or political development. Rather, it is clear that religious fundamentalism arises in reaction to changes in society. This key observation can be deconstructed in order to lay the foundations for policies in response, or anticipation.

The conditions which evoke a fundamentalist reaction may derive from internal or external (to the society) developments, for example, pressures of modernization or globalization (real or perceived), security threats, scarcity of resources including employment, changing political power, demographic shifts. What is common is that there is a rapid change in the *status quo*. Static societies do not produce fundamentalism. The changing conditions are viewed by the fundamentalists as a challenge to their religious values. They may feel uniquely or particularly threatened, excluded, manipulated, exploited or degraded.

Their reaction is to gather together based upon particular interpretations of their religion, retrieving a vision of the past to strengthen the present and build the future. This creates an implicit or explicit divide so as to better protect, and then advance, their own interests. The 'others' are at least different, probably opposed, possibly evil. The fundamentalists insist on the special nature of their 'knowledge' which requires privileged treatment by the state and society. Indeed, ultimately it should apply to all of society. To achieve this they seek political power.

Perhaps it goes without saying that religious fundamentalism can only appear among people who take religion seriously. In societies where religion no longer has (much) meaning or role in the lives of most of the population, religious fundamentalism is unlikely to have a significant impact. However, even in 'post-religious' societies there may and will be sub-groups, whether immigrant or indigenous, for whom religion continues to play an important and perhaps even crucial role, and where fundamentalism can take hold. Even a small fundamentalist group in a largely secular society can have a significant impact if the fundamentalist group either can mobilize sufficient support so that it becomes an important political force, perhaps because of the fractured or divided nature of the society which would allow a small united group to take a leading position, or can formulate policies which resonate with larger portions of the (non-fundamentalist) population.

Essentially, the problem and challenge of fundamentalism are intolerance. If for nothing other than pragmatic reasons, a plural(istic) and non-homogeneous society or state must tolerate a range of beliefs and

231

behaviours. Within broad boundaries which do not allow violence or (implicit) compulsion either within the group or between groups, the actions of others, and certainly their private (religious) values, must be respected, whether they are attractive or repulsive. To do so is to recognize the intrinsic equality of human beings, which each person would insist upon as to him or herself. Not to do so is to invite anger and violence because of (implicit or explicit) disrespect and degradation. It is arguable that at the core of fundamentalism is intolerance, or that at least fundamentalists doubt the equality of those who do not adhere to their views. It may be too provocative to state that intolerance cannot be tolerated. Nonetheless, intolerance certainly cannot be allowed to infiltrate societal or governmental policies at the risk of evoking social instability and civil unrest. Policy actors can defuse the intolerance inherent in religious fundamentalism in a number of ways, as well as limit its potential impact.

Policy responses

The responses which policy actors can make to fundamentalism will necessarily vary widely depending on who the actor is, what role the actor plays, the resources of the actor, how strong the fundamentalist movement is, at what point in the ascent of fundamentalism the policy is considered, and other local details. Among the policies which can be considered are the following.

Separate *religious matters ('church') from secular matters ('state')*

The further religious authorities are from secular or state power, the more difficult it will be for religious fundamentalists to directly influence non-religious matters. Conversely, a religion which has a special or established role in the state, say, through constitutional protection, provides leverage to fundamentalists within it. It would be almost impossible to implement such a basic re-orientation of society as a separation of 'church' and state under fundamentalist pressure. However, preferably before fundamentalism arises, steps can be taken either to increase the distance between religious and secular power or to resist any decrease in that distance. Once fundamentalism is a strong force in a state with an established church or other religious organization, the best that can be hoped for is resistance to any expansion of religious influence in secular affairs.

Understand *grievances and proposals/demands of fundamentalists*

Not to take seriously the growth of fundamentalism is to ensure the absence of preparation and the increase of fundamentalist influence. Ignoring fundamentalism, like any 'problem', is not going to (help) make it go away. Efforts should be made early in the life of fundamentalism for other societal actors to come to grips with what the fundamentalists are 'complaining' about and what they propose to do. By doing so two things are accomplished: (1) these potentially important actors are understood early on and responses to them can be formulated (see immediately below); and (2) the fundamentalists will feel (and be) less isolated and ignored, thereby reducing the legitimacy of the commonly expressed grievance of neglect. This does not mean that they should be given a place, and certainly not a prominent one, at the political 'table'. But it does mean that their 'fringe' status (at that time) is not a reason to either ignore or (even worse) ridicule them.

Address *social disruption*

The analyses in this book have demonstrated that religious fundamentalism arises most often in times of social change. The actors who do not take a fundamentalist approach to these changes are nonetheless also affected by them. If fundamentalism is building up due to social change, other actors should reflect on how the effects of those changes can be either ameliorated or transformed. The 'pain' which is felt by religious fundamentalists is real, at least to them, and taking that pain seriously and dealing with it will at a minimum reduce, and possibly even terminate, the fundamentalist response.

Encourage *multi-religious framework to discuss common problems*

The more religious (and other) actors seek common ground to understand common problems, the less likely they will be to see 'otherness' and the more likely they will be to see commonality. Problems of the family, the environment, crime, drugs, unemployment, etc., usually affect communities without 'discrimination' based upon religion. The fundamentalist viewpoint often is to see themselves as unique in suffering and so justified in a unique, and exclusivist, response. A common platform for (religious) dialogue will reduce this feeling of uniqueness and possibly lead both to mutual understanding and to solutions to the problems.

Accept *that concerns of fundamentalists can be legitimately expressed*

Fundamentalists should neither feel that they are, nor in fact be, excluded from the normal political process. The more they are brought in and expected and required to 'play by the rules', the less likely that they will find excuses or reasons to breach, or argue for the abrogation of, those rules. If they are excluded from normal politics, the normal response would be to act outside politics. If they are co-opted in, they will find it hard to legitimately act outside the bounds. In any event, fundamentalists are citizens whose concerns deserve a fair hearing, and political space should be provided to them as to any other group of citizens.

Resist *special deals or discrimination based upon religious belief*

At the same time, equality of treatment means that no special deals should be made to advantage (or disadvantage) religious fundamentalists. An articulate and well-organized group can make strong demands for special treatment, or that others, not part of their group, should be given less favourable treatment. Allowing such (positive or negative) discrimination is contrary to the principle of respect for all and opens the door to additional demands, on the one hand, and resentment, on the other. Adherence to (fundamentalist) religion should be strongly resisted as a basis for differential treatment.

Expose *(young) fundamentalists to other (positive) experiences*

Many fundamentalist live in closed communities, where their experiences are generated, and mediated, by their co-religionists. While fundamentalists may react against the 'corrupt' or 'evil' world, they may do so in the absence of real experience or knowledge, and on the basis of rhetoric and the repetition of other's statements. They may lack adequate terms of reference to compare and judge situations. It will certainly broaden their horizons, and possibly demonstrate the fallacy of their assumptions, if fundamentalists are exposed to other 'realities'. Such experiences could be at home or abroad, and could include higher academic study. Young (potential) leaders would be a prime group to expose to broader influences. There is of course the risk that such exposure will only reinforce and strengthen the fundamentalist critique, but in any event a better informed leadership is preferable to a narrow-minded one.

Strengthen *democratic resources within fundamentalist community, and generally*

Within any group, even religious fundamentalists, there will be tensions and factions with different, more or less extreme, aims and means in mind. It is preferable that those tendencies which favour (more) democratic responses and solutions should come to the fore and take a leading role. This is also true in society generally, as confrontationalist policies reinforce and magnify each other. The democratic reflex should be inculcated, encouraged and strengthened. Anti-democratic trends should be isolated and devalued. Respect for democracy generally in the society and state is the strongest defence against anti-democratic forces, whether based on religious fundamentalism or otherwise.

Avoid *stereotypes*

While religious fundamentalists have some 'family resemblances', it is clear that fundamentalism appears in very local manifestations. Parallels can rarely be drawn between groups, even within the same state, as local circumstances and leadership vary widely. Portraying fundamentalists as being the same or as sharing the same characteristics does a disservice both to them and to an accurate and appropriate analysis and response. Two stereotypes bear mentioning for the different problems which they throw up. One common misperception is that religious fundamentalists are violent. As has been seen in this book, that is not necessarily so. But portraying them as such may, on the one hand, lead others to react violently against them and, on the other, lead the fundamentalists to adopt violence as a 'self-fulfilling prophecy'. Another misperception is that religious fundamentalists, from their first appearance on the political scene, have an almost magical and irresistible political power. Even leaving aside the various possible policy responses outlined here to reduce their political appeal and power, in fact religious fundamentalists almost always initially reflect a fairly small portion of the population. However, through repetition of this perception of power, politicians and voters may come to believe in the inevitable necessity of submitting to their demands. Religious fundamentalists, like everyone else, deserve and need to be addressed based on their particular reality not on stereotypes.

Ensure *freedom of religion for all, fundamentalist and non-fundamentalist*

As Scott Appleby explains in his chapter, freedom of religion is unquestionably enshrined in international law. Virtually all states are bound by the treaty provisions on freedom of religion, and customary international law on the subject binds all states. An even-handed respect for freedom of religion is due to all. This applies to fundamentalists, who should be allowed to practise their beliefs, as well as to those who do not share their views. Actors inside and outside the society and state can and should act to ensure that this freedom applies at all times. In this way, arguments of victimization by fundamentalists are eliminated and later, if fundamentalists acquire (greater) power, non-fundamentalists will be insulated against calls to adopt fundamentalist beliefs and practices.

Insist *on respect of human rights by and for all*

Respect for freedom of religion at all times for everyone is only a corollary of the basic principle that human rights should be respected by all and for all. Human rights apply to each person on the basis of their common humanity, without distinction based on religion, class, race, etc. The reinforcement of this message, and its practical application, reduce both the chance of fundamentalist ascendancy, by eliminating the cause of many complaints, and the ability of fundamentalists in power to impose their will on others. As Abdullahi An-Na'im points out in his chapter, religious fundamentalists must be reminded that they cannot legitimately insist on their rights while denying the rights of others.

Act *swiftly and decisively on religious violence*

If and when violence occurs around religious fundamentalism, government authorities must act swiftly to investigate and punish. This is true whether it is violence against the fundamentalists, which reinforces their self-view as victims, or by the fundamentalists, which can lead to an aura of impunity. Violence can never be an acceptable way to express political or social dissatisfaction. Violence begets only more violence and intimidation, either in response or when perceived as a successful tool.

Recognize *that governing usually moderates demands*

Experience has shown that when fundamentalists achieve power, usually (initially) in coalition with others, they moderate their demands. The reality that life is lived in shades of grey and not in black and white becomes evident, and the inevitable result is compromise. This moderation may take some time to develop, and it may only do so in response to popular demands. This is not to say that fundamentalists need be invited to power, but it may dull the edge of worry about their ascent to power.

Maintain *perspective*

Finally, and in the worst case, it is (somewhat) comforting to realize that fundamentalism is a cyclical and time-bound phenomenon. Fundamentalism, under some name or another, has appeared and disappeared many times, lasting a longer or shorter period, and is affected by internal and external political, economic, social and even military factors. Patience and understanding can make the experience of living under or with religious fundamentalism more bearable, while the fundamentalists (gradually) come under pressure to moderate and change.

Note

1   Much of the analysis in this chapter is rooted in the policy proposals made by the contributors to this volume, which are set out in the Appendix, and the discussion of those proposals during the Experts Meetings which took place in connection with the original lecture series referred to in the Foreword and Gerrie ter Haar's chapter.

APPENDIX

Policy observations
Islamic fundamentalism and social change

Abdullahi Ahmed An-Na'im

Islamic fundamentalist movements are neither new, prevalent nor permanent in Islamic societies. While these movements tend to draw on Islamic
sacred texts and historical traditions in articulating their vision for social
and political change and strategies of popular mobilization, fundamentalism is not the inevitable outcome of those resources.

Islamic fundamentalism should be seen as an indigenous spontaneous
response to profound social, political and economic crises, rather than
either prevalent among Islamic societies at any given point in time, or
permanent where it does occur. As a product of the interaction of certain
internal and external actors and factors, Islamic fundamentalist movements tends to evolve and change over time in response to changes in its
local and broader context and/or shifting perceptions of its success in
achieving its objectives.

The real issue is how to acknowledge and address the underlying causes
of this phenomenon in each society or community. In the present post-
colonial context in particular, it is important to view Islamic fundamentalism as an expression of the right of Muslim peoples to political, religious
and/or cultural self-determination, whether in terms of demands for the
strict application of *Shari'a* (Islamic law broadly defined) by the state, or
informal communal compliance in social relations and personal life-style.

Islamic fundamentalist movements should neither be dismissed as insignificant in the face of the final global triumph of Western liberalism, nor
exaggerated into a manifestation of permanent confrontation with so-
called Western civilization. A more appropriate response is to seek mediation between imperialistic claims of the permanent hegemony of Western
ideology, on the one hand, and self-fulfilling prophecies of unavoidable
confrontation between different civilizations of the world.

Women and Islamic fundamentalism in Malaysia

Sharifah Zaleha binti Syed Hassan

The observations in my chapter regarding Islamic fundamentalism and its consequences for nation building and women's participation have certain policy implications.

National unity

Islamic fundamentalism encourages Malays to organize into various socio-political groups that are conducive to heightening Malay racial consciousness which in turn can undermine those development programmes in the fields of economics, politics and education aimed at establishing a Malaysian Malaysia. Thus it is imperative for the Malaysian government to do the following:

1   Review its education system so as to emphasize the importance of according respect to other people's religious beliefs and viewpoints and that spiritual improvement is signified by a willingness to give higher priority to public interest than personal interest.
2   Encourage more inter-faith dialogues on the different visions of society, human rights, women and gender relations, etc., among leaders of the various faiths and government officials, development planners and community leaders. It is crucial that the parties to the dialogues should reach agreement on particular development issues based on the plurality of more or less rival religious doctrines.

The integration of women into national development

Islamic fundamentalism fosters varying viewpoints among Malay women about gender relations and the extent of their participation in society which do not help promote the national policy of involving women in all aspects of national development. Thus, it is essential for the Malaysian

239

government to re-examine its education policy so as to ensure that schools and colleges, as active socializing agents in the country, instil values and attitudes among girls to want to be socially and politically engaged at the community, national and international levels.

Religious fundamentalism in Israel

Alice Shalvi

The most important step that needs to be taken by the Israeli legislature is the separation of state and 'church', through the disestablishment of the Orthodox Chief Rabbinate and its subsidiaries and the granting of equal recognition to all denominations. This will be almost impossible so long as there are political parties whose avowed platform is the establishment of a theocracy. Thus there may be a need for legislation barring the existence of non-democratic parties; yet this kind of ban itself appears anti-democratic.

The introduction of civil marriage and divorce may be easier to effect, though it would probably result in the creation of 'second-class' citizens whom the Orthodox would consider ineligible and unacceptable as marital partners because of their 'dubious' Jewishness.

Regarding education, official funding should be withheld from schools that do not guarantee equal educational opportunities to pupils of both sexes. Similarly, all schools should be required to teach a curriculum comprising secular as well as religious subjects.

So long as national service is mandatory for young adults, there should be no exemption for *yeshiva* students as there currently is.

In short, every effort should be made to put into effect the noble aspirations of the Declaration of Independence, which envisioned the creation of a democratic, pluralist state based on the eternal Jewish ideals of social justice that were given such superb poetic expression by the greatest of Israel's prophets. 'Seek justice and pursue it'; 'Love thy neighbour as thyself'; 'Love the stranger in your midst, for you yourselves were strangers in a strange land'. The guidelines are there. All we need to do is to follow them.

Christian fundamentalism and social change

Nancy T. Ammerman

What are the policy dilemmas posed by fundamentalist movements? When violence is threatened, it must be prevented. But it is critical not to expect all fundamentalist movements to be violent, perhaps provoking violence where it might not otherwise have happened.

Fundamentalists often use the liberal rhetoric of tolerance and inclusion to argue for their right to participate as Christians in public life; and, in large measure, I think they are well grounded in making these arguments. Those who wish to oppose their arguments, for whatever reasons, are obligated to mobilize and argue against fundamentalist ideas, not against the fundamentalist right to present those ideas.

When people engage in religiously grounded practices which offend liberal sensibilities (restrictive gender and sexual practices, for instance), there is a necessary public debate to be had about the point at which issues of human rights supersede religious liberty. This is not just an issue raised by fundamentalism, but by many religious traditions around the world.

At this moment in time, some of the assumptions of the secular Enlightenment have been called into question in ways that have provided an opening for fundamentalist movements. The challenge is to take seriously the social critique they offer, carve out habits of civil discourse that make their participation possible, and mount substantive arguments for alternatives to fundamentalist ideas and practices.

Buddhist fundamentalism and social change

H.L. Seneviratne

In Sri Lanka, there has been a breakdown of positive social values and healthy social institutions. The day-to-day crises and problems, including the ethnic crisis, need to be understood within this broad breakdown. Indeed, the ethnic crisis, often understood as an autonomous phenomenon with its own causation, is rather an expression of this general malaise. The process of reconstruction involves the rebuilding of (i) values and (ii) institutions.

The long-term achievement of this goal involves, among other measures, the following:

- a free press;
- independence of the judiciary;
- independence of the public service;
- an independent elections commission;
- abolition of the existing emergency regulations;
- a methodical programme to disarm the people by the establishment and implementation of strict gun laws;
- a comprehensive programme to educate the public in human rights, civic duty and citizenship;
- an enlightened rewriting of the country's history, especially for use in schools, so that the younger generations are taught to appreciate their multi-ethnic heritage and to distinguish between chauvinism and patriotism;
- introduction into the school curriculum of effective ways of inculcating a sense of civility, citizenship, honesty, commitment, tolerance, respect for others, and a sense of duty, honour and dignity in work;
- introduction of a well-conceived system of national service for the attainment of the educational objectives.

243

In implementing these broad objectives, foreign donors can do the following:

- tie foreign aid to specific programmes discussed above;
- fund a comprehensive programme of teaching English universally in the island, including the villages;
- offer foreign travel and opportunities to become acquainted with Western democratic and public institutions to independent or moderately nationalist charismatic figures, including suitable members of the Buddhist clergy, who are likely to have influence over extremist groups;
- offer scholarships to gifted young Buddhist monks to study social science subjects, leading to a PhD degree, even if they are likely to 'derobe' subsequently;
- offer gifted young monks shorter programmes leading to diplomas or MA degrees focusing on human rights and related issues;
- offer short-term scholarships to senior military and police personnel to train in human rights;
- build a pool of people, including politicians, professionals and intellectuals, to methodically carry out a major restructuring of the political culture, introducing a sense of political civility, and to forge a national consensus that would stand above partisan interests.

Implications of *Hindutva*

Chakravarthi Ram-Prasad

There are two different types of anxiety over social change in India. The urban middle-class anxiety is over global competitiveness, India's role as a major player and the consequent economic benefits of enhanced status. *Hindutva* is thought to articulate the vision of a strong state appropriate for these ends. Support is focused on Parliament and calibrated through perceived efficiency. This commands support in the intelligentsia. It dominates the picture of India as supportive of religious ideology. But it does not directly alter the basic realities of conflict, and indeed constrains it through demands of efficiency.

Concerned organizations should not over-estimate the violent consequences of this anxiety. Helpful support following international guidelines for trade and aid, combined with Indian democratic structures, will eventually secure the sort of macro-economic change that will best handle such anxiety.

The wider, semi-urban and rural anxiety is about immediate pressures over scarce resources. *Hindutva* becomes the key to mobilizing Hindus by blaming continued scarcity on the supposedly disproportionate share of resources enjoyed by the 'minorities'. Support is at local and state level, often extra-parliamentary and the locus of violence. Indian-language newspapers, especially in the North, articulate and motivate these forces. Both corrective and preventive activity should focus on these areas, addressing scarcity and inefficiency directly and thereby lessening the otherwise potent ideological appeal of *Hindutva*. Organizations cannot really convince violent activists that Hindu interests are not under threat.

Concerned organizations should offer three types of support to these groups:

1   Logistical (and possibly financial) support for relevant Indian NGOs.
2   Training support for government institutions (for example, the police) in community relations, counselling, etc.
3   Direct work in affected areas, preferably in cooperative ventures with local organizations.

Two general recommendations to foreign organizations would be:

1   To provide support to and work with the institutional concerns of Indian organizations. In particular, to liaise directly with statal bodies like the National Human Rights Commission, which are democratically autonomous but politically and financially constrained.
2   When working to aid the most disadvantaged, who are at the receiving end of social oppression of various sorts, also target sections of the community from which oppressors are generally mobilized – especially if that community is an intermediate one close in status and power to the most disadvantaged.

INDEX

247